EDCO
MATHS
REVISE WISE
JUNIOR CERTIFICATE HIGHER LEVEL

Seamus McCabe

Edco
The Educational Company of Ireland

The Educational Company of Ireland
Ballymount Road
Walkinstown
Dublin 12
A member of the Smurfit Kappa Group
Reprinted October 2010

© Seamus McCabe, 2006

Editor: Antoinette Walker
Interior design: Outburst Design (01) 414 5743
Cover design: Combined Media
Cover photo: www.istockphoto.com

Printed in the Republic of Ireland by ColourBooks Ltd.
0 1 2 3 4 5 6 7 8 9

MATHS
REVISE WISE

Contents

Introduction v
1. Natural Numbers 1
2. Percentages and Income Tax ... 7
3. Estimation and Calculator Use ... 21
4. Indices and Surds 25
5. Ratio and Proportion 38
6. Sets 43
7. Algebra 1: Simplify, Factorise and Evaluate ... 53
8. Algebra 2: Fractions 62
9. Algebra 3: Solving Equations .. 66
10. Algebra 4: Forming Equations ... 78
11. Algebra 5: Changing the Subject of a Formula ... 87
12. Algebra 6: Inequalities 90
13. Functions and Graphs 95
14. Perimeter, Area and Volume ... 110
15. Coordinate Geometry 123
16. Geometry 1: Proofs of the Theorems ... 141
17. Geometry 2: Sample Problems .. 156
18. Geometry 3: Transformations .. 179
19. Geometry 4: The Constructions ... 184
20. Trigonometry 196
21. Statistics 219
22. Examination Section 233
23. Study Plan 239

Introduction

Know which topics to expect
In preparation for your Junior Certificate Maths examination it is essential that you know which topics to expect to appear on each paper. As you will see from the list of contents, topics that appear on Paper 1 are covered in Chapters 1–13 and Paper 2 topics are covered in Chapters 14–21.

Keep doing the examples
Work through the examples in this book regularly. Remember that you might be able to do something in March and have forgotten it by June. If you think you know how to do the question, try it yourself first and then compare your solution with that shown. If you know that you can't do the question, read carefully through the solution and then try it yourself a few days later.

TOP TIPS
Work through the examples in this book regularly.

Memorise material
Certain information must be memorised, for example, formulae, constructions and proofs of theorems. These should be written out at regular intervals from Christmas onwards so that you are aware of how well you know them, and how much additional work you need to do.

Know the format of the papers
Each paper lasts for 2 hours and 30 minutes and in that time you must answer six questions. Every question is worth 50 marks, so roughly the same amount of time (no more than 25 minutes) should be spent on each. Because all questions must be answered, it is a waste of time to read through the entire paper at the start of the examination. Start with your favourite topic. If you get stuck on part of a question, leave a large space and move on to another question. At the end of the examination return to the parts you were stuck on and try them again.

TOP TIPS

Because all questions must be answered, it is a waste of time to read through the entire paper at the start of the examination.

It is essential that you attempt every part of every question! You may make more than one attempt and you will be marked on the best attempt. Rough work should be shown wherever possible. The examiner will only use it to help you get marks. Rough work should not be untidy work!

Good luck!

Seamus McCabe

CHAPTER 1
Natural Numbers

Learning Objectives
- Natural numbers
- Factors (divisors)
- Highest common factor (HCF)
- Prime numbers
- Multiples
- Lowest common multiple (LCM)

Natural numbers

The set of natural numbers, represented by the letter N, contains the positive whole numbers and 0.

i.e. {0,1,2,3,4,5..........}.

The natural numbers can be split into the **even** numbers, 0,2,4,6,8... and the **odd** numbers 1,3,5,7,9...

Factors (divisors)

Every natural number has a set of factors. These are positive whole numbers that divide evenly into the number.

0 is not a factor of any number.
1 is a factor of every number.

Example 1

List all the factors of 12.

It is best to list the factors in pairs: 1 and 12; 2 and 6; 3 and 4.
Answer: 1, 2, 3, 4, 6 and 12.

Example 2

List all the common factors of 16 and 18.

TOP TIPS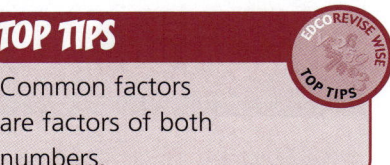
Common factors are factors of both numbers.

Factors of 16: 1, 2, 4, 8, 16
Factors of 18: 1, 2, 3, 6, 9, 18
Common factors: 1 and 2

Highest common factor (HCF)

The highest common factor of two or more numbers is the biggest number that divides evenly into all of the numbers.

To find the HCF:
1 Divide every number by a common factor
2 Divide the answers by a common factor
3 Repeat the above procedure until the only common factor is 1
4 Multiply the numbers you divided by.

Example 3

Find the highest common factor of 24, 40 and 72.

The HCF is 2 × 4 = 8.

2	24	40	72
4	12	20	36
1	3	5	9

Example 4

Find the highest common factor of 120, 180 and 390.

The HCF is 10 × 3 = 30.

10	120	180	390
3	12	18	39
1	4	6	13

Prime numbers

1. A prime number has only two factors, the number itself and 1
2. 1 is not a prime number
3. Some prime numbers are: 2, 3, 5, 7, 11, 13, 17…
4. 2 is the smallest prime number and the only even prime number.

Example 5

Write 4680 as the product of its prime factors.

Solution:
Begin by making a list of prime numbers:
2, 3, 5, 7, 11, 13, 17…

Divide repeatedly by any of these numbers until the answer is 1. *Use your calculator.*

List the numbers you divided by with multiplication signs between them.

Rewrite this using indices.

2	4680
2	2340
2	1170
5	585
3	117
3	39
13	13
	1

$$4680 = 2 \times 2 \times 2 \times 3 \times 3 \times 5 \times 13$$

Answer: $4680 = 2^3 \times 3^2 \times 5 \times 13$

You should check your answer by evaluating this product on the calculator to make sure it gives 4680.

Multiples

A multiple of any whole number can be found by multiplying it by any whole number other than 0.

Example 6

List the first five multiples of 12.

$12 \times 1 = 12$
$12 \times 2 = 24$
$12 \times 3 = 36$
$12 \times 4 = 48$
$12 \times 5 = 60$

Answer: 12, 24, 36, 48 and 60.

Example 7

Find three common multiples of 12 and 18.

Multiples of 12: 12, 24, **36**, 48, 60, **72**, 84, 96, **108**
Multiples of 18: 18, **36**, 54, **72**, 90, **108**
Three common multiples: 36, 72 and 108

Note: Having found a common multiple, any multiple of it will also be a common multiple.

Lowest common multiple (LCM)

The lowest common multiple of a set of numbers is the smallest number that can be divided evenly by each of the numbers.

For example, 12 is the LCM of 3 and 4.

> To find the lowest common multiple of two or more numbers:
> 1 Use the calculator to make a list of the multiples of each number
> 2 The LCM is the first number that appears in each list.

Example 8

Find the lowest common multiple of 16 and 20.

Multiples of 16: 16 32, 48, 64, **80**...
Multiples of 20: 20, 40, 60, **80**...
Lowest common multiple: 80

The above method can sometimes be very long, especially when there are three or more numbers involved. The following are shortcuts.

> **TOP TIPS**
> If the numbers have no common factor apart from 1, then their lowest common multiple is always found by multiplying them.

Example 9

Find the lowest common multiple of 3, 5 and 8.

Solution:
The numbers 3, 5 and 8 have no common factor apart from 1, so their LCM can be found by multiplying them:

$3 \times 5 \times 8 = 120$

Lowest common multiple: 120

1. If two or more numbers have a common prime factor, then divide them by this factor
2. Repeat until there is no longer a common prime factor
3. Multiply the remaining numbers and the prime numbers you divided by together to get the LCM.

Example 10

Find the LCM of 12, 18 and 20.

	12	18	20
2	6	9	10
2	3	9	5
3	1	3	5

LCM = (2)(2)(3)(3)(5) = 180

Example 11

Find the LCM of 45, 54, 64 and 80.

2	45	54	64	80
2	45	27	32	40
2	45	27	16	20
2	45	27	8	10
3	45	27	4	5
3	15	9	4	5
5	5	3	4	5
	1	3	4	1

LCM = (2)(2)(2)(2)(3)(3)(5)(1)(3)(4)(1) = 8640

Key Points

- The set of natural numbers, represented by the letter N, contains the positive whole numbers and 0.
- Every natural number has a set of factors. These are positive whole numbers that divide evenly into the number.
- 0 is not a factor of any number. 1 is a factor of every number.
- The highest common factor (HCF) of two or more numbers is the biggest number that divides evenly into all of the numbers.
- A prime number has only two factors, the number itself and 1. 1 is not a prime number. 2 is the smallest prime number and the only even prime number.
- The highest common factor of a set of numbers is the biggest number that is a factor of all the numbers.
- A multiple of any whole number is found by multiplying it by any whole number other than 0.
- The lowest common multiple (LCM) of a set of numbers is the smallest number that can be divided evenly by each of the numbers.
- If the numbers have no common factor apart from 1, then their lowest common multiple is always found by multiplying them.

CHAPTER 2
Percentages and Income Tax

●●● Learning Objectives

- To convert percentages to decimals
- To convert percentages to fractions
- To find a percentage of a number
- To find a percentage of a number using the unitary method
- Given a percentage of a number, to find the whole number
- Given one percentage of a number, to find another
- To write one number as a percentage of another
- To increase a number by a given percentage
- To reduce a number by a given percentage
- Compound interest
- To calculate total value of investments/withdrawals
- To find any missing figure in an income tax problem.

To convert percentages to decimals

TOP TIPS

To convert a percentage to a decimal, divide it by 100 and leave out the % symbol.

Example 1

Write each of the following as a decimal:
(i) 21%
(ii) 4%
(iii) 2.5%

(i) $21\% = 21 \div 100 = 0 \cdot 21$

(ii) $4\% = 4 \div 100 = 0 \cdot 04$

(iii) $2 \cdot 5\% = 2 \cdot 5 \div 100 = 0 \cdot 025$

To convert percentages to fractions

To convert a percentage to a fraction, put it over 100, leave out the % symbol and simplify.

Example 2

Write each of the following as fractions:

(i) 25% (ii) $33\frac{1}{3}\%$ (iii) $12\frac{1}{2}\%$

(i) $25\% = \frac{25}{100} = \frac{1}{4}$

(ii) $33\frac{1}{3}\% = \frac{33\frac{1}{3}}{100} = \frac{100}{300} = \frac{1}{3}$

(iii) $12\frac{1}{2}\% = \frac{12\frac{1}{2}}{100} = \frac{25}{200} = \frac{1}{8}$

TOP TIPS

The numbers in a ratio must be in the same unit of measure.

To find a percentage of a number

Write the percentage as a decimal or a fraction, then multiply it by the number.

Example 3

Find: (i) 12% of 60   (ii) 5% of 20   (iii) $66\frac{2}{3}\%$ of 1200

(i) $12\% = 12 \div 100 = 0 \cdot 12$ $0 \cdot 12 \times 60 = 7 \cdot 2$

(ii) $5\% = 5 \div 100 = 0 \cdot 05$ $0 \cdot 05 \times 20 = 1$

(iii) $66\frac{2}{3}\% = \frac{66\frac{2}{3}}{100} = \frac{2}{3}$ $\frac{2}{3} \times 1200 = 800$

To find a percentage of a number using the unitary method

An alternative approach is called the **unitary method**. In this case we:
1 Let 100% equal the whole number
2 Divide by 100 to get 1%
3 Multiply by the required percentage.

(i) $100\% = 60$
     $1\% = 0 \cdot 6$
     $12\% = 0 \cdot 6 \times 12 = 7 \cdot 2$

(ii) $100\% = 20$
     $1\% = 0 \cdot 2$
     $5\% = 0 \cdot 2 \times 5 = 1$

(iii) $100\% = 1200$
      $1\% = 12$
      $66\frac{2}{3}\% = 12 \times 66\frac{2}{3} = 800$

Given a percentage of a number, to find the whole number

1 Convert the percentage to a fraction or decimal
2 Divide the given number by the answer.

Example 4

If 42% of a number is 105, find the number.

$$42\% = 0 \cdot 42$$

$$105 \div 0 \cdot 42 = 250$$

Or, using the unitary method:

$$42\% = 105$$
$$1\% = \frac{105}{42} = 2 \cdot 5$$
$$100\% = 250$$

Given one percentage of a number, to find another

1. Write both percentages as decimals
2. Divide the given number by the first percentage to get the whole number
3. Multiply by the required percentage.

Example 5

If 28% of a number is 89.6, find 6% of the same number.

Divide by 0.28 to get the whole number, then multiply by 0.06 to get 6% of it:

$$89 \cdot 6 \div 0 \cdot 28 \times 0 \cdot 06 = 320$$

Answer: 320

Using the unitary method:

$$28\% = 89 \cdot 6$$
$$1\% = \frac{89 \cdot 6}{28} = 3 \cdot 2$$
$$100\% = 320$$

To write one number as a percentage of another

1. Divide the number to be converted to a percentage by the other number
2. Multiply the answer by 100 and include the % symbol.

Example 6

In a test, a student scores 180 out of 250. What percentage is this?

$$\frac{180}{250} \times 100\% = 72\%$$

Example 7

A restaurant bill comes to €112.70, including VAT. If the amount of VAT included in the bill is €14.70, what was the rate of VAT?

TOP TIPS
The VAT is a percentage of the bill before VAT was added, so we must find this first.

$$112 \cdot 70 - 14 \cdot 70 = 98$$

$$\text{VAT rate} = \frac{14 \cdot 70}{98} \times 100\%$$
$$\text{VAT rate} = 15\%$$

Example 8

An estate agent receives commission of €6750 when a house is sold for €450 000. What percentage commission does the estate agent receive?

$$\frac{6750}{450\,000} \times 100\% = 1 \cdot 5\%$$

To increase a number by a given percentage

1. Add 100% to the percentage
2. Divide the answer by 100 to convert to a decimal
3. Multiply by the given number.

Example 9

Increase 70 by 15%.

100% is the whole number. When it is increased by 15%, it becomes 115%, so we are trying to find 115% of 70.

Convert 115% to a decimal and multiply by it:

Answer: $70 \times 1 \cdot 15 = 80 \cdot 5$

Example 10

A car is bought for €2500 and sold at a profit of 8%. Find the selling price.

The selling price is 108%.

$$2500 \times 1 \cdot 08 = 2700$$

Answer: €2700

Example 11

€45 000 is invested for 1 year at an interest rate of 4%. Calculate the value of the investment at the end of the year.

We have to find 104% of 45 000.

$$45000 \times 1 \cdot 04 = 46800$$

Answer: €46 800

Example 12

An article costs €160 excluding VAT. The rate of VAT is 21%. Find the cost including VAT.

$$160 \times 1 \cdot 21 = 193 \cdot 6$$

Answer: €193.6

Example 13

A man borrows €2500. The rate of interest is 8% per annum. How much does he owe after one year?

$$2500 \times 1 \cdot 08 = 2700$$

Answer: €2700

To reduce a number by a given percentage

1. Subtract the percentage from 100%
2. Divide by 100 to convert to a decimal
3. Multiply by the given number.

Example 14

A car when new costs €24 000. It depreciates by 16% in the first year. Find the value of the car after 1 year.

The car has lost 16% of its value, therefore it is worth 84% of its cost price after 1 year.
$$24000 \times 0.84 = 20160$$
Answer: €20 160

Working backwards

Example 15

A boxer increases his weight by 3% while training for a fight. If he weighs 144.2 kg at the end of his training, what did he weigh before?

$$\text{Original weight} \times 1.03 = 144.2$$
$$\text{Original weight} = \frac{144.2}{1.03} = 120$$

Answer: 120 kg

Example 16

A sum of money amounts to €6406.25 after 1 year at 2.5% interest per annum. Find the sum of money.

$$\text{Sum of money} \times 1.025 = 6406.25$$
$$\text{Sum of money} = \frac{6406.25}{1.025} = 6250$$

Answer: €6250

Example 17

A computer costs €907·50, including VAT at 21%. Find the cost of the computer before VAT.

$$\text{Cost before VAT} \times 1\cdot 21 = 907\cdot 50$$
$$\text{Cost before VAT} = \frac{907\cdot 50}{1\cdot 21} = 750$$

Answer: €750

Compound interest

To find the total value of an investment at a fixed rate of compound interest

1. Add 100% to the rate of interest
2. Divide by 100 to convert to a decimal
3. Raise to the power of n, the number of years involved
4. Multiply by the sum involved.

To find the compound interest, proceed as above. Then subtract the initial investment. To calculate the value of an investment involving withdrawals, etc. use the chart in Examples 21 and 22.

Example 18

€8,000 is invested for 3 years at 2·75% per annum, compound interest. Calculate the value of the investment after 3 years, correct to the nearest cent.

$8000 \times 1\cdot 0275^3 = 8678\cdot 316375$

Answer: €8678·32

TOP TIPS
The investment increases by 2·75% every year, so multiply by 1.0275 three times, i.e. $(1\cdot 0275)^3$.

Example 19, Junior Certificate, 2005

There are 25 000 fish in a fish farm. The number of fish in the farm increases by 40% each year. How many fish will be in the farm at the end of 3 years?

$$\text{Number of fish after 3 years} = 25\,000 \times (1\cdot 40)^3$$
$$= 68\,600$$

Working backwards

Example 20

A certain sum of money, invested for 2 years at $4\frac{1}{2}\%$ per annum, compound interest, amounts to €21 840.50. Calculate the sum of money invested.

$$\text{Sum of money} \times 1 \cdot 045^2 = 21840 \cdot 50$$

$$\text{Sum of money} = \frac{21840 \cdot 50}{1 \cdot 045^2} = 20{,}000$$

Answer: €20 000

To calculate total value of investments / withdrawals

Example 21

€3500 is invested for 3 years at 2% per annum, compound interest. At the end of the first year, an additional €1000 is invested. At the end of the second year, €750 is withdrawn. What is the total value of the investment at the end of the third year, correct to the nearest cent?

Year	Start of Year	Rate of Interest	End of Year	Further Investment/Withdrawal
1	3500	2%	3500 × 1·02 = 3570	+1000
2	4570	2%	4570 × 1·02 = 4661·40	−750
3	3911.40	2%	3911.40 × 1·02 = 3989·628	

Answer: €3989.63

Example 22

A man borrows €650 to be repaid over 2 years at 4% per annum, compound interest. The man agrees to repay the loan with two payments, one at the end of the first year and one at the end of the second year.

At the end of the first year, a certain amount of money is repaid. At the end of the second year, he owes €443.04. How much did he repay at the end of the first year?

Year	Start of Year	Rate of Interest	End of Year	Further Investment/Withdrawal
1	650	4%	650 × 1·0 = 676	− x
2	44·3 ÷ 1·04 = 426	4%	443·04	

$676 - x = 426$

$x = 250$

Answer: €250

TOP TIPS

When going from right to left, divide.

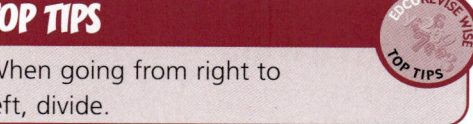

Key Points

- To convert a percentage to a decimal, divide it by 100 and leave out the % symbol.
- To convert a percentage to a fraction, put it over 100, leave out the % symbol and simplify.
- To find a percentage of a number, write the percentage as a decimal or a fraction, then multiply by the number.
- To find a percentage of a number using the unitary method, let 100% equal the whole number, divide by 100 to get 1% and multiply by the required percentage.
- Given a percentage of a number, to find the whole number: convert the percentage to a fraction or decimal, then divide the given number by the answer.
- Given one percentage of a number, to find another percentage: write the percentages as decimals, divide by the first percentage to get the whole number and then multiply by the second percentage.
- To write one number as a percentage of another: divide the number to be converted to a percentage by the other number, and then multiply the answer by 100 and include the % symbol.

Income Tax

Begin all income tax problems that have two rates of tax with the following chart:

Gross income	Standard rate cut-off point	Remainder
	Standard tax rate	Higher tax rate
Gross tax	Standard tax	Higher tax
Tax credits	Net income = gross income − tax paid	
Tax paid		

The chart contains two rows of three figures (heavy border) and three columns of three figures (shading).

Begin all problems that have two rates of tax by filling the given information into the chart. Now look for a row of three or a column of three where two of the figures are given and you should be able to find the third. Continue until the chart is complete.

If a question involves only one rate of tax, then the entire gross income is taxed at that rate and columns 2 and 3 are not needed.

To calculate net income

Example 23

Ross has a gross income of €52 000. The standard rate cut-off point is €28 000. The standard tax rate is 20% and the higher rate is 42%. His tax credits amount to €7500. Calculate his net income.

Begin by filling in the chart overleaf. The shaded sections represent information given in the question.

When you have two figures in a row of three or a column of three, you can find the third. The numbers in boxes show the sequence of calculations.

Gross income €52 000	Standard rate cut-off point €28 000	**1** Remainder €52 000 − €28 000 = €24 000
	Standard tax rate 20%	**3** Higher tax rate 42%
Gross tax €5600 + €10 080 = €15 680	**2** Standard tax €28 000 × 0.20 = €5600	Higher tax €24 000 × 0.42 = €10 080
4 Tax credits €7500	**6** Net income: €52 000 − €8180 = €43 820	
5 Tax paid €15 680 − €7500 = €8180		

Answer: €43 820

Example 24

Joshua pays €8260 in income tax. His tax credits amount to €6200. The standard rate cut-off point is €24 000. The standard tax rate is 20% and the higher rate is 42%.

(a) Calculate his net income.
(b) By how much should his gross income be increased to give him a net income of €40 190?

CHAPTER 2: PERCENTAGES AND INCOME TAX

5 Gross income €23 000 + €24 000 = €47 000	Standard rate cut-off point €24 000	4 Remainder €9660 ÷ 0.42 = €23 000
	Standard tax rate 20%	Higher tax rate 42%
2 Gross tax €6200 + €8260 = €14 460	1 Standard tax €24 000 × 0.20 = €4800	3 Higher tax €14 460 – €4800 = €9660
Tax credits €6200	6 Net income: €47 000 – €8260 = €38 740	
Tax paid €8260		

(a) **Answer:** €38 740

(b) Every euro that is added to his gross income will be taxed at 42%, so he keeps 58% of his increase.

To get a net income of €40 190, his net income must increase by €1450.

€1450 is 58% of his gross increase.

$$\text{Gross increase} \times 0 \cdot 58 = 1450$$

$$\text{Gross increase} = \frac{1450}{0 \cdot 58} = 2500$$

Answer: €2500

Example 25, Junior Certificate 2006

Jill has a gross income of €50 000. Her total income tax payable amounts to €10 460. The standard rate cut-off point is €32 000. The standard rate of tax is 20% and the higher rate is 42%. What are Jill's tax credits for the year?

Gross income €50 000	Standard rate cut-off point €32 000	**1** Remainder €50 000 – €32 000 = €18 000
	Standard tax rate 20%	Higher tax rate 42%
4 Gross tax €6400 + €7560 = €13 960	**2** Standard tax €32 000 × 0.20 = €6400	**3** Higher tax €18 000 × 0.42 = €7560
5 Tax credits €13 960 – €10 460 €3500		
Tax paid €10 460		

Answer: €3500

Key Points

- Memorise the chart and use it if there are two tax rates involved.
- If you have two figures in a row or a column of three, you can find the third.
- If the standard rate cut-off point is less than the gross income, all income is taxed at the lower rate, so gross tax would then be 20% of the gross income, if the standard rate of tax is 20%.

CHAPTER 3
Estimation and Calculator Use

●●● Learning Objectives
- To estimate a number to the nearest whole number
- To estimate a number appropriately
- To estimate a number correct to a specified number of significant figures
- To estimate a number correct to a specified number of decimal places.

Estimation

You may be asked to estimate a number:
- to the nearest whole number
- appropriately
- correct to a specified number of significant figures
- correct to a specified number of decimal places.

Example 1

Estimate each of the following to the **nearest whole number**:

(i) $23 \cdot 49$ (ii) $172 \cdot 712$ (iii) $9 \cdot 6$ (iv) $0 \cdot 28$

1 Check the first digit to the right of the decimal point
2 If it is less than 5, write down the whole number to the left of the decimal point
3 Otherwise, add 1 to this number.

(i) $23 \cdot 49 \approx 23$ (ii) $172 \cdot 712 \approx 173$
(iii) $9 \cdot 6 \approx 10$ (iv) $0 \cdot 28 \approx 0$

TOP TIPS
$\approx$ means 'is approximately equal to'.

Example 2

Estimate each of the following appropriately.

(i) $\sqrt{23 \cdot 2}$ (ii) $\sqrt{52 \cdot 1}$ (iii) $\sqrt[3]{10}$

An estimate should be done without the calculator. In order to estimate the above numbers, we look for the nearest whole number whose square root or (in part iii) whose cube root, we know.

(i) $\sqrt{23 \cdot 2} \approx \sqrt{25} = 5$

(ii) $\sqrt{52 \cdot 1} \approx \sqrt{49} = 7$

(iii) $\sqrt[3]{10} \approx \sqrt[3]{8} = 2$

Significant figures

Reading a number from left to right, the first non-zero digit before the decimal point is the first significant figure.

All digits after this are significant with the exception of zeros at the end of a whole number.

When a digit in a whole number is left out, it **must** be replaced by a 0.

To write 58 379 correct to two significant figures is to write down the number closest to it that has only two significant figures. It is between 58 000 and 59 000 but closer to 58 000, so the answer is 58 000.

Example 3

Estimate each of the following correct to two significant figures.

(i) 123   (ii) 3892   (iii) 70736   (iv) 837

(i) $123 \approx 120$ (ii) $3892 \approx 3900$ (iii) $70736 \approx 71000$
(iv) $837 \approx 840$

Decimal places

Example 4

Estimate each of the following (a) correct to one decimal place and (b) correct to two decimal places.

(i) $24 \cdot 637$ (ii) $0 \cdot 783$ (iii) $9 \cdot 997$ (iv) $6 \cdot 095$

Number	1 Decimal Place	2 Decimal Places
24·637	24·6	24·64
0·783	0·8	0·78
9·997	10·0	10·00
6.095	6·1	6·10

Example 5

By rounding to the nearest whole number, estimate the value of:

$$\frac{131 \cdot 5 - 1 \cdot 73 \times \sqrt{0 \cdot 64}}{35 \cdot 4 - 5 \cdot 1^2}$$

Then, evaluate $\dfrac{131 \cdot 5 - 1 \cdot 73 \times \sqrt{0 \cdot 64}}{35 \cdot 4 - 5 \cdot 1^2}$, correct to two decimal places.

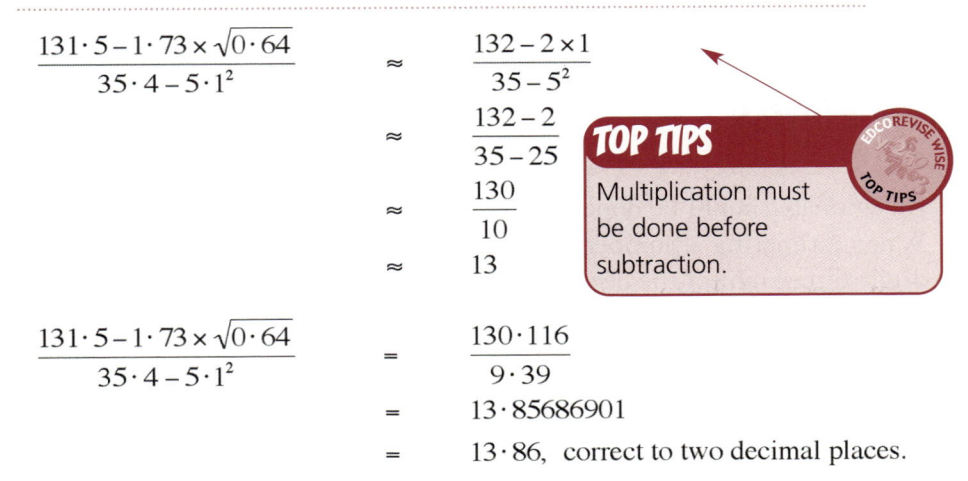

$$\frac{131 \cdot 5 - 1 \cdot 73 \times \sqrt{0 \cdot 64}}{35 \cdot 4 - 5 \cdot 1^2} \approx \frac{132 - 2 \times 1}{35 - 5^2}$$

$$\approx \frac{132 - 2}{35 - 25}$$

$$\approx \frac{130}{10}$$

$$\approx 13$$

TOP TIPS: Multiplication must be done before subtraction.

$$\frac{131 \cdot 5 - 1 \cdot 73 \times \sqrt{0 \cdot 64}}{35 \cdot 4 - 5 \cdot 1^2} = \frac{130 \cdot 116}{9 \cdot 39}$$

$$= 13 \cdot 85686901$$

$$= 13 \cdot 86, \text{ correct to two decimal places.}$$

When using the calculator to evaluate a fraction, always work out the top and bottom separately, as in the above example.

The estimate is a guide to let us know if we have used the calculator incorrectly. Always compare the estimate with the result obtained from the calculator. If there is a big difference between them, check **all** calculations.

Example 6, Junior Certificate Sample Paper 2003

By rounding appropriately, estimate the value of:

$$(4 \cdot 37)^2 + \frac{1}{2 \cdot 05} \times \sqrt{50 \cdot 9}.$$

Then, evaluate $(4 \cdot 37)^2 + \frac{1}{2 \cdot 05} \times \sqrt{50 \cdot 9}.$, correct to two decimal places.

$(4 \cdot 37)^2 + \frac{1}{2 \cdot 05} \times \sqrt{50 \cdot 9} \quad \approx \quad 5^2 + \frac{1}{2} \times \sqrt{49}$

$\approx \quad 25 + \frac{1}{2} \times 7$

$\approx \quad 25 + 3 \cdot 5$

$\approx \quad 28 \cdot 5$

TOP TIPS

49 is the number closest to 50.9, whose square root we know.

$(4 \cdot 37)^2 + \frac{1}{2 \cdot 05} \times \sqrt{50 \cdot 9} \quad = \quad 22 \cdot 57710663, \quad$ using the calculator.

$= \quad 22 \cdot 58, \quad$ correct to two decimal places.

Key Points

- An estimate should be done without the calculator.
- When estimating a number to the nearest whole number, check the first digit to the right of the decimal point. If it is less than 5, write down the whole number to the left of the decimal point, otherwise add 1 to this number
- When estimating a number appropriately, look for the nearest whole number whose square root or whose cube root is known.
- When reading a number from left to right, the first non-zero digit before the decimal point is the first significant figure.
- When a digit in a whole number is left out, it must be replaced by a 0.
- Multiplication must be done before subtraction.
- When using the calculator to evaluate a fraction, always work out the top and bottom separately.
- The estimate is a guide to let us know if we have used the calculator incorrectly. Always compare the estimate with the result obtained from the calculator. If there is a big difference between them, check all calculations.

CHAPTER 4
Indices and Surds

●●●Learning Objectives
- Definition of indices
- Multiplication of indices
- Two indices on the same number
- Division involving indices
- Index or scientific notation
- Simplifying surds
- Adding surds
- Multiplying surds
- Simplifying fractions involving surds.

Definition of indices

$2 \times 2 \times 2$ can be written in a neater way using indices.

$2 \times 2 \times 2 = 2^3$

3 is called the **index** and 2 is the **base**.

Similarly, $5^4 = 5 \times 5 \times 5 \times 5$

Definition: If n is a positive whole number, x^n is another way to write n x's multiplied together.

We will now create some rules that allow us to perform calculations with indices without removing the indices.

Multiplication of indices

$$3^2 \times 3^4 \quad = \quad (3 \times 3)(3 \times 3 \times 3 \times 3)$$
$$= \quad 3^6$$

Rule 1

$$x^a \times x^b = x^{a+b}$$

That is, when multiplying with the same base, keep the base and add the indices.

Example 1

Simplify (i) $2^4 \times 2^3 \times 2$ (ii) $2^x \times 2$

(i) $2^4 \times 2^3 \times 2^1 = 2^{4+3+1} = 2^8$

(ii) $2^x \times 2^1 = 2^{x+1}$

TOP TIPS

$2 = 2^1$

Two indices on the same number

$$(3^4)^2 = (3 \times 3 \times 3 \times 3)(3 \times 3 \times 3 \times 3)$$
$$= 3^8$$

Rule 2

$$\left(x^a\right)^b = x^{ab}$$

That is, when there are two indices on the same number, keep the base and multiply the indices.

Example 2

Simplify (i) $\left(5^3\right)^4$ (ii) $\left(5^x\right)^3$ (iii) $\left(2^x\right)^x$

(i) $\left(5^3\right)^4 = 5^{12}$ (ii) $\left(5^x\right)^3 = 5^{3x}$ (iii) $\left(2^x\right)^x = 2^{x^2}$

Example 3

Simplify (i) $3^2(3^3)^2$ (ii) $x^4(x^2)(x^3)^5$

(i) $3^2(3^3)^2 = 3^2(3^6)$
$= 3^8$

(ii) $x^4(x^2)(x^3)^5 = x^4(x^2)(x^{15})$
$= x^{21}$

TOP TIPS

If there are two indices or a number, begin by multiplying them to get one index.

Division involving indices

$$\frac{2^5}{2^3} = \frac{2\times2\times2\times2\times2}{2\times2\times2} = 2\times2 = 2^2$$

Rule 3

$$\frac{x^a}{x^b} = x^{a-b}$$

That is, when dividing with equal bases, keep the base and subtract the bottom index from the top one.

Example 4

Write $\frac{3^7}{3^2}$ in the form 3^n where $n \in N$

$$\frac{3^7}{3^2} = 3^{7-2} = 3^5$$

Example 5

Simplify (i) $\frac{x^3 \times x^2}{(x^2)^2}$ (ii) $\frac{2^5(2^3)}{(2^2)^3}$

(i) $\frac{x^3 \times x^2}{(x^2)^2} = \frac{x^5}{x^4}$
$= x^{5-4}$
$= x^1$
$= x$

TOP TIPS

Begin by simplifying the top and bottom separately.

(ii) $\frac{2^5(2^3)}{(2^2)^3} = \frac{2^8}{2^6}$
$= 2^{8-6}$
$= 2^2$

We can use Rules 1, 2 and 3 to establish meanings for indices other than positive whole numbers.

$$\frac{x^2}{x^2} = x^{2-2} = x^0$$

But any number divided by itself is 1. Therefore, $x^0 = 1$

Rule 4

$$x^0 = 1$$

$\dfrac{1}{x} = \dfrac{x^0}{x^1} = x^{0-1} = x^{-1}$. Similarly, $\dfrac{1}{x^2} = \dfrac{x^0}{x^2} = x^{0-2} = x^{-2}$

Rule 5

$$x^{-n} = \frac{1}{x^n}$$

Example 6

Express in the form 2^n: (i) $\dfrac{1}{2^5}$ (ii) $\dfrac{2(2^6)}{(2^4)^3}$

(i) $\dfrac{1}{2^5} = 2^{-5}$

(ii) $\dfrac{2(2^6)}{(2^4)^3} = \dfrac{2^7}{2^{12}}$

$= 2^{7-12}$

$= 2^{-5}$

$\left(x^{1/2}\right)^2 = x^1 = x.$ But $\left(\sqrt{x}\right)^2 = x.$ Therefore $x^{1/2} = \sqrt{x}$.

$\left(x^{1/3}\right)^3 = x^1 = x.$ But $\left(\sqrt[3]{x}\right)^3 = x.$ Therefore $x^{1/3} = \sqrt[3]{x}$.

Rule 6

$$x^{1/n} = \sqrt[n]{x}$$

Example 7

(i) $9^{1/2}$ (ii) $8^{1/3}$ (iii) $625^{1/4}$ (iv) $27^{-1/3}$

Simplify

(i) $9^{1/2} = \sqrt{9} = 3$

(ii) $8^{1/3} = \sqrt[3]{8} = 2$

(iii) $625^{1/4} = \sqrt[4]{625} = 5$

(iv) $27^{-1/3} = \dfrac{1}{\sqrt[3]{27}} = \dfrac{1}{3}$

The above problems could also be approached as follows:

(i) $9^{1/2} = (3^2)^{1/2} = 3^1 = 3$

(ii) $8^{1/3} = (2^3)^{1/3} = 2^1 = 2$

(iii) $625^{1/4} = (5^4)^{1/4} = 5^1 = 5$

(iv) $27^{-1/3} = (3^3)^{-1/3} = 3^{-1} = \dfrac{1}{3}$

Example 8

Simplify (i) $16^{3/4}$ (ii) $27^{2/3}$ (iii) $25^{-3/2}$ (iv) $64^{-1\frac{1}{3}}$

(i) $16^{3/4} = (2^4)^{3/4} = 2^3 = 8$

(ii) $27^{2/3} = (3^3)^{2/3} = 3^2 = 9$

(iii) $25^{-3/2} = (5^2)^{-3/2} = 5^{-3} = \dfrac{1}{5^3} = \dfrac{1}{125}$

(iv) $64^{-1\frac{1}{3}} = (4^3)^{-1\frac{1}{3}} = 4^{-4} = \dfrac{1}{4^4} = \dfrac{1}{256}$

TOP TIPS

Remember, when there are two indices on the same number, multiply them.

Example 9, Junior Certificate 2004

Simplify $\dfrac{125^{\frac{1}{3}} \times 5^2}{5^3 \times 25^{\frac{5}{2}}}$ into the form 5^n, where $n \in Z$

It is useful in problems of this type to begin by listing some powers of 5:
$$5^1 = 5, \quad 5^2 = 25, \quad 5^3 = 125, \quad 5^4 = 625 \text{ etc.}$$

$$\dfrac{125^{\frac{1}{3}} \times 5^2}{5^3 \times 25^{\frac{5}{2}}} = \dfrac{(5^3)^{\frac{1}{3}} \times 5^2}{5^3 \times (5^2)^{\frac{5}{2}}}$$

$$= \dfrac{5^1 \times 5^2}{5^3 \times 5^5}$$

$$= \dfrac{5^3}{5^8}$$

$$= 5^{-5}$$

Example 10, Junior Certificate 2004

Simplify $\dfrac{8^{\frac{2}{3}} \times 2^4}{2^3 \times 4^{\frac{3}{2}} \times 2}$ into the form 2^n, where $n \in Z$

$$2^1 = 2, \quad 2^2 = 4, \quad 2^3 = 8$$

$$\dfrac{8^{\frac{2}{3}} \times 2^4}{2^3 \times 4^{\frac{3}{2}} \times 2} = \dfrac{(2^3)^{\frac{2}{3}} \times 2^4}{2^3 \times (2^2)^{\frac{3}{2}} \times 2^1}$$

$$= \dfrac{2^2 \times 2^4}{2^3 \times 2^3 \times 2^1}$$

$$= \dfrac{2^6}{2^7}$$

$$= 2^{-1}$$

Example 11, Junior Certificate 2003

Simplify $\dfrac{\sqrt[3]{27} \times 3}{9^{\frac{1}{2}} \times 3^4}$ into the form 5^n, where $n \in Z$

$$3^1 = 3, \quad 3^2 = 9, \quad 3^3 = 27$$

$$\dfrac{\sqrt[3]{27} \times 3}{9^{\frac{1}{2}} \times 3^4} = \dfrac{3^1 \times 3^1}{(3^2)^{\frac{1}{2}} \times 3^4}$$

$$= \dfrac{3^2}{3^1 \times 3^4}$$

$$= \dfrac{3^2}{3^5}$$

$$= 3^{-3}$$

Index or scientific notation

To write a number using index or scientific notation is to write it in the form:

$$a \times 10^n, \quad \text{where } 1 \leq a < 10 \text{ and } n \in Z$$

Example 12

Express 2300 in the form $a \times 10^n$, where $1 \leq a < 10$ and $n \in Z$

$$2300 = 2 \cdot 3 \times 10^3$$

Note: To check the answer on the calculator press:

| 2 | . | 3 | Exp | 3 | = |

To perform calculations with numbers in index notation, use the calculator.

Example 13, Junior Certificate 2004

Evaluate $(6 \cdot 3 \times 10^9) + (5 \cdot 8 \times 10^{10})$

Express your answer in the form $a \times 10^n$, where $1 \leq a < 10$ and $n \in N$.

6	.	3	Exp	9	+	5	.	8	Exp	1	0	=

Answer: $6 \cdot 43 \times 10^{10}$ will then be displayed on the calculator.

Example 14

Evaluate $(7 \cdot 2 \times 10^5) \div (3 \cdot 6 \times 10^4)$.

Express your answer in the form $a \times 10^n$, where $1 \leq a < 10$ and $n \in N$.

7	.	2	Exp	5	÷	5	3	.	6	Exp	5	=

Answer: $2 \cdot 0 \times 10^1$

Key Points

- In x^n, x is called the base and n is the index.
- If n is a positive whole number, xn is another way to write n x's multiplied together.
- When multiplying with the same base, keep the base and add the indices.
- When there are two indices on the same number, keep the base and multiply the indices.
- When dividing with equal bases, keep the base and subtract the bottom index from the top one.
- To write a number using index or scientific notation is to write it in the form: $a \times 10^n$, where $1 \leq a < 10$ and $n \in Z$
- To perform calculations with numbers in index notation, use the calculator.

Simplifying surds

Look for the biggest square number (4, 9, 16, 25, 36, 49, etc.) that divides evenly into the given surd. Always start with half the given number and work backwards to get the biggest one possible.

Example 15

Simplify: $\sqrt{80}$

$$\sqrt{80} = \sqrt{16 \times 5}$$
$$= \sqrt{16} \times \sqrt{5}$$
$$= 4\sqrt{5}$$

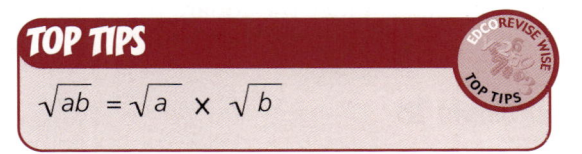

TOP TIPS

$\sqrt{ab} = \sqrt{a} \times \sqrt{b}$

Example 16

Simplify: $\sqrt{72}$

$$\sqrt{72} = \sqrt{36 \times 2}$$
$$= \sqrt{36} \times \sqrt{2}$$
$$= 6\sqrt{2}$$

Adding surds

As in algebra we can only add **like** surds.

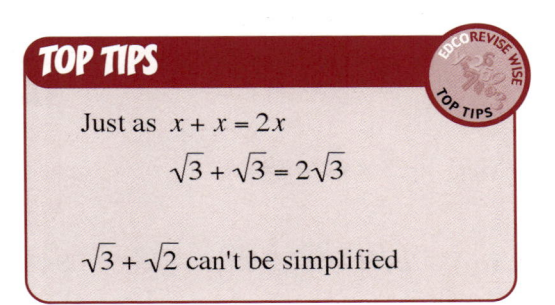

TOP TIPS

Just as $x + x = 2x$

$\sqrt{3} + \sqrt{3} = 2\sqrt{3}$

$\sqrt{3} + \sqrt{2}$ can't be simplified

Example 17

Simplify: $\sqrt{8} + \sqrt{12} + \sqrt{18}$

$\sqrt{8} + \sqrt{12} + \sqrt{18}$
$= \sqrt{4}\sqrt{2} + \sqrt{4}\sqrt{3} + \sqrt{9}\sqrt{2}$
$= 2\sqrt{2} + 2\sqrt{3} + 3\sqrt{2}$
$= 5\sqrt{2} + 2\sqrt{3}$

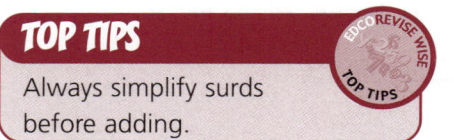

TOP TIPS
Always simplify surds before adding.

Multiplying surds

When multiplying a surd by a whole number, multiply the coefficient. Do not multiply under the square root. For example, $3\sqrt{2} \neq \sqrt{6}$

Example 18

Simplify: $3(2\sqrt{5} + \sqrt{2})$

$3(2\sqrt{5} + \sqrt{2})$
$= 6\sqrt{5} + 3\sqrt{2}$

When multiplying two surds, multiply under the square root and then simplify, if possible.

Example 19

Simplify: (i) $\sqrt{3} \times \sqrt{3}$ (ii) $\sqrt{3} \times \sqrt{2}$ (iii) $2\sqrt{5}(4\sqrt{2} - 3\sqrt{5})$

(i) $\sqrt{3} \times \sqrt{3} = \sqrt{9} = 3$

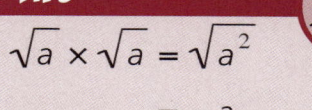

(ii) $\sqrt{3} \times \sqrt{2} = \sqrt{6}$

(iii) $2\sqrt{5}(4\sqrt{2} - 3\sqrt{5})\ =\ 8\sqrt{10} - 6\sqrt{25}$
$= 8\sqrt{10} - 30$

TOP TIPS
$\sqrt{a} \times \sqrt{a} = \sqrt{a^2}$
$\qquad\qquad = a$

Example 20

Simplify: $\sqrt{3}(2 - \sqrt{2} + 4\sqrt{6})$

$\sqrt{3}(2 - \sqrt{2} + 4\sqrt{6})$
$= 2\sqrt{3} - \sqrt{6} + 4\sqrt{18}$
$= 2\sqrt{3} - \sqrt{6} + 12\sqrt{2}$

$\sqrt{18} = \sqrt{9 \times 2}$
$= 3\sqrt{2}$

Example 21

Simplify: $\left(\sqrt{2} + \dfrac{1}{\sqrt{2}}\right)\left(\sqrt{2} - \dfrac{1}{\sqrt{2}}\right)$

$\left(\sqrt{2} + \dfrac{1}{\sqrt{2}}\right)\left(\sqrt{2} - \dfrac{1}{\sqrt{2}}\right) = \sqrt{4} - \dfrac{\sqrt{2}}{\sqrt{2}} + \dfrac{\sqrt{2}}{\sqrt{2}} - \dfrac{1}{\sqrt{4}}$

$= 2 - \dfrac{1}{2}$

$= \dfrac{3}{2}$

Example 22

Simplify: $(1 + \sqrt{7})^2$

$(1 + \sqrt{7})^2 = (1 + \sqrt{7})(1 + \sqrt{7})$
$= 1 + \sqrt{7} + \sqrt{7} + 7$
$= 8 + 2\sqrt{7}$

Example 23, Junior Certificate Paper 1, 2005

Simplify: $\sqrt{3}(2\sqrt{6} - 4\sqrt{3}) - \sqrt{10}(3\sqrt{5} - 2\sqrt{10})$

$$\sqrt{3}(2\sqrt{6} - 4\sqrt{3}) - \sqrt{10}(3\sqrt{5} - 2\sqrt{10})$$
$$= 2\sqrt{18} - 4\sqrt{9} - 3\sqrt{50} + 2\sqrt{100}$$
$$= 2(3\sqrt{2}) - 4(3) - 3(5\sqrt{2}) + 2(10)$$
$$= 6\sqrt{2} - 12 - 15\sqrt{2} + 20$$
$$= 8 - 9\sqrt{2}$$

Simplifying fractions

If the top and bottom have square roots, simplify first, then get the square root:

i.e. $\dfrac{\sqrt{a}}{\sqrt{b}} = \sqrt{\dfrac{a}{b}}$

Example 24

Simplify (i) $\dfrac{\sqrt{8}}{2}$ (ii) $\dfrac{5}{\sqrt{5}}$ (iii) $\dfrac{9}{\sqrt{3}}$

(i) $\dfrac{\sqrt{8}}{2} = \dfrac{\sqrt{8}}{\sqrt{4}} = \sqrt{\dfrac{8}{4}} = \sqrt{2}$

(ii) $\dfrac{5}{\sqrt{5}} = \dfrac{\sqrt{25}}{\sqrt{5}} = \sqrt{\dfrac{25}{5}} = \sqrt{5}$

(iii) $\dfrac{9}{\sqrt{3}} = \dfrac{\sqrt{81}}{\sqrt{3}} = \sqrt{\dfrac{81}{3}} = \sqrt{27} = 3\sqrt{3}$

TOP TIPS

When a whole number, x, appears, replace it with $\sqrt{x^2}$ so that the top and bottom are both surds.

When using the quadratic equation formula, you may have to simplify the answers.

$$x = \frac{-b \pm \sqrt{b^2 - 4ac}}{2a}$$

Example 25

Solve for x: $2x^2 - 2x - 1 = 0$

$a = 2, \ b = -2, \ c = -1$

$\sqrt{b^2 - 4ac} = \sqrt{(-2)^2 - 4(2)(-1)} = \sqrt{12} = 2\sqrt{3}$

$x = \dfrac{2 + 2\sqrt{3}}{4} \ or \ \dfrac{2 - 2\sqrt{3}}{4}$

$x = \dfrac{1 + \sqrt{3}}{2} \ or \ \dfrac{1 - \sqrt{3}}{2}$

TOP TIPS

Divide the top and bottom by 2.

Key Points

- When simplifying surds, look for the biggest square number that divides evenly into the given surd.
- When adding surds, only add like surds.
- When multiplying surds by a whole number, multiply the coefficient. Do not multiply under the square root.
- When multiplying two surds, multiply under the square root and then simplify, if possible.
- When simplifying fractions, if the top and bottom have square roots, simplify first, and then get the square root.

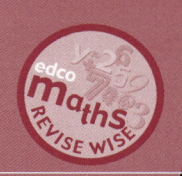

CHAPTER 5
Ratio and Proportion

Learning Objectives
- Ratio
- Direct proportion
- Inverse proportion.

Ratio

Example 1

Simplify the ratio $\dfrac{3}{4} : \dfrac{2}{5} : 1$

$$\dfrac{3}{4} : \dfrac{2}{5} : 1$$
$$= 15 : 8 : 20$$

TOP TIPS
We can multiply or divide every number in a ratio by the same number. In this case, multiply by 20, the common denominator.

Example 2

Simplify the ratio 50 cm : 2 metres

2 metres = 200 cm
50 : 200
= 1 : 4

TOP TIPS
The numbers in a ratio must be in the same unit of measure.

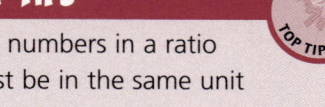

Example 3

The ratio A : B is 4 : 3. The ratio B : C is 2 : 5. Find the ratio A : C.

A	B	B	C
4	3	2	5

We need the same number in the B columns.

The LCM of 3 and 2 is 6, so multiply the first two numbers by 2 and the second two numbers by 3 to get 6 in both B columns.

A	B	B	C
8	6	6	15

Answer: 8 : 15

Example 4

Divide 144 in the ratio 1 : 3 : 5

$$144 \div 9 = 16$$

Now multiply each ratio by 16

Ratio	1	3	5	9
Number	16	48	80	144

TOP TIPS

Put the sum of the ratios here. When each number is divided by the ratio above it, the answer should be the same.

Example 5

When a sum of money is divided between Tom, Dick and Harry in the ratio 2 : 3 : 7, Dick receives €120. How much do Tom and Harry get?

$$120 \div 3 = 40$$

Now multiply each ratio by 40

	Tom	Dick	Harry
Ratio	2	3	7
Money	€80	€120	€280

Example 6

The time spent on homework by Mary and Kate is in the ratio 7 : 4. Mary spends 45 minutes more than Kate. How much time does each spend on their homework?

$$45 \div 3 = 15$$

Now multiply each ratio by 15

	Mary	Kate	Difference
Ratio	7	4	3
Money	105 mins.	60 mins.	45 mins.

TOP TIPS
Put the difference between the ratios here.

Direct proportion

Two quantities are in direct proportion, if dividing one by the other always gives the same answer. If one number is increased, so is the other.

As a result, cross-multiplying also gives the same answer.

Example 7

A car uses 4 litres of petrol on a journey of 32 km. How many litres would it use on a journey of 60 km, at the same rate?

Litres	Km
4	32
x	60

$32x = 240$

$x = \dfrac{240}{32} = 7 \cdot 5$ litres.

Example 8

Convert US$96 to euro if the exchange rate is €1 = US$1·28.

€	US$
1	1.28
x	96

$1 \cdot 28 x = 96$

$x = \dfrac{96}{1 \cdot 28} = 75$

Answer: €75

Example 9

If 15% of a number is 12, find 40% of the same number.

%	Number
15	12
40	x

$15x = 40 \times 12$

$x = \dfrac{40 \times 12}{15} = 32$

See Chapter 2 on percentages for alternative approaches to this type of problem.

Example 10

A hotel room costs €142 for four nights. How much would it cost for seven nights, at the same rate?

€	Nights
142	4
x	7

$4x = 142 \times 7$

$x = \dfrac{142 \times 7}{4} = 248 \cdot 5$

Answer: €248.50

Inverse proportion

Two quantities are in inverse proportion, if multiplying them always gives the same answer. If one number is increased, the other must be reduced.

Example 11

Five men can complete a job in 8 days. How long would it take four men, at the same rate of work?

Men	Days
5	8
4	x

$4x = 5 \times 8$

$x = \dfrac{5 \times 8}{4} = 10$

TOP TIPS

When numbers in the same row are multiplied, the answer is the same.

Answer: 10 days

Example 12

When a prize is shared between six winners, each one receives €120. If there had been five winners, how much would each get?

Winners	Share
6	€120
5	x

$5x = 6 \times 120$

$x = \dfrac{6 \times 120}{5} = 144$

Answer: €144

Key Points

- The numbers in a ratio must be in the same unit of measure.
- We can multiply or divide every number in a ratio by the same number.
- Two quantities are in direct proportion, if dividing one by the other always gives the same answer. As one gets bigger, so does the other.
- Two quantities are in inverse proportion, if multiplying them always gives the same answer. If one gets bigger, the other gets smaller.

CHAPTER 6
Sets

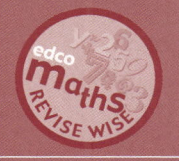

●●● Learning Objectives
- Set symbols
- Listing elements of sets
- Venn diagrams with two sets
- Two-set problems
- Venn diagrams with three sets
- Three-set problems.

Set Symbols

$\in$	'is an element of'
$\notin$	'is not an element of'
$\subset$	'is a subset of'
$\not\subset$	'is not a subset of'
$\emptyset$ or { }	The empty set.
$A \cap B$	**A intersection B:** the set of elements of A that are also in B.
$A \cup B$	**A union B:** a set formed by joining A and B together, without repeating any element.
$A \setminus B$	**A not B:** the set of elements that are in A but are not in B.
#A	**The cardinal number of A:** the amount of elements in the set A.
A'	**The complement of A:** the set of elements that are in the universal set but are not in A.

Listing elements of sets

When listing the elements of a set, put the elements between chain brackets and separate them with commas.

Example 1

$U = \{1,2,3,4,5,6,7,8,9\}$, $A = \{1,3,5,7,9\}$, $B = \{2,3,4,5,6,7\}$ and $C = \{2,4,5,7,8,9\}$.
List the elements of the following sets:

(i) $A \cap B$
(ii) $(B \cup C) \setminus A$
(iii) $C \setminus (A \cap B)$

(iv) $(A \cup C) \cap B$
(v) $[B \cup (A \setminus C)]'$

Solution:

(i) $A \cap B = \{3,5,7\}$ — the elements that are in both sets

(ii) $B \cup C = \{2,3,4,5,6,7,8,9\}$ $\Rightarrow$ $(B \cup C) \setminus A = \{2,4,6,8\}$
— the elements of $B \cup C$ that are not in A

(iii) $C \setminus (A \cap B) = \{2,4,8,9\}$ — the elements of C that are not in $(A \cap B)$

(iv) $A \cup C = \{1,2,3,4,5,7,8,9\}$ $\Rightarrow$ $(A \cup C) \cap B = \{2,3,4,5,7\}$
— the elements of $A \cup C$ that are also in B

(v) $A \setminus C = \{1,3\}$. $B \cup (A \setminus C) = \{1,2,3,4,5,6,7\}$

$[B \cup (A \setminus C)]' = \{8,9\}$

Venn diagrams with two sets

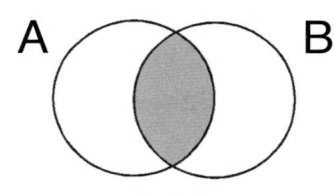

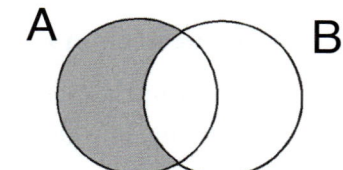

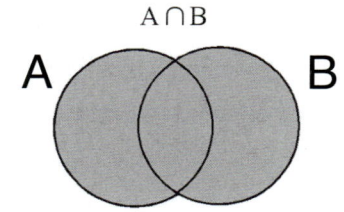

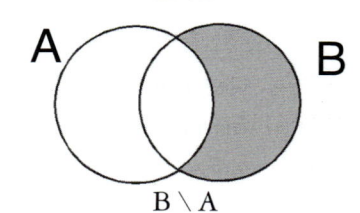

$A \cap B$

$A \setminus B$

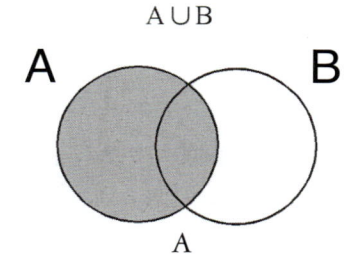

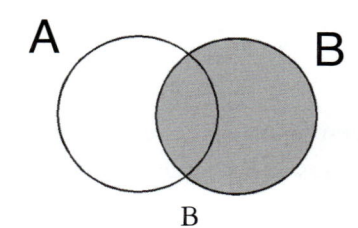

$A \cup B$

$B \setminus A$

A

B

The universal set, U, contains every element that appears in a given question. It is represented on a Venn diagram by a rectangle.

The complement of a set A, written A′, is the set of elements in the universal set that are not in A.

When the universal set is involved, you may be asked to shade the complement of a set. In this case, shade everything **outside** the set.

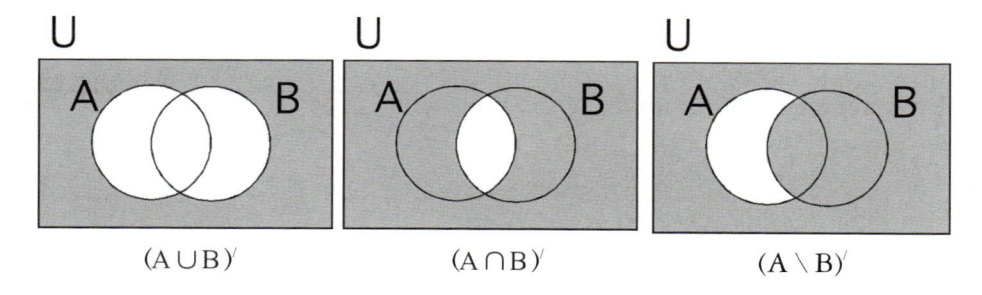

(A ∪ B)′   (A ∩ B)′   (A \ B)′

Two-set problems

Example 2

A group of 30 people were asked if they had a sports channel or a movie channel on their television. Eight people had a sports channel, 12 people had a movie channel and 16 had neither. Show this information on a Venn diagram and calculate how many had both.

Let x represent the number of people who have both.

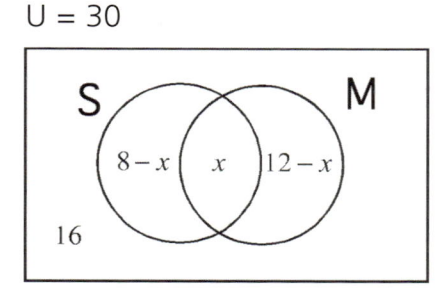

The numbers in the diagram must add up to 30:

$8 - x + x + 12 - x + 16 = 30$
$\qquad 36 - x = 30$
$\qquad 36 - 30 = x$
$\qquad\qquad 6 = x$

U = 30

Example 3

In a survey of geography students, 50 said they had visited the Giant's Causeway and 38 had visited the Aillwee Caves. Three people had visited neither.

What is:
(i) The greatest number that could have been surveyed?
(ii) The smallest number that could have been surveyed?

Let x represent the number of people who visited both.

The total number surveyed is:
$50 - x + x + 38 - x + 3$
$= 91 - x$

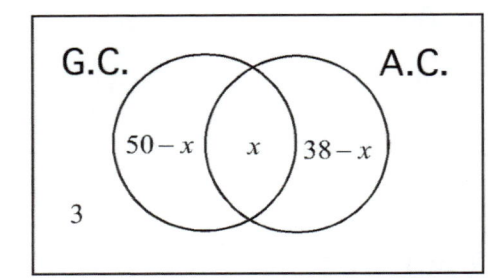

The smallest value that x can have is 0, in which case the number surveyed is 91. The biggest value that x can have is 38 (the smaller of 38 and 50), in which case the total number surveyed is $91 - 38 = 53$.

Answer: (i) 91 (ii) 53

Example 4

$\#A = 7, \#B = 12, \#(A \cap B) = x, \#\left[(A \cup B)'\right] = 0$ and $\#U = u$

Represent this information on an Argand diagram and find the possible values for u.

$u = 7 - x + x = 12 - x$
$u = 19 - x$

Therefore, as x gets bigger, u gets smaller. The smallest value that x can have is 0.
$\Rightarrow \quad u = 19 - 0$
$\quad\quad u = 19$

The biggest value that x can have is 7, the smaller of 7 and 12:
$\Rightarrow \quad u = 19 - 7$
$\quad\quad u = 12$

Therefore, the values of u are always between 12 and 19. The following diagrams demonstrate some possibilities:

U=19

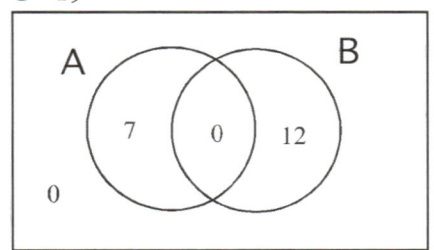

A: 7, A∩B: 0, B: 12, outside: 0

U=17

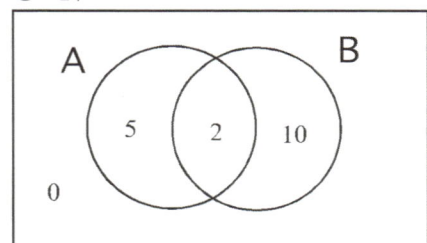

A: 5, A∩B: 2, B: 10, outside: 0

U=14

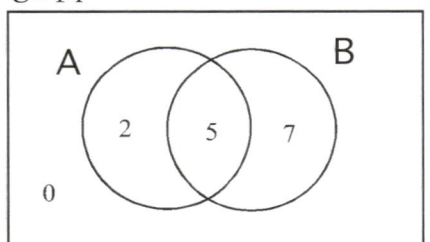

A: 2, A∩B: 5, B: 7, outside: 0

U=12

A: 0, A∩B: 7, B: 5, outside: 0

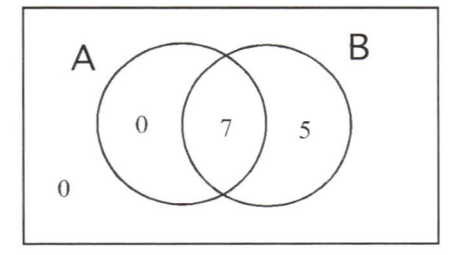

Example 5

$\#A = 7$, $\#B = 12$, $\#(A \cap B) = x$, $\#\left[(A \cup B)\right]' = y$ and $\#U = u$

Represent this information on an Argand diagram and find the possible values for u.

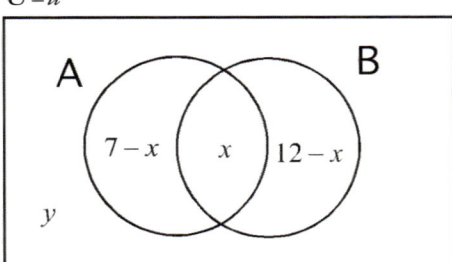

$u = 7 - x + x + 12 - x + y$
$u = 19 + y - x$

When $x = 0$, $u = 19 + y$
When $x = 7$, $u = 12 + y$

In this case, u could have any value between $12 + y$ and $19 + y$.

U=u

A: $7-x$, A∩B: x, B: $12-x$, outside: y

47

Example 6

$\#A = a$, $\#B = b$, $\#(A \cap B) = x$, $\#\left[(A \cup B)'\right] = y$ and $\#U = u$. $b > a$.

Represent this information on an Argand diagram. Show that the smallest value that u can have is $b + y$ and the biggest value that u can have is $a + b + y$.

$u = a - x + x + b - x + y$

$u = a + b + y - x$

Since x cannot be negative, the smallest possible value of x is 0.

When $x = 0$, $u = a + b + y$.

Since $b > a$, the biggest value that x can have is a.

When $x = a$, $u = b + y$

Therefore, $b + y \leq u \leq a + b + y$

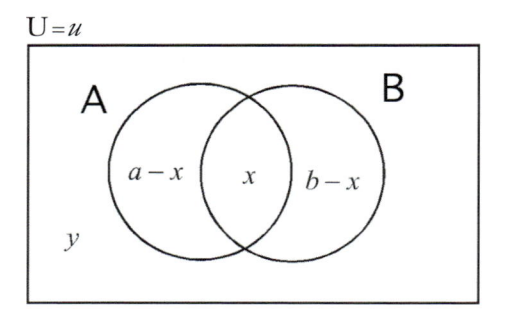

Venn diagrams with three sets

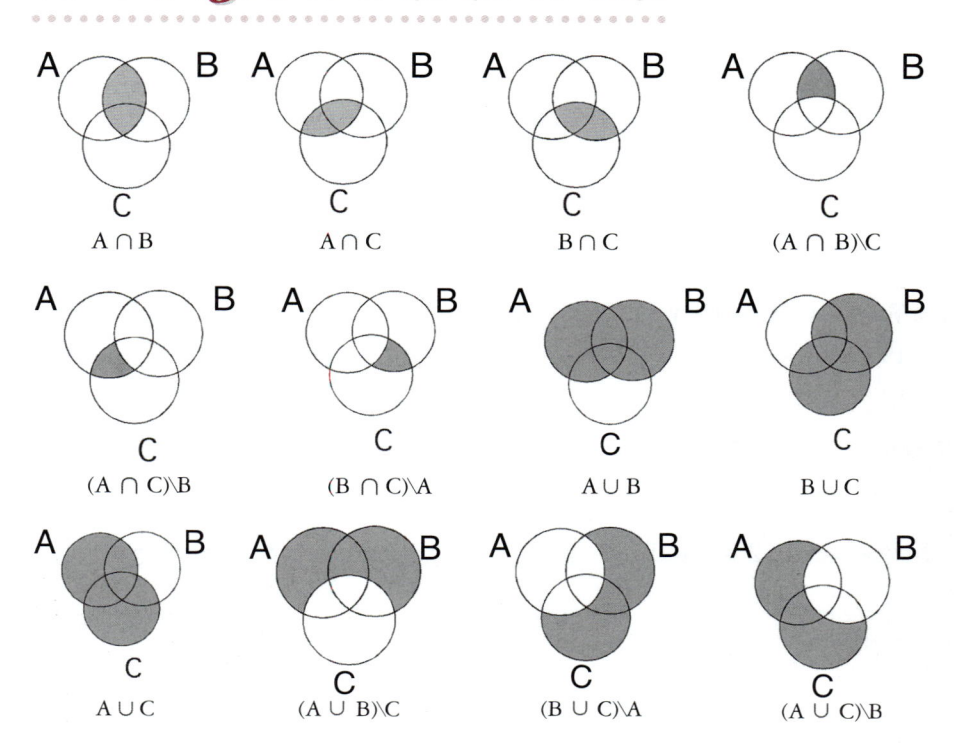

$A \cap B$

$A \cap C$

$B \cap C$

$(A \cap B)\backslash C$

$(A \cap C)\backslash B$

$(B \cap C)\backslash A$

$A \cup B$

$B \cup C$

$A \cup C$

$(A \cup B)\backslash C$

$(B \cup C)\backslash A$

$(A \cup C)\backslash B$

A \ (B ∪ C)

B \ (A ∪ C)

C \ (A ∪ B)

A \ C

A \ B

B \ A

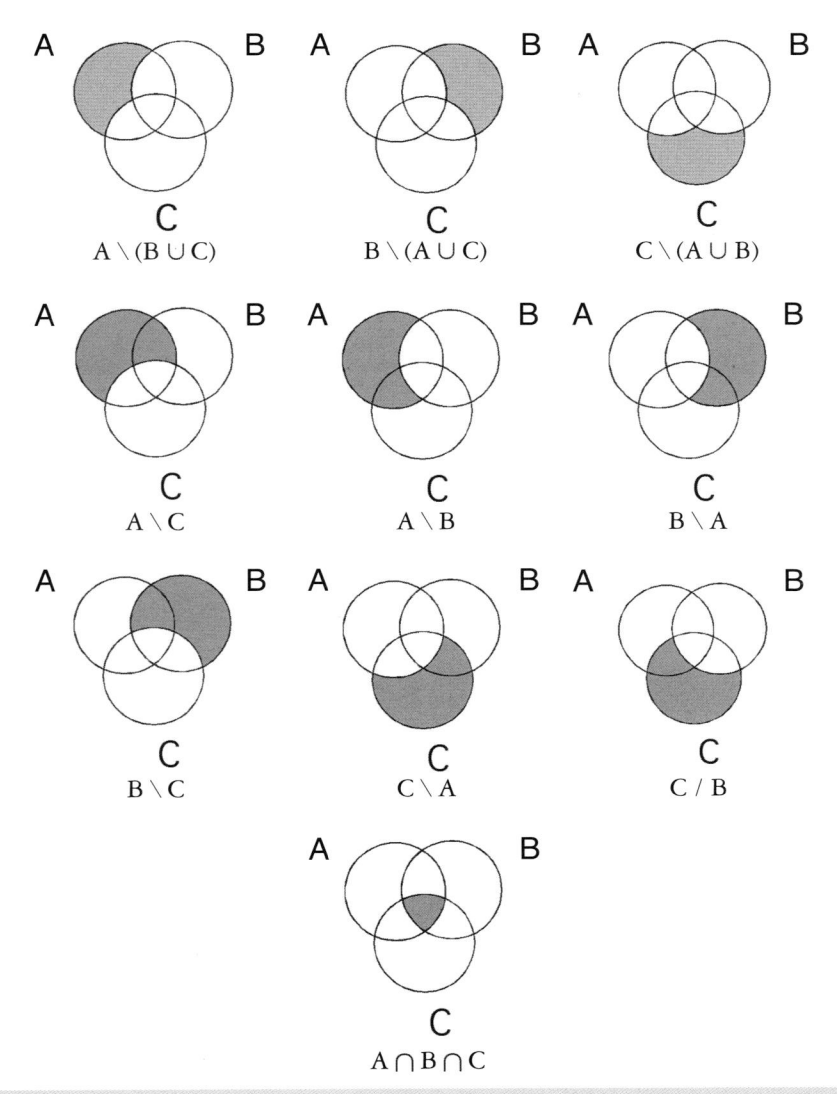

B \ C

C \ A

C / B

A ∩ B ∩ C

When the universal set is involved, you may be asked to shade the complement of a set. In this case, shade everything **outside** the set.

For example:

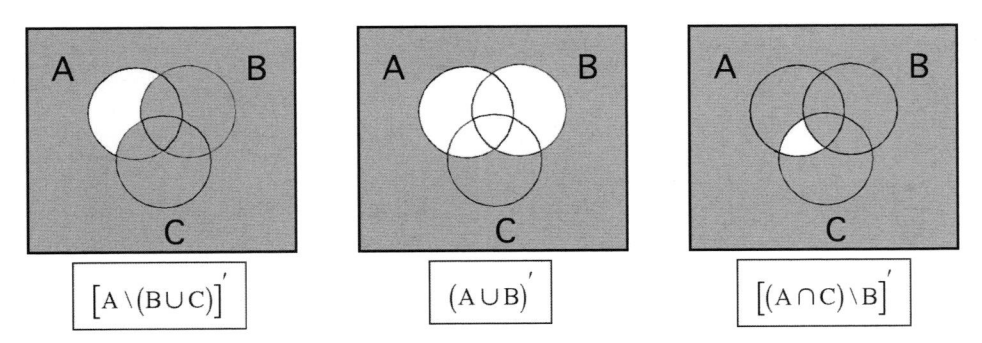

$[A \setminus (B \cup C)]'$

$(A \cup B)'$

$[(A \cap C) \setminus B]'$

Three-set problems

Example 7

Thirty students were asked if they played basketball, soccer or tennis. Everyone played at least one of the sports: 21 played soccer, 10 tennis and 16 basketball. Ten played soccer and basketball. Two played soccer and tennis but not basketball. Four played all three.

Show this information on an Argand diagram and calculate the number who played basketball and tennis but not soccer.

Solution:

Let x be the number who played tennis and basketball but not soccer.

The number in the tennis circle must add up to 10, therefore the number who played tennis only is $4 - x$.

$(4 - x + 2 + 4 + x = 10)$

$U = 30$

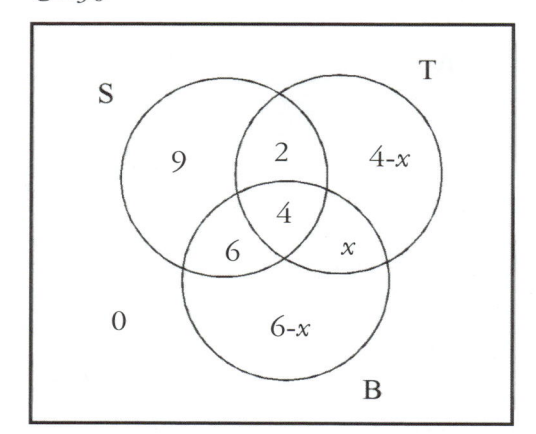

[Venn diagram with three circles S, T, B showing: S only = 9, S∩T only = 2, T only = 4−x, S∩B only = 6, S∩T∩B = 4, T∩B only = x, B only = 6−x, outside = 0]

Similarly, the numbers in the basketball circle add up to 16, so the number who plays basketball only is $6 - x$.

All the numbers in the diagram add up to 30, therefore:

$$31 - x = 30$$
$$31 - 30 = x$$
$$1 = x$$

Example 8

Thirty-seven people were asked if they had visited Scotland, Wales or England.

Sixteen had visited Scotland, 14 had been to Wales and 13 to England. Seven had been to both Scotland and Wales, 8 had visited both Scotland and England and 3 had visited both England and Wales.

The number who had been to none of the countries is five times the number who had visited all three.

Show this information on an Argand diagram and find out how many had visited all three countries.

Solution:

Let x be the number who visited all three countries. Then $5x$ is the number who visited none.
Since 7 people visited both Scotland and Wales, the number who visited Scotland and Wales but not England is $7 - x$.

Similarly, the number who visited Scotland and England but not Wales is $8 - x$ and the number who visited Wales and England but not Scotland is $3 - x$.

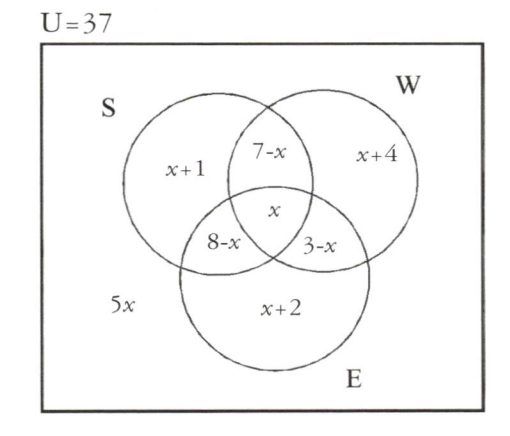

The number who visited Scotland only is $\quad 16 - (15 - x) = x + 1$

The number who visited Wales only is $\quad 14 - (10 - x) = x + 4$

The number who visited England only is $\quad 13 - (11 - x) = x + 2$

The sum of all the numbers in the diagram is 37.

Therefore,
$$9x - 3x + 25 = 37$$
$$6x = 12$$
$$x = 2$$

Key Points

- When listing the elements of a set, put the elements between chain brackets and separate them with commas.
- The universal set U contains every element that appears in a given question. It is represented on a Venn diagram by a rectangle.
- The complement of a set A, written A' is the set of elements in the universal set that are not in A.
- When asked to shade the complement of a set, shade everything outside the set.
- $\#(A \cup B) = \#A + \#B - \#(A \cap B)$
- If $\#A$ and $\#B$ have fixed values, the maximum value for $\#(A \cup B)$ is when $\#(A \cap B) = 0$. The minimum value for $\#(A \cup B)$ is when $\#(A \cap B)$ has its biggest possible value.
- The biggest value for $\#(A \cap B)$ is either $\#A$ or $\#B$, whichever is smaller.
- When completing Venn diagrams with three sets begin with $A \cap B \cap C$ if it is given, and work outwards.
- $\#A$ is the total of all the numbers inside the set A.
- $\#(A \cap B)$ must not be confused with $\#(A \cap B) \backslash C$.

CHAPTER 7
Algebra 1: Simplify, Factorise and Evaluate

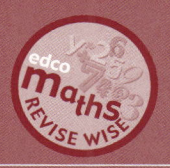

●●● Learning Objectives

- Simplify
- Factorise:
  - Taking out a common factor
  - Grouping to get a common factor
  - Quadratics
  - The difference of two squares
- Evaluate.

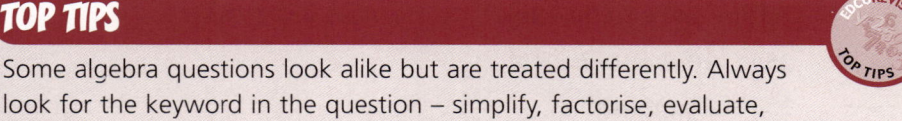

TOP TIPS
Some algebra questions look alike but are treated differently. Always look for the keyword in the question – simplify, factorise, evaluate, etc.

Simplify

Simplify means:
1 Remove brackets
2 Add like terms.

Example 1

Simplify: $3x - 2x(x - 2)$

$$3x - 2x(x - 2)$$
$$= 3x - 2x^2 + 4x$$
$$= 7x - 2x^2$$

TOP TIPS
Like terms must not be added until the brackets have been removed.

Example 2

Simplify: $(3x-2)(x^2-5x+2)$

$$(3x-2)(x^2-5x+2)$$
$$= 3x(x^2-5x+2) - 2(x^2-5x+2)$$
$$= 3x^3 - 15x^2 + 6x - 2x^2 + 10x - 4$$
$$= 3x^3 - 17x^2 + 16x - 4$$

TOP TIPS

Remember to change all signs in this bracket when multiplying by a negative number.

Example 3

Simplify: $(5a-2b)^2$

$$(5a-2b)^2$$
$$= 5a(5a-2b) - 2b(5a-2b)$$
$$= 25a^2 - 10ab - 10ab + 4b^2$$
$$= 25a^2 - 20ab + 4b^2$$

TOP TIPS

Don't take shortcuts for a problem like this – you will make mistakes!

Example 4

Simplify: $6x^2 - (x+4)(3x-1)$

$$6x^2 - (x+4)(3x-1)$$
$$= 6x^2 - x(3x-1) - 4(3x-1)$$
$$= 6x^2 - 3x^2 + x - 12x + 4$$
$$= 3x^2 - 11x + 4$$

TOP TIPS

Notice that the minus sign before the brackets changes **both** signs in the first bracket.

Example 5

Simplify: $5(3x-1)(x+2)$

$$5(3x-1)(x+2)$$
$$= (15x-5)(x+2)$$
$$= 15x(x+2) - 5(x+2)$$
$$= 15x^2 + 30x - 5x - 10$$
$$= 15x^2 + 25x - 10$$

TOP TIPS

Notice that we multiply the first bracket only, by 5. We then multiply the second bracket by the answer.

Example 6

Simplify: $(-3xy)(2x^2)(5y^3)$

$$(-3xy)(2x^2)(5y^3)$$
$$= -30x^3y^4$$

TOP TIPS

Don't confuse this problem with the previous examples that have two terms in a bracket. If there is only one term in each bracket, there is only one term in the answer.

Example 7

Simplify: $(x+1)^2 - (1-x)^2$

$$(x+1)^2 - (1-x)^2$$
$$= x^2 + 2x + 1 - (1 - 2x + x^2)$$
$$= x^2 + 2x + 1 - 1 + 2x - x^2$$
$$= 4x$$

TOP TIPS

Keep the bracket here because of the minus sign before the bracket.

Factorise

When simplifying, we have seen that brackets are removed. When we factorise we create brackets that when multiplied will give the terms in the question.

> There are four different methods used to factorise:
> 1 **Common factor** – any number of terms
> 2 **Grouping to get a common factor** – usually four terms
> 3 **Quadratics** – always three terms
> 4 **Difference of two squares** – always two terms.

Taking out a common factor

Always look for a common factor first. If there is none, then we will know from the number of terms which method to use.

Example 8

Factorise: $3x^2 - 6x^3$

$$3x^2 - 6x^3$$
$$= 3x^2(1 - 2x)$$

TOP TIPS

The highest common factor (HCF) is $3x^2$.

Example 9

Factorise: $x^2y^2 - x^3y^3 - xy^2$

$$x^2y^2 - x^3y^3 - xy^2$$
$$= xy^2(x - x^2y - 1)$$

TOP TIPS

Use the lowest index that appears on each letter when choosing the highest common factor.

Example 10

Factorise: $a(b-c) + c(b-c)$

$$a(b-c) + c(b-c)$$
$$= (b-c)(a+c)$$

TOP TIPS

The highest common factor is $(b - c)$.

Grouping, to get a common factor

Example 11

Factorise: $x^2 - xy - x + y$

$$x^2 - xy - x + y$$
$$= x(x - y) - 1(x - y)$$
$$= (x - y)(x - 1)$$

TOP TIPS

In line 2 the common factor is in the bracket $(x - y)$. The contents of the brackets must be identical if there is to be a common factor.

CHAPTER 7: ALGEBRA 1: SIMPLIFY, FACTORISE AND EVALUATE

Example 12

Factorise: $a^2b - 2dc - ac + 2abd$

$\quad a^2b - 2dc - ac + 2abd$
$=\quad a^2b - ac + 2abd - 2dc$
$=\quad a(ab - c) + 2d(ab - c)$
$=\quad (ab - c)(a + 2d)$

TOP TIPS

Change the order so that the first two terms have a common factor. Remember that the brackets must be identical.

Example 13

Factorise: $a(b - c) - b(c - b)$

$\quad a(b - c) - b(c - b)$
$=\quad a(b - c) + b(b - c)$
$=\quad (b - c)(a + b)$

TOP TIPS

The second bracket contains the same letters as the first but both signs are different. We can change the signs inside a bracket if we also change the sign before the bracket.

Example 14, Junior Certificate 2005

Factorise: $3p - c + 3pc - c^2$

$\quad 3p - c + 3pc - c^2$
$=\quad 3p + 3pc - c - c^2$
$=\quad 3p(1 + c) - c(1 + c)$
$=\quad (1 + c)(3p - c)$

Quadratics

Example 15

Factorise: $2x^2 + 11x + 12$

These must give $2x^2$ when they are multiplied → $2x$ and x (from $2x^2$)

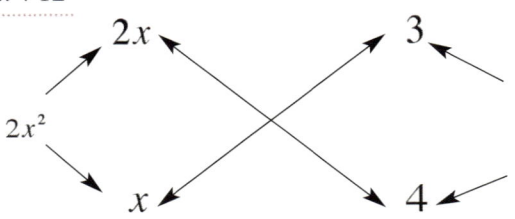

These numbers must give $+12$ when they are multiplied → 3 and 4

When you cross-multiply and add, you should get $+11x$: $8x + 3x = +11x$

Answer: $(2x + 3)(x + 4)$

Example 16

Factorise: $2x^2 - 5x - 12$

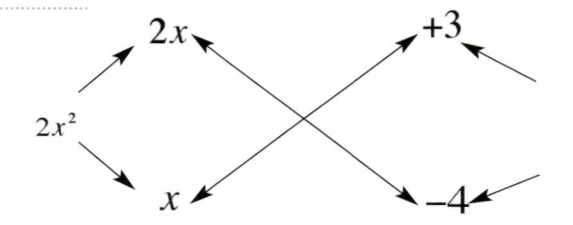

These must give $2x^2$ when they are multiplied

$2x^2$ → $2x$, x

These numbers must give -12 when they are multiplied

$+3$, -4

When you cross-multiply and add, you should get $-5x$: $-8x + 3x = -5x$

Answer: $(2x + 3)(x - 4)$

Alternative method for factorising quadratics

The following is an alternative method for factorising quadratics where we convert the problem to four terms and use grouping to get a common factor.

Example 17, Junior Certificate 2005

Factorise: $3x^2 + 8x - 3$

$$3x^2 + 8x - 3$$
$$= 3x^2 + 9x - 1x - 3$$
$$= 3x(x + 3) - 1(x + 3)$$
$$= (x + 3)(3x - 1)$$

TOP TIPS

The idea is to split $8x$ into two parts using numbers that have the same product as the end numbers.

$3(-3) = -9$ We must use $+9$ and -1 rather
$9(-1) = -9$ than -9 and $+1$ so that they give $+8$ when added.

Example 18

Factorise: $12x^2 + x - 6$

$$12x^2 + x - 6$$
$$= 12x^2 + 9x - 8x - 6$$
$$= 3x(4x + 3) - 2(4x + 3)$$
$$= (4x + 3)(3x - 2)$$

TOP TIPS

$12(-6) = -72$
$9(-8) = -72$
and $+9 - 8 = +1$

Example 19, Junior Certificate 2004

Factorise: $6x^2 - 7x - 24$

$$\begin{aligned} & 6x^2 - 7x - 24 \\ = \ & 6x^2 - 16x + 9x - 24 \\ = \ & 2x(3x - 8) + 3(3x - 8) \\ = \ & (3x - 8)(2x + 3) \end{aligned}$$

TOP TIPS

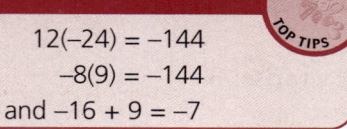

$12(-24) = -144$
$-8(9) = -144$
and $-16 + 9 = -7$

The method is particularly useful in a problem like this one where the end numbers are not prime numbers. Because 24 has lots of factors, the first method can take a long time.

Difference of two squares

Example 20

Factorise: $4x^2 - 9y^2$

$$\begin{aligned} & 4x^2 - 9y^2 \\ = \ & (2x - 3y)(2x + 3y) \end{aligned}$$

TOP TIPS

There is no common factor. This is the difference of two squares so we use the formula:
$a^2 - b^2 = (a - b)(a + b)$

Example 21

Factorise: $x^2 - (5y - 2x)^2$

$$\begin{aligned} & x^2 - (5y - 2x)^2 \\ = \ & [x - (5y - 2x)][x + (5y - 2x)] \\ = \ & (x - 5y + 2x)(x + 5y - 2x) \\ = \ & (3x - 5y)(5y - x) \end{aligned}$$

TOP TIPS

Difference of two squares again. The square brackets are not needed when the round brackets are removed.

Sometimes there is a common factor followed by another method. Watch out for a clue. The question should say: factorise **fully**.

Example 22

Factorise: $3x^2 - 12y^2$

$$3x^2 - 12y^2$$
$$= 3(x^2 - 4y^2)$$
$$= 3(x - 2y)(x + 2y)$$

TOP TIPS

Here the common factor is followed by the difference of two squares.

Always read the question carefully. The following problem involves the difference of two squares but you are not asked to factorise!

Example 23, Junior Certificate 2005

Simplify: $(2x - 1)^2 - (x - 1)^2$

$$(2x - 1)^2 - (x - 1)^2$$
$$= 4x^2 - 4x + 1 - (x^2 - 2x + 1)$$
$$= 4x^2 - 4x + 1 - x^2 + 2x - 1$$
$$= 3x^2 - 2x$$

Evaluate

To evaluate an expression is to replace the variables (letters) with numbers and then reduce what you get to a single number.

To evaluate an expression:
1 Replace each letter with a number in a bracket
2 Now use the calculator.

Example 24

Evaluate: $-3x^2 y$ if $x = -1$ and $y = 3$

$$-3x^2 y$$
$$= -3(-1)^2(3)$$
$$= -9$$

CHAPTER 7: ALGEBRA 1: SIMPLIFY, FACTORISE AND EVALUATE

Example 25

Evaluate: $2x(x-4y)^3$ if $x = 3$ and $y = -2$

$2x(x-4y)^3$

$2(3)[(3) - 4(-2)]^3 = 7986$

TOP TIPS

Existing brackets are replaced by square brackets to avoid confusion. The same key is used on the calculator for both a round bracket and a square bracket.

Example 26, Junior Certificate 2004

Evaluate: $\dfrac{2x+1}{4} - \dfrac{3x-4}{3}$, when $x = \dfrac{1}{2}$

Express your answer in the form $\dfrac{a}{b}$, where $a, b \in \mathbb{N}$.

$$= \dfrac{2x+1}{4} - \dfrac{3x-4}{3}$$

$$= \dfrac{2(\tfrac{1}{2})+1}{4} - \dfrac{3(\tfrac{1}{2})-4}{3} = \dfrac{2}{4} - \dfrac{(-2\tfrac{1}{2})}{3}$$

$$= \dfrac{1}{2} + \dfrac{5}{6}$$

$$= \dfrac{4}{3}$$

Key Points

- When simplifying an expression, remove the brackets and add like terms.
- When factorising an expression, create brackets that when multiplied will give the terms in the question.
- There are four ways to factorise: common factor, grouping to get a common factor, quadratics, and the difference of two squares.
- Always look for a common factor first. There may be a common factor no matter how many terms are in the question.
- Grouping can be used to get a common factor. This type of problem usually has four terms.
- Quadratics always have three terms.
- The difference of two squares always has two terms.
- When evaluating an expression, replace the variables (letters) with numbers and then use the calculator to reduce what you get to a single number.

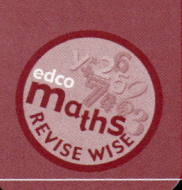

CHAPTER 8
Algebra 2: Fractions

●●● Learning Objectives
- Simplifying fractions
- Multiplying / dividing fractions
- Adding / subtracting fractions.

Simplifying fractions

The first step is to factorise the top and bottom, if necessary, to see if they have a common factor. If they do, then we divide the top and bottom by the highest common factor.

Example 1

Simplify $\dfrac{3x^2 y^3 z}{6xy^4}$

The top and bottom are products, so there is no need to factorise. The highest common factor is $3xy^3$. Divide the top and bottom by this number.

$$\dfrac{3x^2 y^3 z}{6xy^4} = \dfrac{3xy^3(xz)}{3xy^3(2y)}$$
$$= \dfrac{xz}{2y}$$

TOP TIPS
Never cancel in a fraction before factorising.

Example 2

Simplify $\dfrac{2x^2 + 5x - 3}{4x^2 - 1}$

The top and bottom are sums, so we must begin by factorising.

$$\dfrac{2x^2 + 5x - 3}{4x^2 - 1}$$
$$= \dfrac{(2x-1)(2x+3)}{(2x-1)(2x+1)}$$
$$= \dfrac{2x+3}{2x+1}$$

TOP TIPS
The highest common factor is $2x - 1$. Divide the top and bottom by this number.

Multiplying fractions

If the top or bottom are sums, begin by factorising.

We then multiply the top by the top and the bottom by the bottom and simplify, if possible.

Example 3

Simplify $\dfrac{3x^2y}{4z} \times \dfrac{2x^2z^2}{y^3}$

$\quad \dfrac{3x^2y}{4z} \times \dfrac{2x^2z^2}{y^3}$

$= \dfrac{6x^4yz^2}{4y^3z}$

$= \dfrac{2yz(3x^4z)}{2yz(2y^2)}$

$= \dfrac{3x^4z}{2y^2}$

Example 4

Simplify $\dfrac{x^2 - 3x}{x+1} \times \dfrac{x^2 + 2x + 1}{x^2 - 9}$

The top and bottom are sums, so we will begin by factorising.

$\dfrac{x^2 - 3x}{x+1} \times \dfrac{x^2 + 2x + 1}{x^2 - 9} = \dfrac{x(x-3)}{(x+1)} \times \dfrac{(x+1)(x+1)}{(x-3)(x+3)}$

$\phantom{\dfrac{x^2 - 3x}{x+1} \times \dfrac{x^2 + 2x + 1}{x^2 - 9}} = \dfrac{x(x-3)(x+1)(x+1)}{(x+1)(x-3)(x+3)}$

$\phantom{\dfrac{x^2 - 3x}{x+1} \times \dfrac{x^2 + 2x + 1}{x^2 - 9}} = \dfrac{x(x+1)}{x+3}$

Dividing fractions

Turn the fraction on the right (the divisor) upside down, then multiply.

Example 5

Simplify $\dfrac{4x^2 - 2x}{x + 1} \div \dfrac{4x^2 - 1}{x^2 - 2x - 3}$

$$\dfrac{4x^2 - 2x}{x + 1} \div \dfrac{4x^2 - 1}{x^2 - 2x - 3}$$

$$= \dfrac{4x^2 - 2x}{x + 1} \times \dfrac{x^2 - 2x - 3}{4x^2 - 1}$$

$$= \dfrac{2x(2x-1)}{(x+1)} \times \dfrac{(x-3)(x+1)}{(2x+1)(2x-1)}$$

$$= \dfrac{2x(x-3)}{2x+1}$$

Adding / subtracting fractions

To add or subtract fractions we need a common denominator, i.e. the bottom numbers must be the same.

Example 6

Simplify $\dfrac{2x+1}{3} + \dfrac{3x-1}{4}$

The common denominator is 12.

$$\dfrac{2x+1}{3} + \dfrac{3x-1}{4}$$

$$= \dfrac{4(2x+1) + 3(3x-1)}{12}$$

$$= \dfrac{8x + 4 + 9x - 3}{12}$$

$$= \dfrac{17x + 1}{12}$$

TOP TIPS

The brackets on top are very important.

Example 7

Simplify $\dfrac{2}{x+1} - \dfrac{3}{x-4}$

$\dfrac{2}{x+1} - \dfrac{3}{x-4}$

$= \dfrac{2(x-4) - 3(x+1)}{(x+1)(x-4)}$

$= \dfrac{2x - 8 - 3x - 3}{(x+1)(x-4)}$

$= \dfrac{-x - 11}{(x+1)(x-4)}$

> **TOP TIPS**
>
> Do not 'cancel' in your answer unless there is a common factor on top and bottom.

Key Points

- When simplifying fractions, factorise the top and bottom to see if they have a common factor. Then divide the top and bottom by the highest common factor.
- When multiplying fractions, if the top or bottom are sums, factorise them. Then multiply the top by the top and the bottom by the bottom and simplify, if possible.
- To divide fractions, turn the divisor upside down and multiply.
- When adding or subtracting fractions, a common denominator is needed.

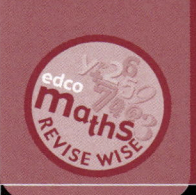

CHAPTER 9
Algebra 3: Solving Equations

Learning Objectives
- Simple equations
- Quadratic equations solved by factors
- Quadratic equations solved by formula
- Rational equations
- Simultaneous equations in two variables.

Equations

Equations are easy to recognise – there is an equal sign (=) in the question and you will be asked to solve for some variable (letter). This means that you must find out what number the variable represents.

There are five different types of equation to consider.

1 Simple equations

How to recognise them:
- There is only one variable involved
- There are no indices
- If there are fractions, the variable will usually be on top.

> How to solve them:
> 1. **Remove fractions**, if they appear
> 2. **Remove brackets**, if they appear
> 3. **Simplify** each side by adding like terms
> 4. **'Switch sides'** so that the terms which involve letters are on one side and the numbers are on the other side
> 5. **Simplify** again
> 6. **Divide** both sides by the number before the letter.

Example 1

Solve for x: $\dfrac{2x-1}{3} - 4 = \dfrac{3(x-2)}{2} + x - 5$

$$\dfrac{(2x-1)}{3} - \dfrac{(4)}{1} = \dfrac{3(x-2)}{2} + \dfrac{(x-5)}{1}$$

$$2(2x-1) - 6(4) = 9(x-2) + 6(x-5)$$

$$4x - 2 - 24 = 9x - 18 + 6x - 30$$

$$4x - 26 = 15x - 48$$

$$-26 + 48 = 15x - 4x$$

$$22 = 11x$$

$$\dfrac{22}{11} = \dfrac{11x}{11}$$

$$2 = x$$

TOP TIPS

In order to remove fractions accurately, it is best to write each term as a fraction with a bracket on top.

TOP TIPS

To remove the fractions, multiply each fraction by 6, the common denominator. To do this, divide each bottom number into 6 and multiply the answer, outside the bracket, on top.

TOP TIPS

When switching sides, keep the letters on the side that has the bigger number before x. Don't forget to change the signs of the terms you move.

2 Quadratic equations solved by factors

How to recognise them:
- There is only one letter involved
- At least one term will contain that letter squared.

How to solve them:
1. **Remove fractions**, if they appear
2. **Remove brackets**, if they appear
3. **Simplify** each side by adding like terms
4. **'Switch sides'** so that that all terms are together with the squared term positive
5. If possible, **divide** each term by the same number
6. **Factorise**
7. **Put each factor equal to zero** (= 0) and solve the resulting simple equations.

Example 2

Solve for x: $12x^2 - 2 = 5x$

$$12x^2 - 2 = 5x$$
$$12x^2 - 5x - 2 = 0$$
$$(3x - 2)(4x + 1) = 0$$

$3x - 2 = 0$	or	$4x + 1 = 0$
$3x = 2$		$4x = -1$
$x = \dfrac{2}{3}$		$x = -\dfrac{1}{4}$

TOP TIPS
If a product is equal to zero, then one of the factors must be zero.

TOP TIPS
If the answer is a fraction, the number before x is always on the bottom.

A quadratic equation usually produces two different solutions but will produce two identical solutions if the two factors are identical.

Example 3

Solve for x: $3x^2 = 4x$

$$3x^2 - 4x = 0$$
$$x(3x - 4) = 0$$

$x = 0$	or	$3x - 4 = 0$
		$3x = 4$
		$x = \dfrac{4}{3}$

TOP TIPS
Get all terms on one side.

TOP TIPS
Take out x as a common factor.

Example 4

Solve for x: $2x^2 - 18 = 0$

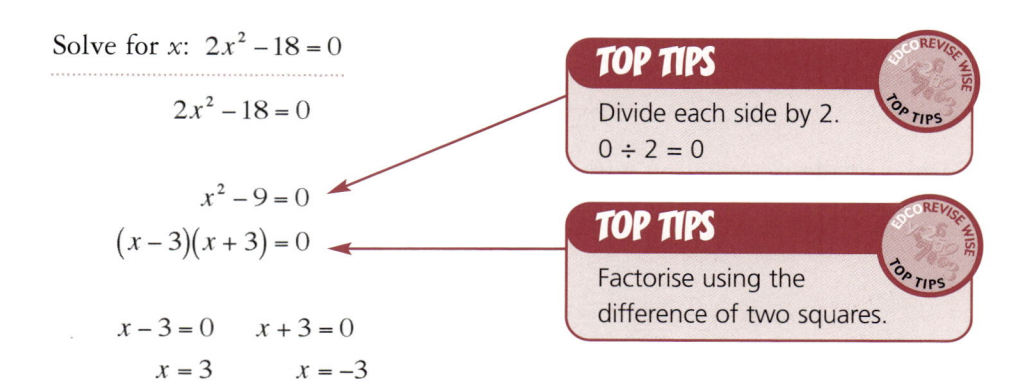

$$2x^2 - 18 = 0$$

$$x^2 - 9 = 0$$

$$(x-3)(x+3) = 0$$

$x - 3 = 0 \qquad x + 3 = 0$

$x = 3 \qquad x = -3$

TOP TIPS
Divide each side by 2.
$0 \div 2 = 0$

TOP TIPS
Factorise using the difference of two squares.

Sometimes, we use the solution to one quadratic equation to solve another:

Example 5

Solve for x: $x^2 + 3x - 54 = 0$

Hence, solve for t: $(2t+1)^2 + 3(2t+1) - 54 = 0$

$$x^2 + 3x - 54 = 0$$
$$(x+9)(x-6) = 0$$
$$x + 9 = 0 \quad \text{or} \quad x - 6 = 0$$
$$x = -9 \quad \text{or} \quad x = 6$$

The equation $(2t+1)^2 + 3(2t+1) - 54 = 0$ is identical to the equation $x^2 + 3x - 54 = 0$ except that x has been replaced by $(2t+1)$.

In the solution we also replace x with $2t + 1$, and then solve for t:

$$2t + 1 = -9 \quad \text{or} \quad 2t + 1 = 6$$
$$2t = -9 - 1 \quad \text{or} \quad 2t = 6 - 1$$
$$2t = -10 \quad \text{or} \quad 2t = 5$$
$$t = -5 \quad \text{or} \quad t = \frac{5}{2}$$

Sometimes we are given the solutions (roots) of a quadratic equation and asked to form the equation. In this case, work backwards, as in the following example.

Example 6

Form a quadratic equation with roots -4 and $\dfrac{2}{5}$.

$$x = -4 \qquad x = \dfrac{2}{5}$$

$$x + 4 = 0 \qquad 5x = 2$$
$$5x - 2 = 0$$

$$(x + 4)(5x - 2) = 0$$
$$x(5x - 2) + 4(5x - 2) = 0$$
$$5x^2 - 2x + 20x - 8 = 0$$
$$5x^2 + 18x - 8 = 0$$

3 Quadratic equations solved by formula

How to recognise them:
- There is only one letter involved
- At least one term will contain that letter squared
- You will be asked to give your answer correct to one or two decimal places, or else you will be asked to give your answer in surd form (involving a square root).

How to solve them:
1 **Rewrite the equation** in the form $ax^2 + bx + c = 0$, with positive a

2 Use the formula: $x = \dfrac{-b \pm \sqrt{b^2 - 4ac}}{2a}$

3 Either use the calculator and round off the answers or give your answer in surd form.

Example 7

Solve for x: $3 - x(2x+5) = 4$
Give your answers correct to two decimal places.

$$3 - x(2x+5) = 4$$
$$3 - 2x^2 - 5x = 4$$
$$0 = 2x^2 + 5x + 1$$

$a = 2 \quad b = 5 \quad \text{and} \quad c = 1$

$\therefore \quad b^2 - 4ac \ = \ 25 - 4(2)(1)$
$ = \ 25 - 8$
$ = \ 17$
$\sqrt{b^2 - 4ac} \ = \ \sqrt{17}$

TOP TIPS
Always find the value of $b^2 - 4ac$ first

TOP TIPS
If this number is negative, then you have made a mistake since the square root of a negative number is not on your course.

$x = \dfrac{-5 + \sqrt{17}}{4}$ or $x = \dfrac{-5 - \sqrt{17}}{4}$

$x = \dfrac{-0 \cdot 876894374}{4}$ or $x = \dfrac{-9 \cdot 123105626}{4}$

$x = -0 \cdot 219223593$ or $x = -2 \cdot 280776406$

$x = -0 \cdot 22$ or $x = -2 \cdot 28$, correct to 2 decimal places

Example 8

Solve for x: $4x^2 + 2x - 1 = 0$
Write your answer in its simplest surd form.

$4x^2 + 2x - 1 = 0$

$a = 4$, $b = 2$ and $c = -1$

$b^2 - 4ac = (2)^2 - 4(4)(-1)$
$ = 20$

$\sqrt{b^2 - 4ac} = \sqrt{20} = 2\sqrt{5}$

$x = \dfrac{-2 + 2\sqrt{5}}{8}$ or $x = \dfrac{-2 - 2\sqrt{5}}{8}$

$x = -\dfrac{2}{8} + \dfrac{2\sqrt{5}}{8}$ or $x = -\dfrac{2}{8} - \dfrac{2\sqrt{5}}{8}$

$x = -\dfrac{1}{4} + \dfrac{\sqrt{5}}{4}$ or $x = -\dfrac{1}{4} - \dfrac{\sqrt{5}}{4}$

TOP TIPS
This step is important if the answer is to be simplified.

TOP TIPS
Separate into two fractions before simplifying.

4 Rational equations

How to recognise them:
- There is only one letter involved
- There will be at least one fraction with a letter on the bottom.

> How to solve them:
> 1 **Remove fractions**, by multiplying by the common denominator
> 2 **Remove brackets**
> 3 **Simplify** each side by adding like terms
> 4 At this stage you will have either a simple equation or a quadratic equation, so proceed as appropriate
> 5 **Check** that your answers do not make the bottom of the original fractions equal to zero. If this is the case, then that number is **not** a solution.

Example 9

Solve for x: $\dfrac{4}{2x-3} - \dfrac{2}{x} = \dfrac{1}{9}$

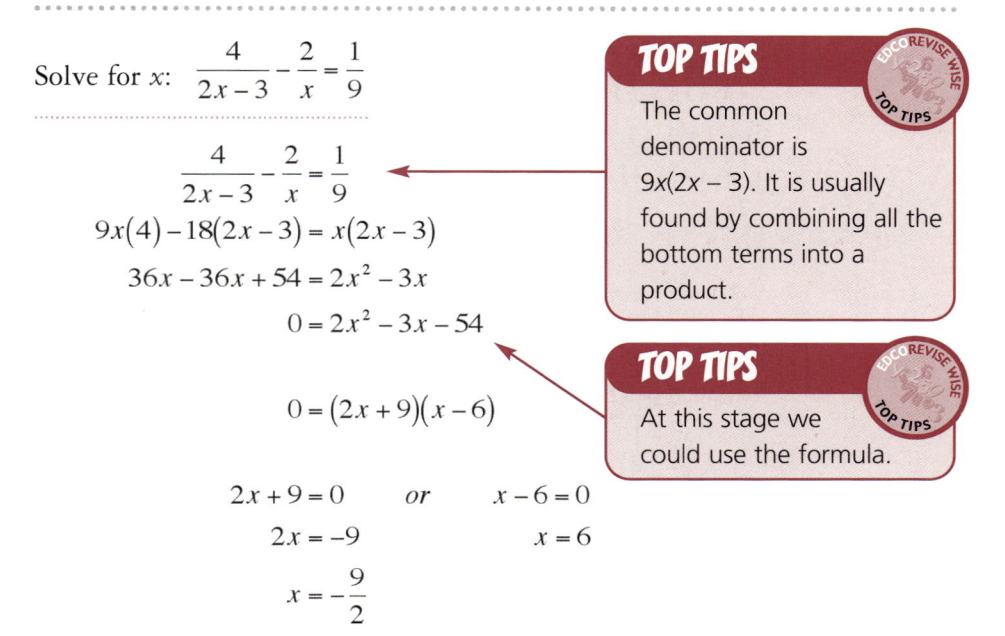

$\dfrac{4}{2x-3} - \dfrac{2}{x} = \dfrac{1}{9}$

$9x(4) - 18(2x-3) = x(2x-3)$

$36x - 36x + 54 = 2x^2 - 3x$

$0 = 2x^2 - 3x - 54$

$0 = (2x+9)(x-6)$

$2x + 9 = 0 \quad \text{or} \quad x - 6 = 0$

$2x = -9 \qquad\qquad\quad x = 6$

$x = -\dfrac{9}{2}$

TOP TIPS
The common denominator is $9x(2x-3)$. It is usually found by combining all the bottom terms into a product.

TOP TIPS
At this stage we could use the formula.

These numbers are both solutions because they do not make the bottom of the fractions equal to zero.

Alternative approach
The following in an alternative approach where we convert the left side to a single fraction and then cross-multiply to remove the fractions.

Example 10, Junior Certificate 2005

(i) Express in its simplest form: $\dfrac{1}{x-1} + \dfrac{1}{x+1}$

(ii) Hence, or otherwise, solve the equation: $\dfrac{1}{x-1} + \dfrac{1}{x+1} = 3$

Express your answer in the form $a \pm b\sqrt{10}$, where $a, b \in Q$.

(i) $\dfrac{1}{x-1} + \dfrac{1}{x+1}$

$= \dfrac{1(x+1) + 1(x-1)}{(x-1)(x+1)}$

$= \dfrac{x+1+x-1}{x^2 - x + x - 1}$

$= \dfrac{2x}{x^2 - 1}$

(ii) $\dfrac{1}{x-1} + \dfrac{1}{x+1} = 3$

$\Rightarrow \dfrac{2x}{x^2 - 1} = \dfrac{3}{1}$

$3x^2 - 3 = 2x$

$3x^2 - 2x - 3 = 0$

$a = 3, \; b = -2, \; c = -3 \quad \Rightarrow \quad \sqrt{b^2 - 4ac} = \sqrt{(-2)^2 - 4(3)(-3)} = \sqrt{40}$

$\sqrt{40} = \sqrt{4(10)} = 2\sqrt{10}$

$x = \dfrac{2 + 2\sqrt{10}}{6} \quad or \quad x = \dfrac{2 - 2\sqrt{10}}{6}$

$x = \dfrac{2}{6} + \dfrac{2\sqrt{10}}{6} \quad or \quad x = \dfrac{2}{6} - \dfrac{2\sqrt{10}}{6}$

$x = \dfrac{1}{3} + \dfrac{1}{3}\sqrt{10} \quad or \quad x = \dfrac{1}{3} - \dfrac{1}{3}\sqrt{10}$

5 Simultaneous equations in two variables

How to recognise them:
- There will be two equations to solve
- One or both equations will contain two letters.

How to solve them:
1 **Rewrite each equation**, if necessary, with the variables on one side and the constants on the other.
2 **Multiply** one or both equations by numbers that will make the coefficients of y identical, but opposite in sign.
3 **Add** the resulting equations to eliminate y.
4 **Solve** the new equation to find x.
5 **Substitute** this value for x into any of the equations to find y.

Example 11

Solve for x and y: $5x - 3y = 2$ and $2x - 4y = 3$

$A:$ $\quad 5x - 3y = 2$
$B:$ $\quad 2x - 4y = 3$

$4A:$ $\quad 20x - 12y = 8$
$-3B:$ $\quad -6x + 12y = -9$

Add: $\quad 14x = -1$

$\quad\quad x = -\dfrac{1}{14} =$

> **TOP TIPS**
> The coefficients of y must be equal but opposite in sign before adding to remove y.

> **TOP TIPS**
> Use the calculator, when working with fractions.

$B:$ $\quad 2x - 4y = 3 \Rightarrow 2x - 4\left(\dfrac{-1}{14}\right) = 3$

$\quad\quad\Rightarrow \quad 2x + \dfrac{2}{7} = 3$

$\quad\quad\Rightarrow \quad 2x = 3 - \dfrac{2}{7}$

$\quad\quad\Rightarrow \quad 2x = \dfrac{19}{7}$

$\quad\quad\Rightarrow \quad x = \dfrac{19}{14}$

Example 12, Junior Certificate 2003

(i) Solve the simultaneous equations: $\quad\begin{aligned} 3x + 4y &= -1 \\ 2x + 9 &= -6y \end{aligned}$

(ii) By graphing the two lines on a single coordinate diagram, check your answer to part (i).

Solution:

$2x + 9 = -6y \Rightarrow \quad 2x + 6y = -9 \quad\quad\quad 3x + 4y = -1$
$\quad\quad\quad\quad\quad \Rightarrow \quad 6x + 18y = -27 \quad \Rightarrow \quad -6x - 8y = 2$

$$-6x - 8y = 2$$
$$6x + 18y = -27$$
Add $\Rightarrow$ $\quad 10y = -25$

$$y = -\frac{25}{10} = -\frac{5}{2}$$

$$3x + 4y = -1$$
$$3x + 4\left(-\frac{5}{2}\right) = -1$$
$$3x - 10 = -1$$
$$3x = 9$$
$$x = 3$$

Answer: $x = 3$, $y = -2\frac{1}{2}$

(ii) To draw the lines we need two points on each line.

$3x + 4y = -1$:

Let $y = 0$ $\Rightarrow$ $3x = -1$
$$x = -\frac{1}{3}$$

Let $x = 0$ $\Rightarrow$ $4y = -1$
$$y = -\frac{1}{4}$$

$\left(-\frac{1}{3}, 0\right)$ and $\left(0, -\frac{1}{4}\right)$ are points on the line $3x + 4y = -1$

$2x + 6y = -9$:

Let $x = 0$ $\Rightarrow$ $6y = -9$
$$y = -\frac{9}{6} = -1\frac{1}{2}$$

Let $y = 0$ $\Rightarrow$ $2x = -9$
$$x = -\frac{9}{2} = -4\frac{1}{2}$$

$\left(0, -1\frac{1}{2}\right)$ and $\left(-4\frac{1}{2}, 0\right)$ are points on the line $2x + 6y = -9$

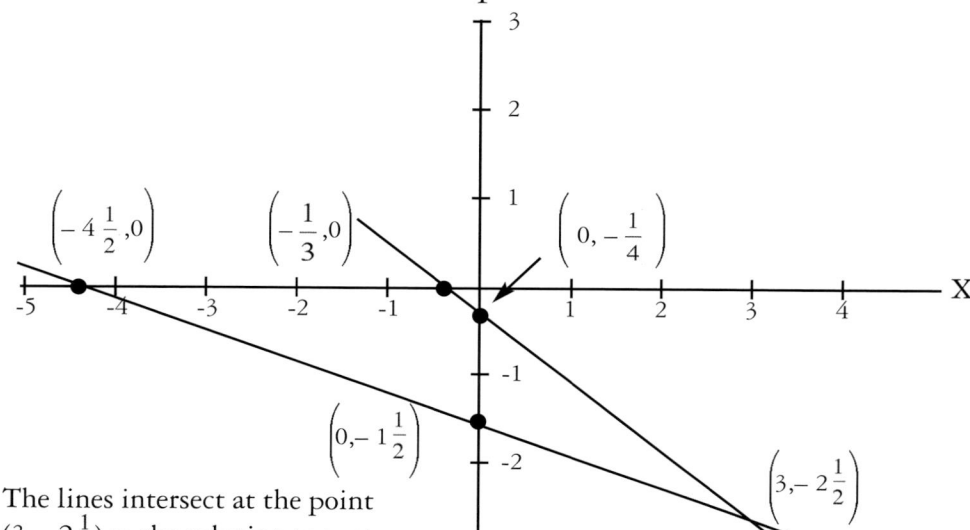

The lines intersect at the point $(3, -2\frac{1}{2})$ so the solution to part (i) is correct.

Key Points

- An equation is recognised by an equal sign (=) in the question and you are asked to solve for some letter.
- There are five different types of equation: simple equations, quadratic equations solved by factors, quadratic equations solved by formula, rational equations, and simultaneous equations in two variables.
- Simple equations have only one variable involved. There are no indices and if there are fractions, the variable will usually be on top.
- Quadratic equations solved by factors have only one letter involved. At least one term will contain that letter squared.
- Quadratic equations solved by formula have only one letter involved. At least one term will contain that letter squared. Answers must be given correct to one or two decimal places, or else given in surd form (involving a square root).
- Rational equations have only one letter involved. There will be at least one fraction with a letter on the bottom.
- Simultaneous equations in two variables have two equations to solve. One or both equations will contain two letters. The solution represents the point of intersection of two lines.

CHAPTER 10
Algebra 4: Forming Equations

Learning Objectives
- Problems leading to a linear equation
- Problems leading to a quadratic equation
- Problems leading to simultaneous equations
- Two-part problems leading to an equation with fractions.

Forming Equations

These problems can be split into four categories:

1. Problems leading to a linear equation
2. Problems leading to a quadratic equation
3. Problems leading to simultaneous equations
4. Two-part problems leading to an equation involving fractions.

1 Problems leading to a linear equation

Example 1

A man is five times as old as his daughter. In 6 years' time he will be only three times as old as her. What age is his daughter now?

Let x represent the daughter's age now.

	Now	In 6 Years
Daughter's age	x	$x+6$
Father's age	$5x$	$5x+6$

TOP TIPS
Use these numbers to form the equation.

In 6 years: Father's age = 3(daughter's age)

$$5x + 6 = 3(x + 6)$$
$$5x + 6 = 3x + 18$$
$$5x - 3x = 16 - 6$$
$$2x = 12$$
$$x = 6$$

Answer: The daughter is 6 years old now.

Example 2

A bag contains 27 discs, all of which are either red, yellow or blue. There are twice as many blue discs as red. The number of yellow is five less than the number of red.

If x is the number of yellow discs, form an equation involving x and find out how many discs of each colour are in the bag.

Yellow Discs	Red Discs	Blue Discs
x	$x + 5$	$2(x + 5)$

$$x + (x + 5) + 2(x + 5) = 27$$
$$x + x + 5 + 2x + 10 = 27$$
$$4x + 15 = 27$$
$$4x = 12$$
$$x = 3$$

Answer: There are 3 yellow discs, 8 red and 16 blue.

Example 3, Junior Certificate 2005

Seven shirts and two sweaters cost €202.50. A sweater costs the same as four shirts. Find the cost of one shirt.

Let x represent the cost of a shirt. The cost of a sweater is $4x$.

Cost of Seven Shirts	Cost of Two Sweaters
$7x$	$8x$

Total cost = 202·5

$$7x + 8x = 202\cdot 5$$
$$15x = 202\cdot 5$$
$$x = \frac{202\cdot 5}{15} = 13\cdot 50$$

Answer: The cost of one shirt is €13.50.

2 Problems leading to a quadratic equation

Example 4

When a number is added to twice the square of the number, the answer is 105. Find two possible values for the number.

Let x represent the number. The square of the number is x^2.

$$2x^2 + x = 105$$
$$2x^2 + x - 105 = 0$$
$$(2x + 15)(x - 7) = 0$$
$$2x + 15 = 0 \quad or \quad x - 7 = 0$$
$$2x = -15 \quad or \quad x = 7$$
$$x = -7\tfrac{1}{2}$$

Answer: The number could be 7 or $-7\tfrac{1}{2}$

Example 5

When a prize of €104 is divided equally between x winners, they receive € $(2x - 3)$ each. Find the share received by each winner.

When the number of winners is multiplied by their share of the prize, we get the total prize.

$$x(2x-3) = 104$$
$$2x^2 - 3x - 104 = 0$$

$a = 2,\ b = -3,\ c = -104 \quad \Rightarrow \quad \sqrt{b^2 - 4ac} = \sqrt{(-3)^2 - 4(2)(-104)} = 29$

$x = \dfrac{3 + 29}{4}$ or $x = \dfrac{3 - 29}{4}$

$x = 8$ or $x = -\dfrac{13}{2}$

TOP TIPS

Ignore the negative value of x in this case since the number of winners cannot be negative.

Answer: The share each winner received is €$(2x - 3)$, i.e. €13.

3 Problems leading to simultaneous equations

Example 6

Two apples and five oranges cost €4.69, while three apples and four oranges cost €4.76. Find the cost of one apple and one orange.

Let x cent be the cost of an apple and y cent be the cost of an orange.

$$2x + 5y = 469$$
$$3x + 4y = 476$$

$$6x + 15y = 1407$$
$$-6x - 8y = -952$$
Add: $\quad 7y = 455$
$$y = 65$$

$$2x + 5(65) = 469$$
$$2x + 325 = 469$$
$$2x = 144$$
$$x = 72$$

Answer: An apple costs 72 cent and an orange costs 65 cent.

TOP TIPS

If we represent the cost of an apple and an orange in cent, we must represent the total cost in cent, so 4.69 becomes 469.

Example 7, Junior Certificate 2005

Helen buys stamps costing 48 cent and 60 cent. She buys a total of 50 stamps costing €25·68.

(i) Taking x to be the number of 48-cent stamps and y to be the number of 60-cent stamps, write down two equations in x and y to represent this information.

(ii) Solve the equations to find the number of each type of stamp that Helen has purchased.

(i) $x + y = 50$ and $48x + 60y = 2568$

(ii)
$$48x + 60y = 2568$$
$$-48x - 48y = -2400$$
Add: $12y = 168$
$$y = 14$$

$$x + y = 50$$
$$x + 14 = 50$$
$$x = 36$$

Example 8

There are 30 students in a class. If the number of boys was doubled and the number of girls was halved, then there would be 42 students. How many boys and how many girls are in the class?

Let x be the number of boys and $2y$ the number of girls.
$x + 2y = 30$ and $2x + y = 42$

$$x + 2y = 30$$
$$-4x - 2y = -84$$
$$-3x = -54$$
$$x = 18$$

$$18 + 2y = 30$$
$$2y = 12$$

Answer: There are 18 boys and 12 girls in the class.

> **TOP TIPS**
> Since the number of girls is halved, let $2y$ be the number of girls and we avoid fractions.

CHAPTER 10: ALGEBRA 4: FORMING EQUATIONS

Example 9

Find two numbers that satisfy the following conditions. Two-thirds the bigger number added to three-quarters of the smaller number is 58. When half of the smaller number is taken from one-third of the bigger number, the answer is 8.

Let x be the bigger number and y the smaller.

> **TOP TIPS**
> Try this problem with $6x$ = bigger number and $12y$ = smaller.

$$\frac{2x}{3} + \frac{3y}{4} = 58 \quad \text{and} \quad \frac{x}{3} - \frac{y}{2} = 8$$

$$\Rightarrow \quad 8x + 9y = 696 \quad \text{and} \quad 2x - 3y = 48$$

$$8x + 9y = 696 \qquad\qquad 8x + 9y = 696$$
$$6x - 9y = 144 \qquad\qquad 8(60) + 9y = 696$$
$$\text{Add:} \quad 14x = 840 \qquad\qquad 480 + 9y = 696$$
$$x = 60 \qquad\qquad\qquad 9y = 216$$
$$\qquad\qquad\qquad\qquad\qquad y = 24$$

4 Two-part problems

Example 10

A prize of €600 is shared between x winners. If there had been two fewer winners then they would each have got an extra €10. Find x, the number of winners.

	Situation 1	Situation 2
Total prize	€600	€600
Number of winners	x	$x - 2$
Winnings	€$\frac{600}{x}$	€$\frac{600}{x-2}$

> **TOP TIPS**
> We are given the difference between these numbers. This allows us to form an equation, but be careful to put the bigger number first.

> **TOP TIPS**
> The prize has gone up, so this is the bigger number. (You can see which one is bigger by replacing x with any number bigger than 2).

$$\frac{600}{x-2} - \frac{600}{x} = 10$$

$$\frac{600x - 600(x-2)}{x^2 - 2x} = \frac{10}{1}$$

$$\frac{1200}{x^2 - 2x} = \frac{10}{1}$$

$$10x^2 - 20x = 1200$$

$$10x^2 - 20x - 1200 = 0$$

$$x^2 - 2x - 120 = 0$$

$$(x-12)(x+10) = 0$$

$$x - 12 = 0 \quad or \quad x - 10 = 0$$

$$x = 12 \quad or \quad x = -10$$

> **TOP TIPS**
> See rational equations for instructions to solve equations of this type.

The number of winners can't be negative, so there were 12 winners.

Example 11, Junior Certificate 2003

A cinema takes in €400 each time that all the seats are sold. Next week, eight seats will be removed to make room for a new emergency exit. The price per seat will have to be increased by €2.50 in order to keep the takings at €400.

(i) Taking x to be the number of seats now in the cinema, write an equation in x to represent the above information.

(ii) Solve the equation to find the number of seats now in the cinema and the price per seat now.

	Situation 1	Situation 2
Takings	€400	€400
Number of seats	x	$x-8$
Price per seat	€$\frac{400}{x}$	€$\frac{400}{x-8}$

> **TOP TIPS**
> We are given that the difference between these numbers is 2.5

> **TOP TIPS**
> The price has increased, so this is the bigger number.

(i) $$\frac{400}{x-8} - \frac{400}{x} = 2\cdot5$$

(ii) $$\frac{400}{x-8} - \frac{400}{x} = \frac{5}{2}$$
$$\frac{400x - 400(x-8)}{x^2 - 8x} = \frac{5}{2}$$
$$\frac{400x - 400x + 3200}{x^2 - 8x} = \frac{5}{2}$$
$$\frac{3200}{x^2 - 8x} = \frac{5}{2}$$
$$5x^2 - 40x = 6400$$
$$5x^2 - 40x - 6400 = 0$$
$$x^2 - 8x - 1280 = 0$$
$$(x - 40)(x + 32) = 0$$
$$x - 40 = 0 \quad \text{or} \quad x + 32 = 0$$
$$x = 40 \quad \text{or} \quad x = -32$$

> **TOP TIPS**
>
> Write 2.5 as $\frac{5}{2}$ to avoid decimals.

Since x cannot be negative, the number of seats now in the cinema is 40.

The price per seat now is €$\frac{400}{40}$ = €10

Example 12, Junior Certificate 2004

A youth club is organising an outing to a park. The total cost of entry for club members to the park is €42.

(i) Taking x to be the number of club members, write an expression in x to represent the cost of entry per member. If two club members decided not to go on the outing, the total cost of entry to the park would be €35.

(ii) Write an expression in x to represent the cost of entry per member in this case. The cost of entry per member, in this case, would be increased by €1.

(iii) Write an equation in x to represent the above information.

(iv) Solve this equation to find the number of members in the club.

	Situation 1	Situation 2
Total cost	€42	€35
Number of members	x	$x - 2$
Cost per member	€ $\dfrac{42}{x}$	€ $\dfrac{35}{x-2}$

(i) € $\dfrac{42}{x}$ (ii) € $\dfrac{35}{x-2}$ (iii) $\dfrac{35}{x-2} - \dfrac{42}{x} = 1$

(iv)
$$\dfrac{35}{x-2} - \dfrac{42}{x} = \dfrac{1}{1}$$
$$\dfrac{35x - 42(x-2)}{x^2 - 2x} = \dfrac{1}{1}$$
$$\dfrac{84 - 7x}{x^2 - 2x} = \dfrac{1}{1}$$
$$x^2 - 2x = 84 - 7x$$
$$x^2 + 5x - 84 = 0$$
$$(x + 12)(x - 7) = 0$$
$$x + 12 = 0 \quad \text{or} \quad x - 7 = 0$$
$$x = -12 \quad \text{or} \quad x = 7$$

TOP TIPS
The cost has increased, so this is the bigger number.

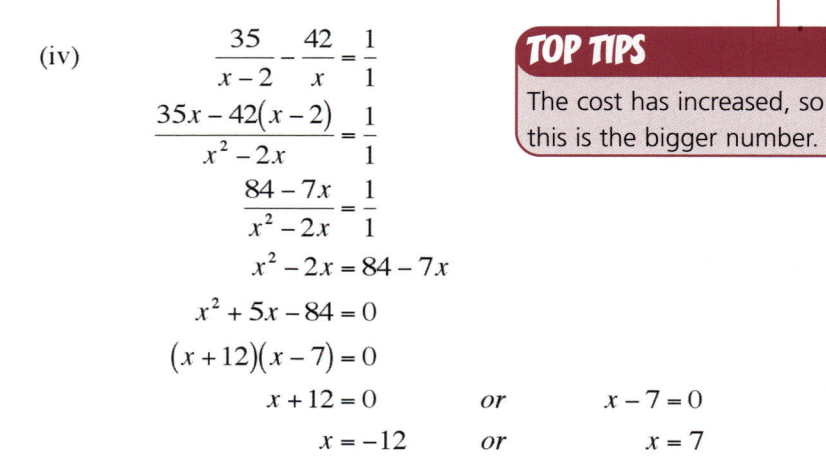

Since x cannot be negative, the number of members in the club is 7.

Key Points

- Fives times x is written: $5x$.
- When 5 is added to x we get $x + 5$ or $5 + x$.
- When 5 is taken from x we get $x - 5$, **not** $5 - x$.
- When representing an unkown number; using $2x$ or $6x$, etc. instead of x can help to avoid fractions.
- Try to avoid decimals. €2.50 = 250 cent and $2.5 = \dfrac{5}{2}$

- When subtracting to form an equation, always put the bigger number first.

CHAPTER 11
Algebra 5: Changing the Subject of a Formula

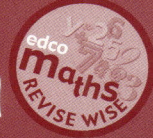

● ● ● Learning Objectives
- Changing the subject of a formula.

Changing the subject of a formula

Proceed as follows:
1. Remove fractions
2. Remove brackets
3. Rearrange, so that terms containing the required letter are together and all other terms are on the other side
4. If the required letter appears more than once, take it out as a common factor
5. Divide both sides by the other factor.

Example 1

Express b in terms of a and c if: $2a - b = a(3b + c)$

$$2a - b = a(3b + c)$$
$$2a - b = 3ab + ac$$
$$2a - ac = 3ab + b$$
$$2a - ac = b(3a + 1)$$
$$\frac{2a - ac}{3a + 1} = b$$

TOP TIPS

If the required letter appears twice, take it out as a common factor.

Example 2

Express x in terms of y and z if: $\frac{1}{y} = \frac{2}{x} + \frac{3}{z}$

$$\frac{1}{y} = \frac{2}{x} + \frac{3}{z}$$
$$xz = 2yz + 3xy$$
$$xz - 3xy = 2yz$$
$$x(z - 3y) = 2yz$$
$$x = \frac{2yz}{z - 3y}$$

TOP TIPS

Multiply each side by xyz to remove the fractions.

87

Example 3, Junior Certificate 2004

Given that $2(2q - 7p) = q(3p - q)$, express p in terms of q.

$$2(2q - 7p) = q(3p - q)$$
$$4q - 14p = 3pq - q^2$$
$$q^2 + 4q = 3pq + 14p$$
$$q^2 + 4q = p(3q + 14)$$
$$\frac{q^2 + 4q}{3q + 14} = p$$

Example 4, Junior Certificate 2004

Given that $2s - 3t = \dfrac{s+t}{t}$, express s in terms of t.

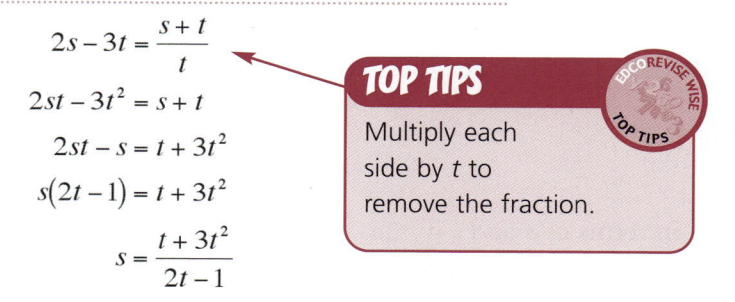

$$2s - 3t = \frac{s+t}{t}$$
$$2st - 3t^2 = s + t$$
$$2st - s = t + 3t^2$$
$$s(2t - 1) = t + 3t^2$$
$$s = \frac{t + 3t^2}{2t - 1}$$

TOP TIPS

Multiply each side by t to remove the fraction.

If the required letter is under a $\sqrt{}$, isolate the term containing the $\sqrt{}$ first and then square both sides.

Example 5

Given that $a = b + \sqrt{\dfrac{c+1}{2}}$, express c in terms of a and b.

$$a = b + \sqrt{\frac{c+1}{2}}$$
$$a - b = \sqrt{\frac{c+1}{2}}$$
$$(a - b)^2 = \frac{c+1}{2}$$
$$2(a - b)^2 = c + 1$$
$$2(a - b)^2 - 1 = c$$

Key Points

- Remove fractions.
- Remove brackets.
- Rearrange, so that terms containing the required letter are together and all other terms are on the other side.
- If the required letter appears more than once, take it out as a common factor.
- Divide both sides by the other factor.
- If the required letter is under a $\sqrt{}$, isolate the term containing the $\sqrt{}$ first and then square both sides.

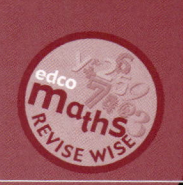

CHAPTER 12
Algebra 6: Inequalities

Learning Objectives
- Simple inequalities
- Compound inequalities
- Graphing the solution set on a number line.

Types of inequalities

There are two types of inequalities on the Maths course:

1. Simple inequalities containing only one inequality symbol
2. Compound inequalities containing two inequality symbols.

Simple inequalities

These are solved just like simple equations with one exception – if you multiply or divide by a negative number the inequality symbol must be reversed.

Example 1, Junior Certificate 2005

Find the solution set of the inequality: $6 - 2x \leq 12$, $x \in R$.

$$6 - 2x \leq 12$$
$$-2x \leq 12 - 6$$
$$-2x \leq 6$$
$$x \geq -3, \quad x \in R$$

TOP TIPS
Dividing by –2 causes the symbol $\leq$ to be reversed to $\geq$.

Alternative approach
$$6 - 2x \leq 12$$
$$6 - 12 \leq 2x$$
$$-6 \leq 2x$$
$$-3 \leq x$$

TOP TIPS
Read the solution from left to right, if x is on the right, i.e. x is greater than or equal to –3.

Example 2

Solve for x: $\ 3 - 2(4x+1) \leq x - 3(2x-1), \quad x \in \mathbb{R}.$

$$3 - 2(4x+1) \leq x - 3(2x-1), \quad x \in \mathbb{R}.$$
$$3 - 8x - 2 \leq x - 6x + 3$$
$$1 - 8x \leq -5x + 3$$
$$-8x + 5x \leq 3 - 1$$
$$-3x \leq 2$$
$$x \geq -\frac{2}{3}, \qquad x \in \mathbb{R}$$

Compound inequalities

1. There are three parts involved: to the left of the first inequality symbol, between the symbols, and to the right of the second symbol
2. You must get x on its own in the middle
3. Whatever you do to one part must be done to all three parts.

Example 3

Write the solution set for: $\ 7 \leq 2x - 1 \leq 13, \qquad x \in \mathbb{N}.$

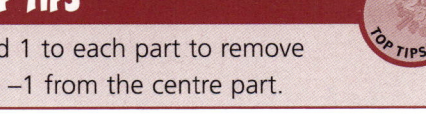

$7 \leq 2x - 1 \leq 13, \qquad x \in \mathbb{N}$
$7 + 1 \leq 2x \leq 13 + 1$
$8 \leq 2x \leq 14$
$4 \leq x \leq 7$

Solution set: $\{4, 5, 6, 7\}$

TOP TIPS
Add 1 to each part to remove the −1 from the centre part.

TOP TIPS
Divide each part by 2 to remove the 2 from the centre part.

TOP TIPS
The answers must be positive whole numbers since x must be a natural number.

Example 4

Write the solution set for: $-7 < 3x + 2 \leq 8, \ x \in Z$

$-7 < 3x + 2 \leq 8, x \in Z$
$-9 < 3x \leq 6$
$-3 < x \leq 2$

TOP TIPS
−3 is not included in the solution since x must be biggger than −3.

Solution set: {−2, −1, 0, 1, 2}

Graphing the solution set on a number line

Example 5

Graph on a number line:
(i) $x \leq 3, \ x \in N$ (ii) $x \leq 3, \ x \in Z$
(iii) $x \leq 3, \ x \in R$ (iv) $x < 3, \ x \in R$

(i) $x \leq 3, \ x \in N$

Place dots on the positive whole numbers less than or equal to 3, including 0. N (the natural numbers) does not include negative numbers.

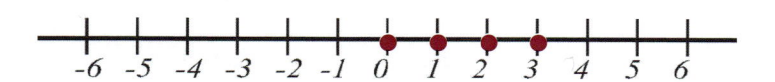

(ii) $x \leq 3, \ x \in Z$

Place dots on the whole numbers less than or equal to 3, including negative numbers. The arrow indicates that the solution set is infinite.

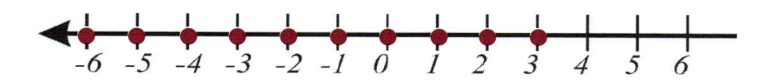

(iii) $x \leq 3$, $x \in R$

Use a heavy line to show every number less than or equal to 3. The dot on 3 shows that 3 is included and the arrow indicates that the solution set is infinite.

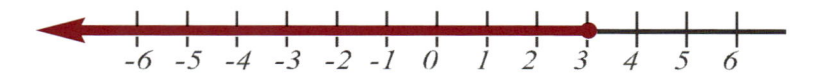

(iv) $x < 3$, $x \in R$

As in part (iii) except that the ring on 3 shows that 3 is not included in the solution set.

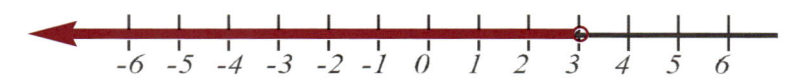

Example 6, Junior Certificate 2004

Graph on the number line the solution set of $-9 \leq 2x - 5 < 7$, $x \in Z$

$-9 \leq 2x - 5 < 7$, $x \in Z$
$-9 + 5 \leq 2x < 7 + 5$
$\quad -4 \leq 2x < 12$
$\quad -2 \leq x < 6$

TOP TIPS

Always check which set x belongs to. This will influence the numbers you show on the number line.

$x \in Z$, so we place dots on the whole numbers between -2 and 6. Notice that -2 must be included in the solution set but not 6.

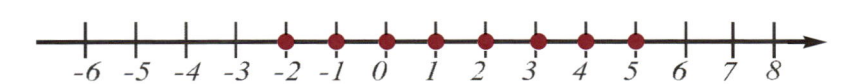

Example 7, Junior Certificate Sample Paper 2003

Show on a number line the solution of the inequality: $3x + 2 \geq x - 4$, $x \in R$

$$3x + 2 \geq x - 4, \qquad x \in R$$
$$3x - x \geq -4 - 2$$
$$2x \geq -6$$
$$x \geq -3$$

Since $x \in R$ we must use a heavy line to show the solution set. -3 is included so we place a dot on it.

Key Points

- Simple inequalities are solved like simple equations, except if you multiply or divide by a negative number, the inequality symbol must be reversed.
- Switching terms from one side to the other does not cause the inequality sign to be reversed.
- There are three parts involved in compound inequalities: to the left of the first inequality symbol, between the symbols, and to the right of the second symbol. You must get x on its own in the middle. Whatever you do to one part must be done to all three parts.
- When graphing the solution set on a number line, always check which set x belongs to. This will influence the numbers you show on the number line.

CHAPTER 13
Functions and Graphs

Learning Objectives
- Functions definitions
- Arrow diagrams
- Graphing linear functions
- Graphing quadratic functions
- Functions with missing coefficients.

Definitions

1. A relation is a set of couples
2. The set of first components is called the domain
3. The set of second components is called the range
4. A function is a set of couples that satisfies **two** conditions: (1) every couple has a different first component; (2) every element of the domain has an image
5. If you are asked to identify a number for which a function is not defined, the answer is usually a number which would give 0 on the bottom of a fraction, since division by 0 is not defined.

It may be helpful to think of a function as a machine that changes numbers. We use x to represent a number that goes into the machine and $f(x)$ to represent the number that comes out. Therefore, $f(-1)$ is the number produced by the function $f(x)$ when x is replaced by the number -1.

When a function is defined, it is usually written in the form:

$$f: x \rightarrow \text{some expression involving } x.$$

The expression tells us what to do to x to calculate the number that comes out of the function.

Example 1

$f: x \to 3x^2 - 1$ is a function. Find $f(-2)$.

Solution: $f(-2) = 3(-2)^2 - 1$
$= 3(4) - 1$
$= 12 - 1$
$= 11$

Example 2

$f: x \to \dfrac{x}{x+2}$ is a function.

Find   (i) $f(\tfrac{2}{3})$ (ii) $f(h)$ (iii) $f(x+1)$ and   (iv) $f(2y-3)$

For what value of x is $f(x)$ undefined?

Solution: (i) $f(\tfrac{2}{3}) = \dfrac{\tfrac{2}{3}}{\tfrac{2}{3} + 2}$

$= \dfrac{\tfrac{2}{3}}{\tfrac{8}{3}}$

$= \dfrac{2}{8}$

$= \dfrac{1}{4}$

TOP TIPS
Use the calculator for calculations involving fractions.

(ii) $f(h) = \dfrac{h}{h+2}$ — replace x with h

(iii) $f(x+1) = \dfrac{x+1}{(x+1)+2}$ — replace x with $x+1$

$= \dfrac{x+1}{x+3}$

(iv) $f(2y-3) = \dfrac{2y-3}{(2y-3)+2}$ — replace x with $2y-3$

$= \dfrac{2y-3}{2y-1}$

The function is undefined for $x = -2$ since this value of x would result in division by 0, which is undefined in mathematics.

Example 3

$f:x \rightarrow 2 - 3x^2$ is a function.

Find (i) $f(4)$
(ii) $f(-4)$
(iii) $f(2k)$
(iv) $f(2k-1)$

(i) $f(4) = 2 - 3(4)^2$
$f(4) = 2 - 3(16)$
$f(4) = 2 - 48$
$f(4) = -46$

(ii) $f(-4) = 2 - 3(-4)^2$
$f(-4) = 2 - 3(16)$
$f(-4) = 2 - 48$
$f(-4) = -46$

TOP TIPS

In each of these problems the first calculation was to square the number in the bracket. Notice that we kept the answer in a bracket. This is especially important in part (iv).

(iii) $f(2k) = 2 - 3(2k)^2$
$f(2k) = 2 - 3(4k^2)$
$f(2k) = 2 - 12k^2$

(iv) $f(2k-1) = 2 - 3(2k-1)^2$
$f(2k-1) = 2 - 3(4k^2 - 4k + 1)$
$f(2k-1) = 2 - 12k^2 + 12k - 3$
$f(2k-1) = -12k^2 + 12k - 1$

$\begin{aligned}(2k-1)^2 &= (2k-1)(2k-1) \\ &= 2k(2k-1) - 1(2k-1) \\ &= 4k^2 - 2k - 2k + 1 \\ &= 4k^2 - 4k = 1\end{aligned}$

Arrow diagrams

A function may be represented by an arrow diagram. This consists of two ovals; the one on the left representing the domain and the one on the right representing the range.

We then draw arrows connecting each element of the domain with its corresponding element in the range.

Example 4

The function f is defined as follows:

$f : x \rightarrow x^2 - 1, \ x \in \{-3, -2, -1, 0, 1\}$.

(i) Show f on an arrow diagram.
(ii) Write f as a set of couples.

x	$x^2 - 1$	$f(x)$
-3	$(-3)^2 - 1$	8
-2	$(-2)^2 - 1$	3
-1	$(-1)^2 - 1$	0
0	$(0)^2 - 1$	-1
1	$(1)^2 - 1$	0

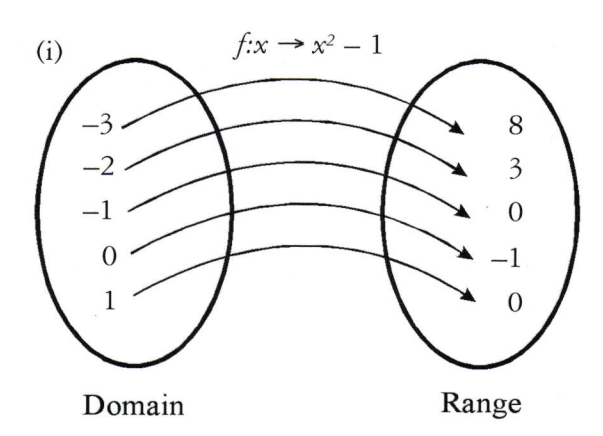

(i) $f : x \rightarrow x^2 - 1$

Domain: $\{-3, -2, -1, 0, 1\}$ → Range: $\{8, 3, 0, -1, 0\}$

(ii) Couples of f: $\{(-3, 8), (-2, 3), (-1, 0), (0, -1), (1, 0)\}$

Graphing linear functions

Since a function produces a set of couples, these couples may be represented by dots plotted using an X and a Y axis. By joining the dots we get a graph of the function.

A linear function is in the form $f: x \rightarrow ax + b$, where a and b are real numbers. It is called linear because its graph is always a straight line.

Example 5

Draw a graph of the function $f : x \rightarrow 2x + 1$, $-3 \leq x \leq 3, x \in R$

Since the graph will be a straight line, we need only find two points on it. These are found by substituting -3 and 3 for x (the end numbers in the domain).

x	$2x + 1$	$f(x)$
-3	$2(-3) + 1$	-5
3	$2(3) + 1$	7

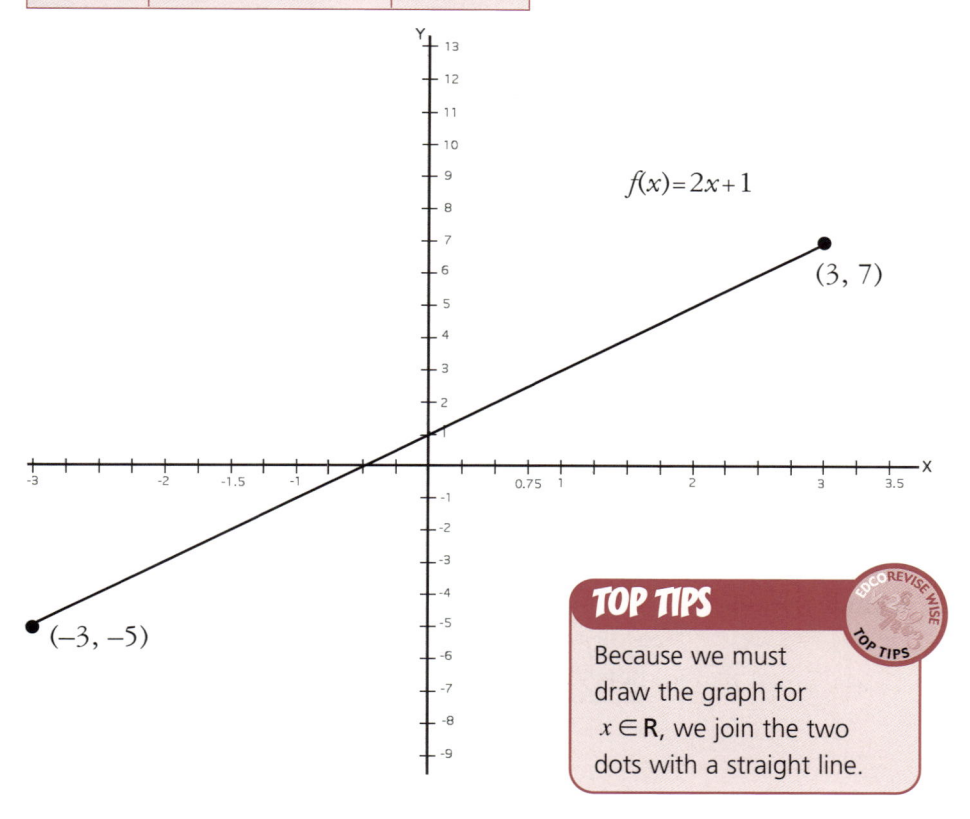

TOP TIPS

Because we must draw the graph for $x \in R$, we join the two dots with a straight line.

Graphing quadratic functions

A quadratic function is in the form $f : x \to ax^2 + bx + c$, where a, b and c are real numbers.

> To graph a quadratic function we need a number of points. These are usually found by substituting whole numbers in the given domain, for x. It can be useful to substitute some decimals as well.

Example 6

Draw a graph of the function $f : x \to 2x^2 - 3x - 20$, $\quad -2 \le x \le 2, x \in R$

- The domain of the function is every real number between -2 and 2, inclusive. This means that when finding couples of the function, we can use any number between -2 and 2 for x, not just whole numbers.

- When graphing a function in the form $ax^2 + bx + c$, it is useful to include the number $-\dfrac{b}{2a}$ for x, since this is always the x-coordinate of the point where the graph turns. In this case $a = 2$ and $b = -3$ $\Rightarrow$ $-\dfrac{b}{2a} = \dfrac{3}{4} = 0 \cdot 75$

- Construct a chart as follows to identify couples of the function:

x	$2x^2 - 3x - 2$	$f(x)$
-2	$2(-2)^2 - 3(-2) - 2$	12
-1	$2(-1)^2 - 3(-1) - 2$	3
0	$2(0)^2 - 3(0) - 2$	-2
0·75	$2(\cdot 75)^2 - 3(\cdot 75) - 2$	$-3 \cdot 125$
1	$2(1)^2 - 3(1) - 2$	-3
2	$2(2)^2 - 3(2) - 2$	0
3	$2(3)^2 - 3(3) - 2$	7

- Because the points $(-2, 12)$ and $(-1, 3)$ are so far apart, it would help to include $x = -1.5$.

$-1 \cdot 5$	$2(-1 \cdot 5)^2 - 3(-1 \cdot 5) - 2$	7

- Now plot the points and draw the graph.

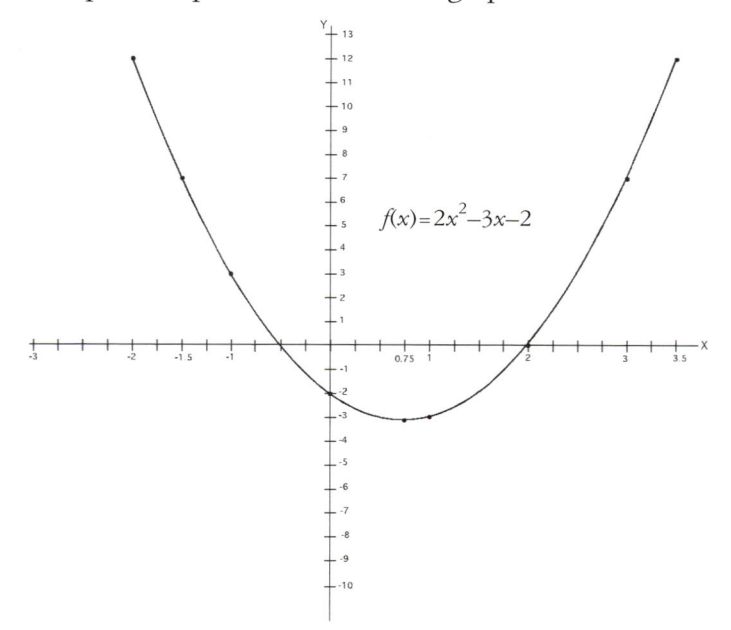

$f(x) = 2x^2 - 3x - 2$

The graph can now be used to answer questions about the function.

Questions about quadratic functions

In most cases one coordinate of a point or set of points is identified and the graph must be used to identify the other coordinate(s).

Question 1

Find $f(-1.75)$.

To find $f(-1.75)$ is to identify the y-coordinate of the point on the graph that has an x-coordinate of -1.75.

Locate -1.75 on the X axis. Draw a vertical line up or down until it hits the graph. Now from the point where it hits the graph draw a horizontal line to the Y axis as shown.

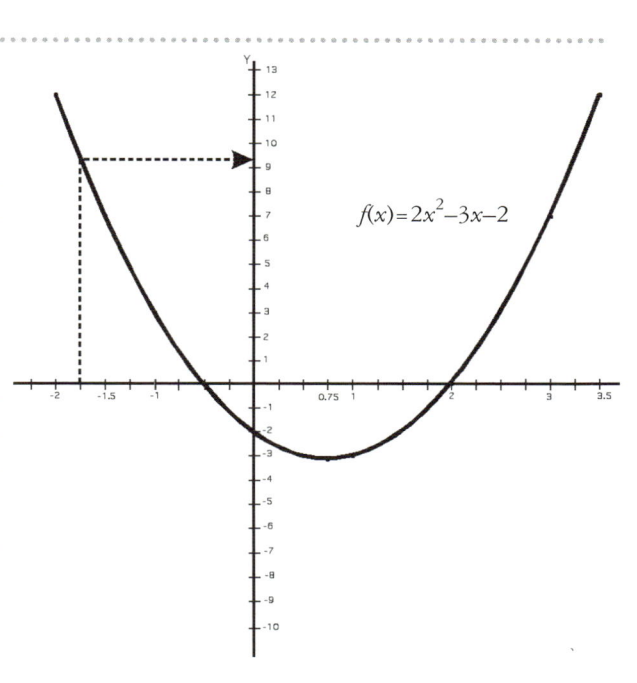

$f(x) = 2x^2 - 3x - 2$

The number on the Y axis (where the arrow is pointing) is $f(-1\cdot 75)$.

In this case, $f(-1\cdot 75) = 9\cdot 25$.

Question 2

Solve for x: $f(x) = 5$

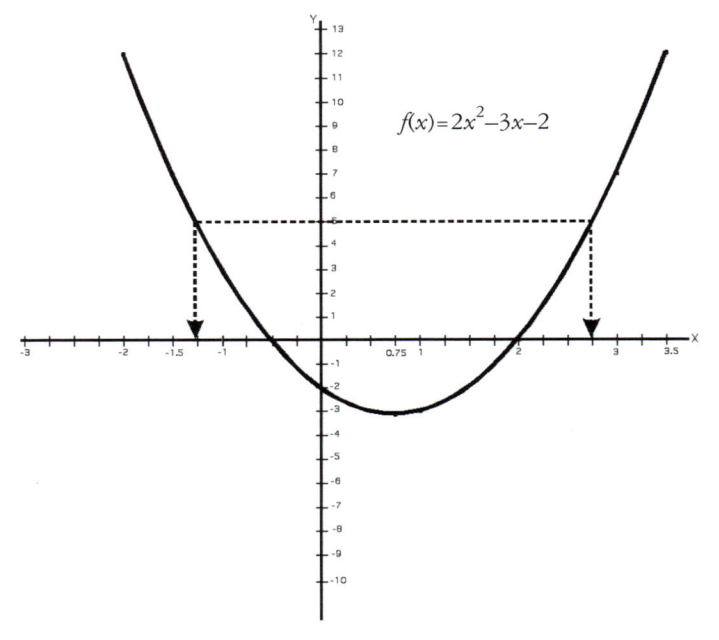

$f(x) = 2x^2 - 3x - 2$

To solve for x the equation $f(x) = 5$, we must identify points on the graph with a y-coordinate of 5 and write down the x-coordinate.

Locate 5 on the Y axis and draw a horizontal line to cut the graph twice. Draw vertical lines from these points to the X axis.

The numbers on the X axis (where the arrows are pointing) are the x values we want, in this case, $-1\cdot 25$ and $2\cdot 75$.

Question 3

Write down the equation of the axis of symmetry of the graph.

The axis of symmetry of the graph is a vertical line through the point where the graph turns. The equation of the axis of symmetry is always

$$x = -\frac{b}{2a}$$

In this case, the equation of the axis of symmetry is

$$x = \frac{3}{4}$$

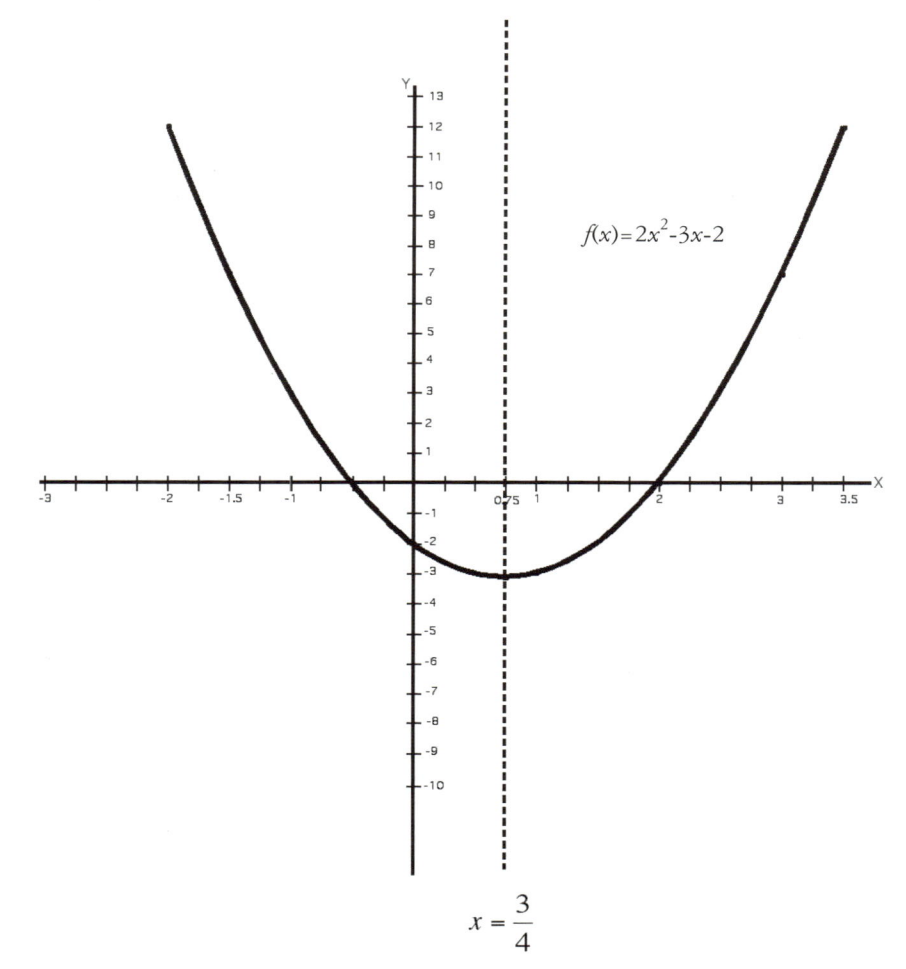

We are sometimes asked to draw the graph of a linear function and the graph of a quadratic function on the same axes. Having done so, you should always identify the x coordinates of the points where the graphs intersect.

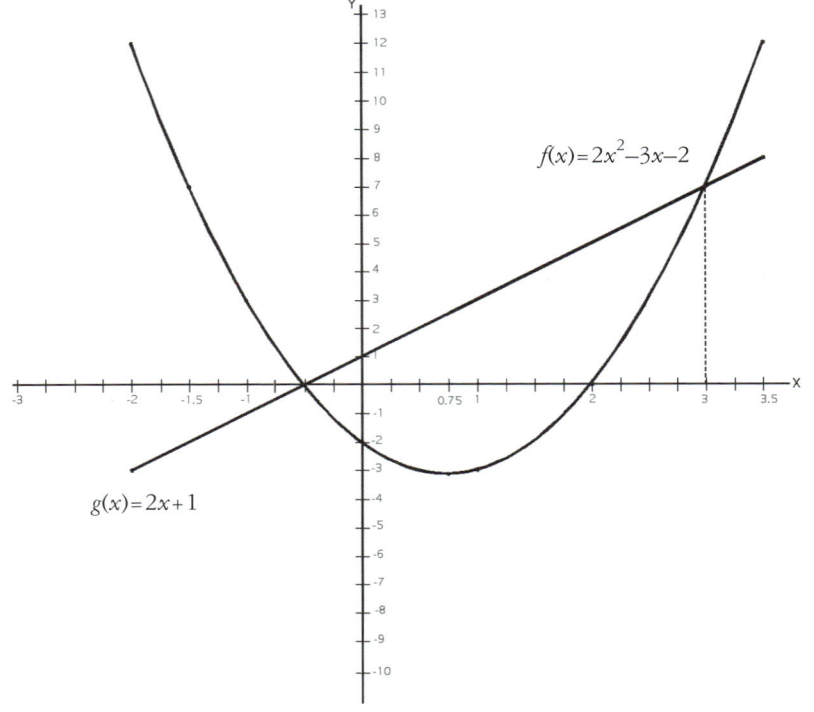

The graph above shows the functions $f(x) = 2x^2 - 3x - 2$ and $g(x) = 2x + 1$ for $-2 \leq x \leq 3.5$. The graphs intersect at $x = -0.5$ and $x = 3$.

Having drawn the two graphs, the most likely questions to be asked are:

(i) Solve for x: $f(x) = g(x)$

Solution: $x = -0.5$ and $x = 3$.

These are the x-coordinates of the points where the line cuts the curve.

(ii) Write down the range of values of x for which $f(x) \geq g(x)$.

Solution: $f(x) \geq g(x)$ for $-2 \leq x \leq -0.5$ and $3 \leq x \leq 3.5$.

These are the x-coordinates of the points where the curve is above the line.

(iii) Write down the range of values of x for which $f(x) \leq g(x)$.

Solution: $f(x) \leq g(x)$ for $-0.5 \leq x \leq 3$.

These are the *x*-coordinates of the points where the curve is below the line.

The graph may represent some 'real life' quantity. For instance, in 2005 the function students were asked to graph represented the area of a rectangle with *x* representing the length of a side.

Example 7

The perimeter of a rectangle is 14 m. The width of the rectangle is x m.

(a) Write an expression in x for the length of the triangle.

Solution:
Let y be the length.

$2x + 2y = 14$
$x + y = 7$
$y = 7 - x$

(b) (i) Show that the area, in m², of the rectangle is $7x - x^2$.

(ii) Let f be the function $f : x \rightarrow 7x - x^2$.
Draw the graph of f for $0 \leq x \leq 7$, $x \in R$.

(i) Area = xy — length × width
= $x(7 - x)$
= $7x - x^2$

(ii) When making out the table it is easier to use $f(x) = x(7 - x)$.

$$\frac{-b}{2a} = \frac{-7}{-2} = 3 \cdot 5$$

x	$x(7-x)$	$f(x)$
0	0(7)	0
1	1(6)	6
2	2(5)	10
3	3(4)	12
3.5	3.5(3.5)	12.25
4	4(3)	12
5	5(2)	10
6	6(1)	6
7	7(0)	0

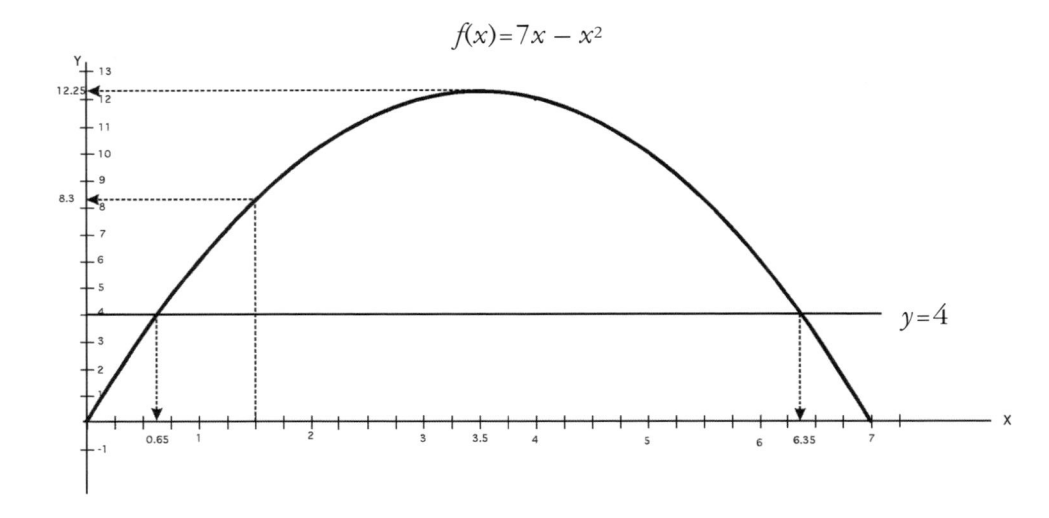

$$f(x) = 7x - x^2$$

(iii) Use your graph to estimate
   (a) the area of the rectangle when the width is 1·5 m
   (b) the maximum possible area of the rectangle
   (c) the two possible values of the width of the rectangle when the area is 4 m².

Solution:
(i) We need the y-coordinate when $x = 1·5$. Area = 8·3
(ii) We must identify the y-coordinate of the highest point on the graph. Maximum area = 12·25
(iii) We need the x-coordinates of the two points on the graph whose y-coordinate is 4.

The two possible values are: 0·65 and 6·35.

Functions with missing coefficients

When a function of x has a missing coefficient, we will be given a couple of the function. This gives us an equation from which the missing coefficient may be found.

> **To form the equation:**
> 1 Replace x with the number on the left of the couple.
> 2 Put the result equal to the number on the right.

If there are two coefficients missing, then we will be given two couples. We then use simultaneous equations.

Note: Each of the following is a different way to tell us that when we replace x in the function with 3, the answer is equal to 0:

- $(3, 0)$ is a couple of the function f
- $f(3) = 0$
- The graph of f crosses the X axis at the point where $x = 3$
- The point $(3, 0)$ is on the graph of f
- Given a graph of the function showing the point $(3, 0)$ on it.

Example 8

Let f be the function $f : x \to x^2 + bx + c$, $x \in R$ and $b, c \in Z$.
The graph of f cuts the X axis at the points where $x = -3$ and $x = 2$.
Find the value of b and the value of c.

$(-3, 0)$ and $(2, 0)$ are couples of the function.

$\Rightarrow \quad (-3)^2 + b(-3) + c = 0 \qquad$ and $\qquad (2)^2 + b(2) + c = 0$
$\qquad \qquad 9 - 3b + c = 0 \qquad$ and $\qquad 4 + 2b + c = 0$
$\qquad \qquad -3b + c = -9 \qquad$ and $\qquad 2b + c = -4$

$\qquad \qquad \qquad \qquad 3b - c = 9$
$\qquad \qquad \qquad \qquad 2b + c = -4 \qquad \qquad 2(1) + c = -4$
add $\qquad \qquad \qquad 5b = 5 \qquad \qquad \qquad c = -4 - 2$
$\qquad \qquad \qquad \qquad b = 1 \qquad \qquad \qquad \quad c = -6$

Example 9

Let f be the function $f : x \rightarrow x^2 + bx + c$, $x \in R$ and $b, c \in Z$.
The points $(2,-6)$ and $(0,6)$ lie on the graph of f.

(i) Find the value of b and the value of c.
(ii) k is a positive real number and $(k,-k)$ is a point on the graph.
Find the two possible values of k.

$f(2) = -6 \Rightarrow (2)^2 + b(2) + c = -6$ $\qquad$ $f(0) = 6 \Rightarrow (0)^2 + b(0) + c = 6$
$\qquad\qquad\qquad 4 + 2b + c = -6$ $\qquad\qquad\qquad\qquad\qquad\qquad c = 6$
$\qquad\qquad\qquad\quad 2b + c = -10$

$\qquad\qquad$ But $c = 6 \quad \Rightarrow \quad 2b + 6 = -10$
$\qquad\qquad\qquad\qquad\qquad\qquad\quad 2b = -10 - 6$
$\qquad\qquad\qquad\qquad\qquad\qquad\quad 2b = -16$
$\qquad\qquad\qquad\qquad\qquad\qquad\quad\; b = -8$

$f(x) = x^2 - 8x + 6$

$(k,-k)$ is a couple of $f \quad \Rightarrow \quad f(k) = -k$

$\qquad\qquad\qquad\qquad (k)^2 - 8(k) + 6 = -k$
$\qquad\qquad\qquad\qquad k^2 - 8k + k + 6 = 0$
$\qquad\qquad\qquad\qquad\quad k^2 - 7k + 6 = 0$
$\qquad\qquad\qquad\qquad\; (k-1)(k-6) = 0$

$\qquad\qquad k - 1 = 0 \quad$ or $\quad k - 6 = 0$
$\qquad\qquad\quad\; k = 1 \quad$ or $\quad\quad k = 6$

Key Points

- A relation is a set of couples.
- The set of first components is called the domain.
- The set of second components is called the range.
- A function is a set of couples that satisfies two conditions: (1) every couple has a different first component; (2) every element of the domain has an image.
- If you are asked to identify a number for which a function is not defined, the answer is usually a number which would give 0 on the bottom of a fraction, since division by 0 is not defined.
- A function may be represented by an arrow diagram. This consists of two ovals, the one on the left representing the domain and the one on the right representing the range. Arrows are used to connect elements of the domain with corresponding elements of the range.
- Since a function produces a set of couples, these couples may be represented by dots plotted using an X and a Y axis. By joining the dots we get a graph of the function.
- The graph of a function in the form: $f:x \rightarrow ax + b$ is always a straight line.
- A quadratic function is in the form $f:x \rightarrow ax^2 + bx + c$, where a, b and c are real numbers.
- To graph a quadratic function we need a number of points. These are usually found by substituting whole numbers in the given domain, for x. It can be useful to substitute some decimals as well.
- When a function of x has a missing coefficient, we will be given a couple of the function. This gives us an equation from which the missing coefficient may be found.

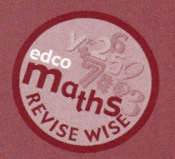

CHAPTER 14
Perimeter, Area and Volume

●●● Learning Objectives

- **Two-dimensional objects:** how to get the perimeter and area of a rectangle, a square, a parallelogram, a triangle, a circle, a sector of a circle and any object formed by combining these objects
- **Three-dimensional objects:** how to get the surface area and volume of a rectangular box, a cube, a cylinder, a sphere, a hemisphere and a cone
- Surface area questions
- Volume questions.

Two-dimensional objects

You should know how to get the perimeter and area of a rectangle, a square, a parallelogram, a triangle, a circle, a sector of a circle and any object formed by combining these objects.

Object	Perimeter	Area
Rectangle	2(length + width) = $2(x + y)$	length × width = xy
Square	4(length of a side) = $4x$	(length of a side)^2 = x^2
Parallelogram	Sum of the sides = $2(x + y)$	base × perpendicular height = xh
Triangle	Sum of the sides = $x + y + z$	$\frac{1}{2}$(base × perpendicular height) $\frac{1}{2}xh$
Circle	2π(radius) = $2\pi r$	π(radius)^2 = πr^2
Sector	sum of the sides = $2r + l$ ($l = \frac{\theta}{360} \times 2\pi r$)	$\frac{\theta}{360}$ × area of the circle = $\frac{\theta}{360} \times \pi r^2$

CHAPTER 14: PERIMETER, AREA AND VOLUME

Example 1

The sides of a rectangle are in the ratio 4:3. The perimeter is 56 cm. Find the lengths of the sides.

Let $4x$ and $3x$ be the lengths of the sides. The perimeter is $2(4x + 3x) = 14x$.

$14x = 56$

$x = 4$

$\Rightarrow \quad 4x = 16$ and $3x = 12$

Therefore, the lengths are 16 cm and 12 cm.

Example 2

The area of a square is 64 cm². Find the perimeter.

Let x be the length of one side.

$\quad x^2 = 64$

$\Rightarrow \quad x = 8$

$\Rightarrow \quad 4x = 32$

The perimeter is 32 cm.

Example 3

The area of a circle is 254.34 cm². Find the length of the radius. (Use $\pi = 3 \cdot 14$)

$\pi r^2 = $ Area

$3 \cdot 14 r^2 = 254.34$

$r^2 = \dfrac{254.34}{3 \cdot 14}$

$r^2 = 81$

$r = 9$

> **TOP TIPS**
>
> Always write the formula so that the letter you are trying to find is on the left.

The radius is 9 cm.

Example 4

The radius of the circle shown is 8 cm. Find the area of the shaded region, correct to the nearest cm².

The area of the whole circle is $\pi(8)^2 = 64\pi$.

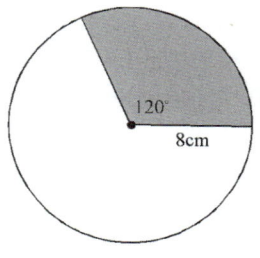

The area of the shaded sector $= \dfrac{120}{360} \times 64\pi$

$= 67.02$

$= 67 \text{ cm}^2$

Note 1: You should use the π key on the calculator, unless you are given a value to use for π.

Note 2: When told to give your answer **in terms of π**, do not substitute any value for π.

Note 3: When rounding, only the final answer should be rounded off.

Example 5

Find l, the length of the arc. $\pi = 3\cdot 14$

Let C be the length circumference of the circle.

$C = 2\pi r$
$C = 2(3\cdot 14)(12)$
$C = 75\cdot 36$

$l = \dfrac{60}{360} \times 75\cdot 36$

$l = 12\cdot 56 \text{ cm}$

Example 6

Find the area of the parallelogram. (All measurements are in cm.)

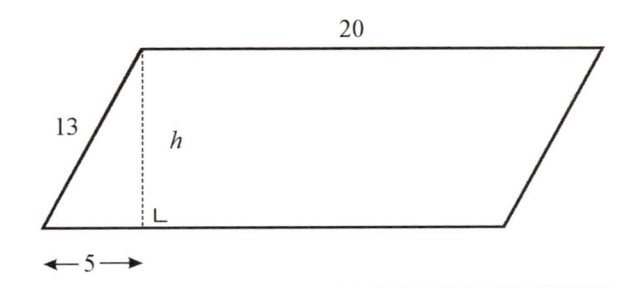

Area = base × perpendicular height.
⇒ We need to find the height, h.

By Pythagoras' theorem
$$h^2 + 5^2 = 13^2$$
$$h^2 = 169 - 25$$
$$h^2 = 144$$
$$h = 12$$

Area = $20h$
Area = $20(12)$
Area = 240 cm^2

Example 7

The figure shows a semi-circle of diameter 12 cm surmounted by an isosceles triangle.

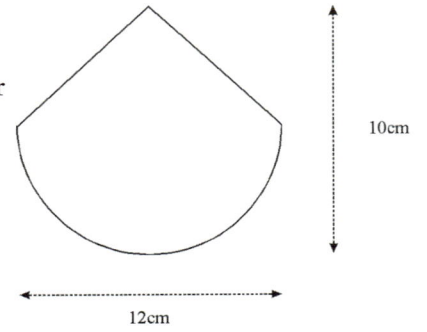

The total height of the figure is 10 cm. Find the area in terms of π.

The radius of the semi-circle is 6 cm, therefore the height of the triangle is 4 cm.

Area of triangle: $\frac{1}{2}(12)(4) = 24$ cm^2

Area of semi-circle: $\frac{1}{2}\pi(6)^2 = 18\pi$ cm^2

Total area: $(18\pi + 24)$ cm^2

Three-dimensional objects

You should know how to get the surface area and volume of a rectangular box, a cube, a cylinder, a sphere, a hemisphere and a cone.

Object	Surface Area	Volume
Rectangular box	$2(lw + lh + wh)$	lwh
Cube	$6x^2$	x^3
cylinder	Curved: $2\pi rh$ Total: $2\pi r^2 + 2\pi rh$ $= 2\pi r(r + h)$	$\pi r^2 h$
sphere	$4\pi r^2$	$\dfrac{4}{3}\pi r^3$
hemisphere	Curved: $2\pi r^2$ Total: $3\pi r^2$	$\dfrac{2}{3}\pi r^3$
cone	Curved: πrl Total: $\pi r^2 + \pi rl$ $= \pi r(r + l)$	$\dfrac{1}{3}\pi r^2 h$

Surface area questions

A three-dimensional object may have a number of surfaces. The surfaces may be flat or curved. For example, a solid rectangular block has six flat surfaces, each of which is a rectangle. A solid cylinder has three surfaces, two discs and the curved surface.

TOP TIPS

In questions to do with surface area, always check if you need the total surface area or just the curved surface area.

Example 8

Calculate, in terms of π the total surface area of a solid cylinder with diameter 6 cm and height 8 cm.

Solution:
Because the cylinder is solid it has three surfaces:

- The top, which is a disc
- The bottom, which is an identical disc
- The curved surface.

$$r = 3\text{cm} \quad - \quad \text{half the diameter}$$
$$h = 8\text{cm}$$

$$\begin{aligned}\text{Total surface area} &= 2\pi r(r + h) \\ &= 2\pi(3)(11) \\ &= 66\pi \text{ cm}^2\end{aligned}$$

Example 9

The surface area of a cube is 54 cm². Find the length of a side.

Solution:
Let x be the length of a side.

$$6x^2 = \text{surface area}$$
$$6x^2 = 54$$
$$x^2 = 9$$
$$x = 3 \text{ cm}$$

Example 10

Find, in terms of π, the total surface area of a cone with height 15 cm and diameter 16 cm.

Solution:
We need l, the slant height.

Using Pythagoras' theorem:

$l^2 = 15^2 + 8^2$

$l^2 = 225 + 64$

$l^2 = 289$

$l = \sqrt{289} = 17$

Total surface area	=	$\pi r(r + l)$
	=	$\pi(8)(8+17)$
	=	$200\pi \text{ cm}^2$

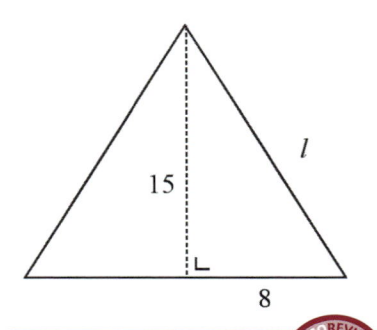

TOP TIPS

The height, radius and slant height form a right-angled triangle.

Example 11

The surface area of a rectangular block of metal is 62 cm². If the length is 5 cm and the width is 3 cm, find the height.

$2(lw + lh + wh) = $ surface area

$2(15 + 5h + 3h) = 62$

$15 + 8h = 31$

$8h = 16$

$h = 2$ cm

Example 12, Junior Certificate 2005

(i) A solid metal cylinder has height 20 cm and diameter 14 cm. Find its curved surface area in terms of π.

$h = 20$, $r = 7$

curved surface area $= 2\pi rh$

curved surface area $= 2\pi(7)(20)$

curved surface area $= 280\pi \text{ cm}^2$

(ii) A hemisphere with diameter 14 cm is removed from the top of this cylinder, as shown. Find the total surface area of the remaining solid, in terms of π.

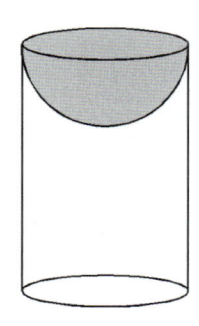

CHAPTER 14: PERIMETER, AREA AND VOLUME

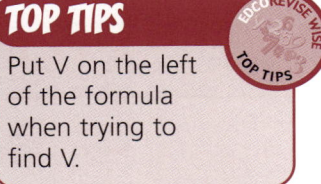

Solution:
The solid that remains has three surfaces:
(a) The base, which is a disc
(b) The outer curved surface, which was calculated in part (i)
(c) The inner surface resulting from the removal of the hemisphere, which is equal to the curved surface area of a hemisphere.

The areas are as follows:

(a) $\pi r^2 = 49\pi$
(b) 280π
(c) $2\pi r^2 = 98\pi$

Therefore, the total surface area is $427\pi \, \text{cm}^2$.

Volume questions

Example 13

A cone and a cylinder have the same volume. The cylinder has height 8 cm and radius 6 cm. The radius of the cone is 4 cm. Find the height of the cone.

In problems where two objects have the same volume, do not replace π with a number.

The cylinder:

$r = 6$, $h = 8$

$V = \pi r^2 h$
$V = \pi (6)^2 (8)$
$V = 288\pi$

TOP TIPS
Put V on the left of the formula when trying to find V.

Answer: $h = 54$ cm

The cone:

$r = 4$, $V = 288\pi$

$\frac{1}{3}\pi r^2 h = V$

$\frac{1}{3}\pi (4)^2 h = 288\pi$

$\frac{16\pi h}{3} = 288\pi$

$16\pi h = 864\pi$

$h = 54$

TOP TIPS
Put V on the right of the formula when trying to find r or h.

Example 14

A cylinder has height x cm and radius $2x$ cm. A second cylinder has height $2x$ cm and radius x cm. Find the ratio of the volume of the first cylinder to the volume of the second.

First cylinder: $h = x, r = 2x$

$$V = \pi r^2 h$$
$$V = \pi(2x)^2(x)$$
$$V = 4x^3\pi$$

Second cylinder: $h = 2x, r = x$

$$V = \pi r^2 h$$
$$V = \pi(x)^2(2x)$$
$$V = 2x^3\pi$$

$$\frac{\text{First}}{\text{Second}} = \frac{4x^3\pi}{2x^3\pi} = \frac{2}{1}$$

Answer: 2:1

Example 15, Junior Certificate 2003

A solid rectangular metal block has length 12 cm and width 5 cm. The volume of the block is 90 cm³.

(i) Find the height of the block in cm.
(ii) Find the total surface area of the block in cm².
(iii) Each cm³ of the metal has mass 8.4 g. The total mass of a number of these metals is 113.4 kg. How many blocks are there?

(i)
$$lwh = V$$
$$(12)(5)h = 90$$
$$60h = 90$$
$$h = \frac{90}{60} = 1 \cdot 5 \text{cm}$$

TOP TIPS

Length is measured in mm, cm, m or km. Area is measured in mm², cm², m² or km². Volume is measured in mm³, cm³, m³ or km³.

(ii) Total surface area = $2(lw + lh + wh)$
= $2(60 + 18 + 7 \cdot 5)$
= $2(85 \cdot 5)$
= 171 cm^2

(iii) 1 cm³ has mass $8 \cdot 4$ g

90 cm³ has mass $90(8 \cdot 4)\text{g} = 756$ g.

Therefore, the mass of 1 block is 756 g.

$113 \cdot 4 \text{ kg} = 113400$ g

TOP TIPS

The total mass and the mass of one block must be in the same units before dividing.

The number of blocks is $\dfrac{113400}{756} = 150$

Converting units:

1 km = 1000 m	1 km² = 1,000,000 m²	1 km³ = 1,000,000,000 m³
1 m = 100 cm	1 m² = 10,000 cm²	1 m³ = 1,000,000 cm³
1 cm = 10 mm	1 cm² = 100 mm²	1 cm³ = 1000 mm³

Example 16

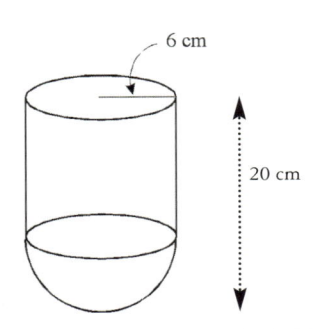

A container is in the shape of a cylinder on top of a hemisphere, as shown. The cylinder has a radius of 6 cm and the container has a height of 20 cm.

Calculate the volume of the container in terms of π.

Solution:

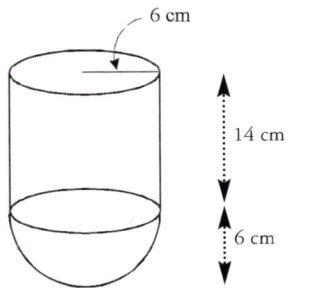

Cylinder:
$h = 14, r = 6$

$V = \pi r^2 h$
$V = \pi(6)^2(14)$
$V = 504\pi$

Hemisphere:
$r = 6$

$V = \dfrac{2}{3}\pi r^3$
$V = \dfrac{2}{3}\pi(6)^3$
$V = 144\pi$

Volume of the container: $648\pi \text{ cm}^3$

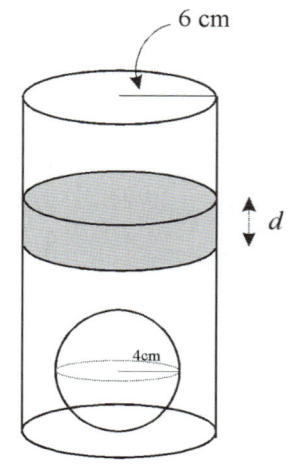

(ii) One-third of the volume of the container is filled with water. Calculate d, the depth of the water in the container.

Solution:
It is easier to find h, the height of the empty part of the container since it involves only one object, a cylinder. Then $d = 20 - h$.

The volume of the empty part is $\frac{2}{3}(648\pi) = 432\pi$.
The radius is 6.

$$\pi r^2 h = V$$
$$\pi(6)^2 h = 432\pi$$
$$h = \frac{432\pi}{36\pi} = 12$$

$d = 20 - 12$
$d = 8 \text{ cm}$

Example 17

A cylinder of radius 6 cm contains liquid. A sphere of radius 4 cm is totally submerged in the liquid so that the liquid rises without overflowing. Find d, the height that the liquid rises, correct to one decimal place.

Solution:

Sphere

$$V = \frac{4}{3}\pi r^3$$
$$V = \frac{4}{3}\pi(4)^3$$
$$V = \frac{256\pi}{3}$$

Cylinder of risen liquid

$$V = \frac{256\pi}{3}, r = 6$$
$$\pi r^2 h = V$$
$$\pi(6)^2 d = \frac{256\pi}{3}$$
$$36\pi d = \frac{256\pi}{3}$$
$$108 d = 256$$
$$d = \frac{256}{108}$$
$$d = 2 \cdot 4 \text{ cm, correct to 1 decimal place.}$$

Example 18

Water flows through a cylindrical pipe of radius 2 cm at the rate of 50 cm/sec. The water flows into a cylindrical container of radius 10 cm. What height will the water have reached in the container after 4 seconds?

> **TOP TIPS**
> The volume of the liquid that rises is equal to that of the submerged object.

> **TOP TIPS**
> The rising liquid takes the shape of the container i.e. in this case, a cylinder.

Solution:
The volume of water passing through the pipe per second is that of a cylinder with radius 2 cm and height 50 cm:

$V = \pi r^2 h$
$V = \pi(2)^2(50)$
$V = 200\pi$

Therefore, the volume of water in the container after 4 seconds is:
$4(200\pi) = 800\pi \text{ cm}^3$

The water in the container is in the shape of a cylinder with radius 10 cm and volume $800\pi \text{ cm}^3$.

$\pi r^2 h = V$
$\pi(10)^2 h = 800\pi$
$100h = 800$
$h = 8 \text{ cm}$

Key Points

- Know where to find the appropriate formula in the mathematical tables.
- Know how to get the perimeter and area of two-dimensional objects such as a rectangle, a square, a parallelogram, a triangle, a circle, a sector of a circle and any object formed by combining these objects.
- Know how to get the surface area and volume of three-dimensional objects such as a rectangular box, a cube, a cylinder, a sphere, a hemisphere and a cone.
- A three-dimensional object may have a number of surfaces. The surfaces may be flat or curved. A solid rectangular block has six flat surfaces, each of which is a rectangle. A solid cylinder has three surfaces, two discs and the curved surface.
- In questions to do with surface area, always check if you need the total surface area or just the curved surface area.
- In problems where two objects have the same volume, do not replace π with a number.
- When asked for the answer in terms of π, do not replace π with a number.
- Length is measured in mm, cm, m or km. Area is measured in mm^2, cm^2, m^2 or km^2. Volume is measured in mm^3, cm^3, m^3 or km^3.
- Before multiplying or dividing measurements, ensure that they are in the same units.
- When an object is totally immersed in a liquid, the volume of the liquid that rises is equal to that of the submerged object.

CHAPTER 15
Coordinate Geometry

Learning Objectives

- Plotting points
- The distance formula
- The midpoint formula
- The slope formula
- The equation of a line
- When given the equation of a line
- Transformations.

The X and Y axes

We begin by drawing a horizontal number line called the X-axis. Then, through the number 0, draw a vertical number line called the Y-axis. The point where the lines intersect is called the **origin**.

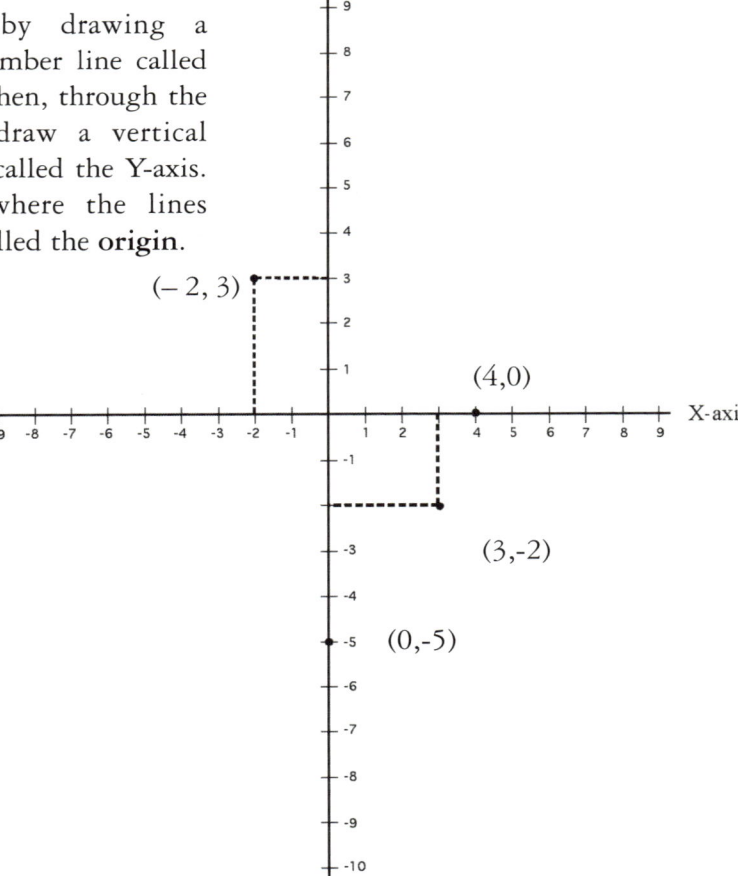

The plane is made up of an infinite set of points. We can now identify the location of any of these points by using two numbers, which we call the coordinates of the point.

The first number is the *x*-coordinate and the second number is the *y*-coordinate. The coordinates are always in round brackets with a comma between them.

The diagram on the previous page shows some points and their coordinates. When dealing with two unknown points we usually call them (x_1, y_1) and (x_2, y_2).

The distance formula

The formula: $\sqrt{(x_2 - x_1)^2 + (y_2 - y_1)^2}$

gives the distance between any two points (x_1, y_1) and (x_2, y_2).

Example 1

Find the distance between the points $a(-3, 2)$ and $b(5, -4)$.

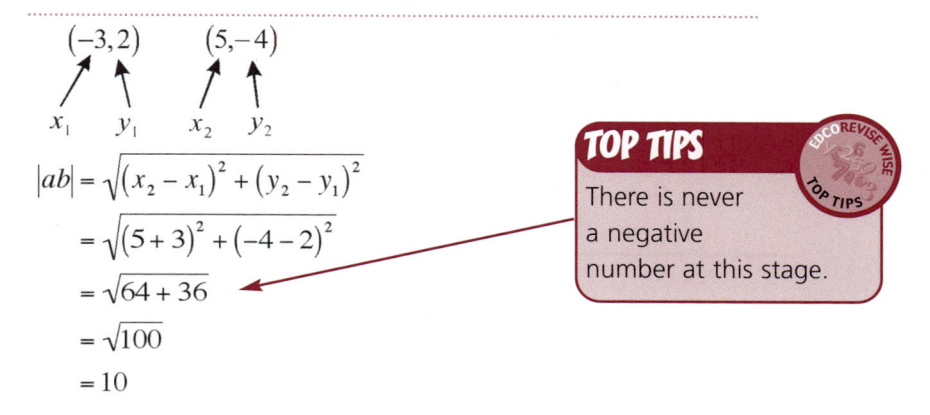

$(-3, 2)$ $(5, -4)$
x_1 y_1 x_2 y_2

$|ab| = \sqrt{(x_2 - x_1)^2 + (y_2 - y_1)^2}$
$= \sqrt{(5 + 3)^2 + (-4 - 2)^2}$
$= \sqrt{64 + 36}$
$= \sqrt{100}$
$= 10$

TOP TIPS
There is never a negative number at this stage.

We can use the distance formula in any problem that can be solved using the lengths of line segments.

Some of the more common problems are:

- **To prove that line segments are equal in length** – find the length of each one, as above.

- **To prove that a triangle is isosceles or equilateral** – find the length of each side. If only two lengths are equal, the triangle is isosceles. If all three sides are equal in length, the triangle is equilateral.

- **To prove that a quadrilateral is a parallelogram** – find the length of each side. Both pairs of opposite sides should be equal in length.

- **To find the radius of a circle** – find the distance from the centre to any point on the circumference.

The midpoint formula

The formula: $\left(\dfrac{x_1 + x_2}{2}, \dfrac{y_1 + y_2}{2}\right)$ gives us the coordinates of the point that is exactly halfway between (x_1, y_1) and (x_2, y_2) and in the same line.

Example 2

Find the midpoint of the line segment $[ab]$, where a is the point $(-5, -1)$ and b is the point $(3, -2)$.

$$\underset{x_1 \quad y_1}{(-5,-1)} \quad \underset{x_2 \quad y_2}{(3,-2)}$$

midpoint: $\left(\dfrac{-5+3}{2}, \dfrac{-1-2}{2}\right)$

$= \left(\dfrac{-2}{2}, \dfrac{-3}{2}\right)$

$= \left(-1, -\dfrac{3}{2}\right)$

Note: Watch out for questions that require the use of the midpoint formula, even though there may be no reference to midpoint in the question!

For example:
- The point b is the image of the point a under central symmetry in the point p. Find the co-ordinates of the point p.
- Find the coordinates of the centre of a circle, given the end points of a diameter.

The slope formula

It is important to remember the following basics concerning slope:

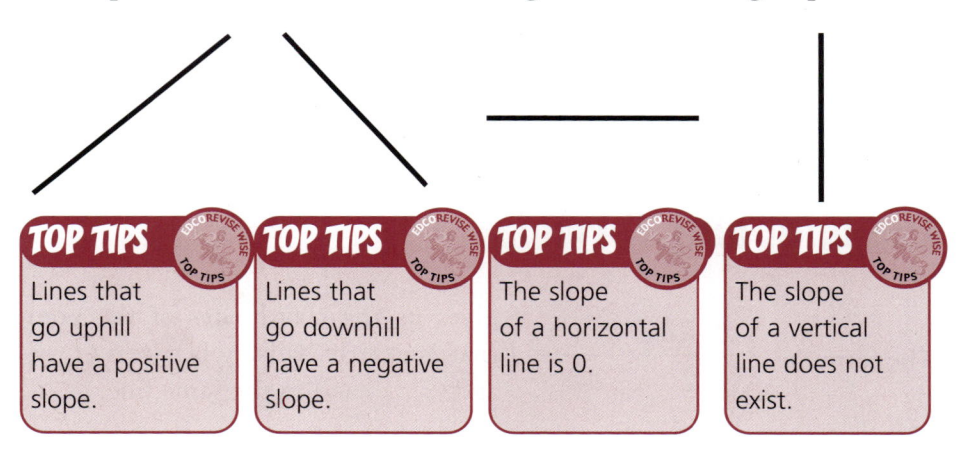

TOP TIPS: Lines that go uphill have a positive slope.

TOP TIPS: Lines that go downhill have a negative slope.

TOP TIPS: The slope of a horizontal line is 0.

TOP TIPS: The slope of a vertical line does not exist.

In coordinate geometry we use the letter m to represent slope.

The formula: $$m = \frac{y_2 - y_1}{x_2 - x_1}$$

gives the slope of the line that passes through the points (x_1, y_1) and (x_2, y_2).

Example 3

Find the slope of the line ab where a is the point $(-5, -1)$ and b is the point $(3, -2)$.

$(-5, -1) \quad (3, -2)$
$x_1 y_1 x_2 y_2$

$$m = \frac{-2 + 1}{3 + 5}$$
$$= -\frac{1}{8}$$

The following are important things to remember about slope:
- Parallel lines have the same slope
- Perpendicular lines have slopes that give −1 when multiplied
- Given the slope of a line, we can obtain the slope of a perpendicular line by turning the given slope upside down and changing the sign.

e.g. $\dfrac{2}{3}$ and $-\dfrac{3}{2}$ represent the slopes of perpendicular lines.

- The slope of a line is the tan of the angle that the line makes with the positive sense of the X-axis.

$m = \tan A$

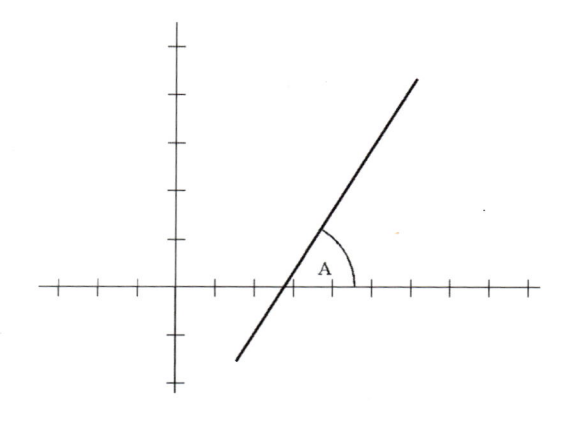

Example 4

Investigate if the triangle abc is right angled, where $a(-1, 3)$, $b(2, 5)$ and $c(4, 2)$.

If the triangle is right angled, then two sides are perpendicular. Begin by finding the slope of each side.

$m_{ab} = \dfrac{5-3}{2+1} = \dfrac{2}{3}$

$m_{ac} = \dfrac{3-2}{-1-4} = -\dfrac{1}{5}$

$m_{bc} = \dfrac{5-2}{2-4} = -\dfrac{3}{2}$

$m_{ab} \times m_{bc} = \dfrac{2}{3} \times -\dfrac{3}{2}$
$= -1$

$\therefore ab \perp bc$

The triangle is right angled at b.

The equation of a line

The formula: $y - y_1 = m(x - x_1)$

gives us the equation of a line when we know:

- a point on the line (x_1, y_1)
- the slope of the line, m.

Example 5

Find the equation of the line through the point (−4, 3) whose slope is $-\dfrac{3}{5}$

The formula is: $\quad y - y_1 = m(x - x_1)$

$$x_1 = -4,\ y_1 = 3,\ m = -\dfrac{3}{5}$$

$$y - 3 = -\dfrac{3}{5}(x + 4)$$
$$5(y - 3) = -3(x + 4)$$
$$5y - 15 = -3x - 12$$
$$3x + 5y - 15 + 12 = 0$$
$$3x + 5y - 3 = 0$$

TOP TIPS

Multiply both sides by 5 to remove the fraction.

The formula cannot be used to get the equation of a vertical line since its slope does not exist. The equation of a vertical line is always $x =$ some number.

For example, the equation of a vertical line through is (−1, −3) is $x = -1$.

When given the equation of a line

1 We can test if a given point is on the line

Substitute the coordinates of the point for x and y in the equation. If the two sides are equal, then the point is on the line, otherwise it is not.

Example 6

Investigate if the point $(3, -4)$ is on the line $5x + 4y + 1 = 0$.

$$\begin{aligned} \text{Is } 5(3) + 4(-4) + 1 &= 0? \\ 15 - 16 + 1 &= 0? \\ 16 - 16 &= 0 \end{aligned}$$

∴ the point is on the line.

2 We can find the coordinates of a point on the line

Substitute any number for either x or y, then solve the resulting equation to find the other letter. Combine the answers to make a point, being careful to put x before y.

Example 7

Find the coordinates of any point on the line $2x - 3y + 8 = 0$.

Let $y = 2$:
$$\begin{aligned} 2x - 3(2) + 8 &= 0 \\ 2x - 6 + 8 &= 0 \\ 2x + 2 &= 0 \\ 2x &= -2 \\ x &= -1 \end{aligned}$$

The point $(-1, 2)$ is on the line $2x - 3y + 8 = 0$.

3 We can find the coordinates of the point where a line crosses the X axis

On the X axis, the *y*-coordinate of every point is 0. Substitute 0 for *y* and solve the resulting equation for *x*.

Note: The equation of the X axis is $y = 0$.

Example 8

Find the coordinates of the point where the line $2x - 3y + 8 = 0$ crosses the X axis.

Let $y = 0$:
$$2x - 3(0) + 8 = 0$$
$$2x + 8 = 0$$
$$2x = -8$$
$$x = -4$$

The line crosses the X axis at $(-4, 0)$.

4 We can find the coordinates of the point where a line crosses the Y axis

On the Y axis, the *x*-coordinate of every point is 0. Substitute 0 for *x* and solve the resulting equation for *y*.

Note: The equation of the Y axis is $x = 0$.

Example 9

Find the coordinates of the point where the line $2x - 3y + 8 = 0$ crosses the Y axis.

Let $x = 0$:
$$2(0) - 3y + 8 = 0$$
$$-3y + 8 = 0$$
$$8 = 3y$$
$$\frac{8}{3} = y$$

The line crosses the Y axis at $\left(0, \frac{8}{3}\right)$.

5 We can find the slope of the line

Rearrange the equation so that y is on its own. The coefficient of x is the slope.

Example 10

Find the slope of the line $3x + 4y - 1 = 0$.

$$3x + 4y - 1 = 0$$
$$\Rightarrow \quad 4y = -3x + 3$$
$$\Rightarrow \quad y = -\frac{3}{4}x + \frac{1}{4}$$

The slope of the line is $-\dfrac{3}{4}$

Note: The slope of the line $ax + by + c = 0$ is always $-\dfrac{a}{b}$, using the above method.

6 We can find a missing coefficient, if we know the slope of a line

Write down the slope of the line in terms of the missing coefficient. Put this equal to the given slope. Solve this equation.

Example 11

The slope of the line $3x - ty - 2 = 0$ is $-\dfrac{2}{5}$. Find the value of t.

The slope of $3x - ty - 2 = 0$ is $\dfrac{3}{t}$ $\quad \left(-\dfrac{a}{b}\right)$

$$\frac{3}{t} = -\frac{2}{5}$$
$$-2t = 15$$
$$t = -7\frac{1}{2}$$

> **TOP TIPS**
>
> When two fractions are equal we can cross-multiply to remove the fractions.

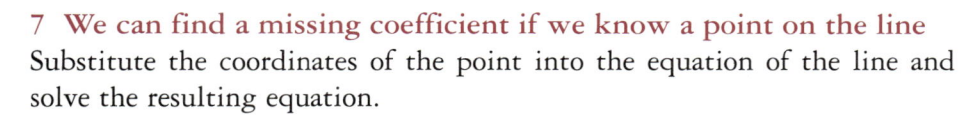

7 We can find a missing coefficient if we know a point on the line

Substitute the coordinates of the point into the equation of the line and solve the resulting equation.

Example 12

Find the value of p if the point $(-1, 3)$ is on the line $x - 5y + p = 0$.

$$(-1) - 5(3) + p = 0$$
$$-1 - 15 + p = 0$$
$$-16 + p = 0$$
$$p = 16$$

8 We can find the equation of a parallel line through a given point
Find the slope of the given line. Using the same slope and the given point, apply the formula $y - y_1 = m(x - x_1)$.

Example 13

Find the equation of the line through $(2, -1)$ that is parallel to the line $x - 4y + 2 = 0$.

The slope of $x - 4y + 2 = 0$ is $\dfrac{1}{4}$. Parallel lines have the same slope.

$$x_1 = 2, \ y_1 = -1 \text{ and } m = \frac{1}{4}$$

The equation is:
$$y + 1 = \frac{1}{4}(x - 2)$$
$$4y + 4 = x - 2$$
$$0 = x - 4y - 2 - 4$$
$$x - 4y - 6 = 0$$

9 We can find the equation of a perpendicular line, through a given point
Find the slope of the given line. Turn the slope upside down and change the sign to get the slope of a perpendicular line. Using this slope and the given point, apply the formula $y - y_1 = m(x - x_1)$.

Example 14

Find the equation of the line through (2, −1) that is perpendicular to the line $x - 4y + 2 = 0$.

The slope of $x - 4y + 2 = 0$ is $\frac{1}{4}$. The slope of a perpendicular line is -4.

$$x_1 = 2, \ y_1 = -1 \text{ and } m = -4$$

The equation is:
$$y + 1 = -4(x - 2)$$
$$y + 1 = -4x + 8$$
$$4x + y - 8 + 1 = 0$$
$$4x + y - 7 = 0$$

10 We can find the point of intersection of two lines (the point where they cross), if we have the equations of both lines

Use simultaneous equations.

Example 15

Find the coordinates of the point of intersection of the lines $3x + 4y - 11 = 0$ and $2x + 7y - 3 = 0$.

$$-6x - 8y + 22 = 0 \qquad\qquad 2x + 7(-1) - 3 = 0$$
$$6x + 21y - 9 = 0 \qquad\qquad 2x - 7 - 3 = 0$$
$$13y + 13 = 0 \qquad\qquad 2x - 10 = 0$$
$$13y = -13 \qquad\qquad 2x = 10$$
$$y = -1 \qquad\qquad x = 5$$

The point of intersection is: $(5, -1)$

11 We can draw a graph of the line
If the equation contains both x and y, we need to find two points on it. If the equation contains only x, it is vertical. If the equation contains only y, it is horizontal.

Example 16

Draw graphs of each of the following lines:
L: $4x - 3y + 6 = 0$; M: $x + 3 = 0$; N: $y - 4 = 0$

To draw L, we need to find two points on it:

Let $x = 0$ $\Rightarrow$ $4(0) - 3y + 6 = 0$
$0 - 3y + 6 = 0$
$6 = 3y$
$2 = y$

Let $y = -2$ $\Rightarrow$ $4x - 3(-2) + 6 = 0$
$4x + 6 + 6 = 0$
$4x = -12$
$x = -3$

$(0, 2)$ is on L.

$(-3, -2)$ is on L.

M is vertical since the equation contains only x.

M: $x + 3 = 0$
  $\Rightarrow$ $x = -3$

N is horizontal since the equation contains only y.

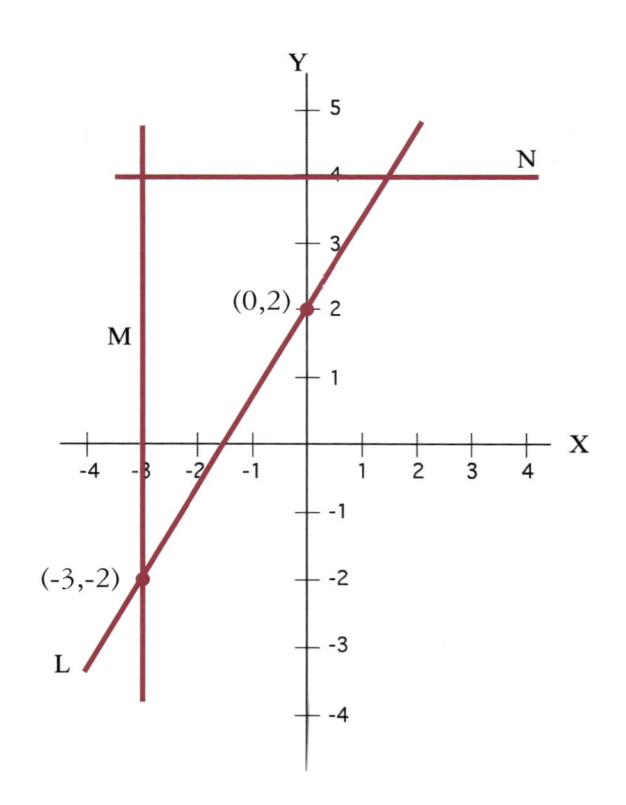

N: $y - 4 = 0$
  $\Rightarrow$ $y = 4$

Transformations

1 Translations

Example 17

Find the image of the point (−5, 6) under the translation $\overrightarrow{ab}$, where a is the point (−3, −1) and b is the point (4, −4).

Solution:
When we perform a translation, we add numbers (sometimes negative numbers) to the x and y coordinates.

In this case, in going from a to b, we have added 7 to x and −3 to y. To find the image of (−5, 6), we again add 7 to x and −3 to y.
(−5, 6) → (2, 3)

Answer: (2, 3)

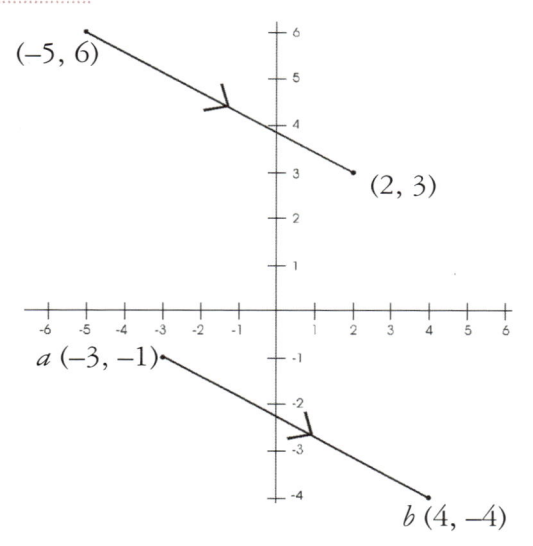

Given the image point, the translation must be applied 'backwards'.

Example 18

The point (−3, 2) is the image of the point a under the translation $\overrightarrow{pq}$, where $p(4, −1)$ and $q(6, 0)$. Find the coordinates of a.

a is the image of (−3, 2) under the translation $\overrightarrow{qp}$.

$$\Rightarrow \begin{array}{c} (6,0) \to (4,-1) \\ \text{add } -2 \text{ to } x \text{ and add } -1 \text{ to } y. \\ (-3,2) \to (-5,1) \end{array}$$

Answer: The coordinates of a are $(-5, 1)$.

A translation is used when we are given three vertices of a parallelogram in order to find the fourth vertex.

Note: Always draw a sketch of the parallelogram first.

Example 19

$abcd$ is a parallelogram, $a(-1, 5)$, $b(0, -1)$ and $c(2, -5)$. Find the coordinates of d.

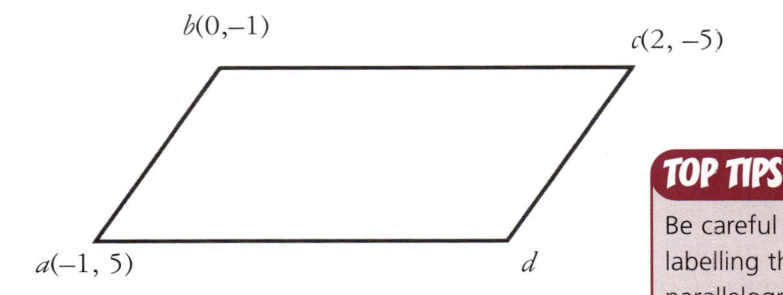

d is the image of a under the translation $\overrightarrow{bc}$.

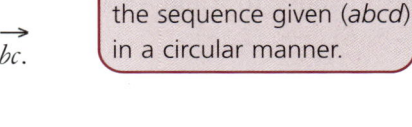

TOP TIPS
Be careful when labelling the parallelogram to follow the sequence given ($abcd$) in a circular manner.

$$(0,-1) \to (2,-5)$$
$\Rightarrow$ add 2 to x and add -4 to y.
$$(-1,5) \to (1,1)$$

Answer: The coordinates of d are $(1,1)$.

2 Central symmetry

Example 20

Find the image of the point $(-2, 5)$ under central symmetry in the point $(3, -1)$.

$$(-2,5) \to (3,-1)$$
$\Rightarrow$ add 5 to x and add -6 to y.
$$(3,-1) \to (8,-7)$$

TOP TIPS
Proceed, as with a translation, with the point we are going through appearing twice – in the top right and the bottom left.

Answer: $(8, -7)$

For central symmetry in the origin (0,0), there is a shortcut. Change the signs of both coordinates.

Example 21

Find the image of (4, −2) under central symmetry in the origin.

Answer: (−4, 2)

3 Axial symmetry

- **Axial symmetry in the X axis:** Change the sign of y, leave x as it is.
- **Axial symmetry in the Y axis:** Change the sign of x, leave y as it is.
- **Axial symmetry in a vertical or horizontal line:** Use a diagram.
- **Axial symmetry in a diagonal line:** See Example 23.

Example 22

Write down the image of (3, −2) under
(i) axial symmetry in the X axis
(ii) axial symmetry in the line $x = 1$
(iii) axial symmetry in the line $y = 1$.

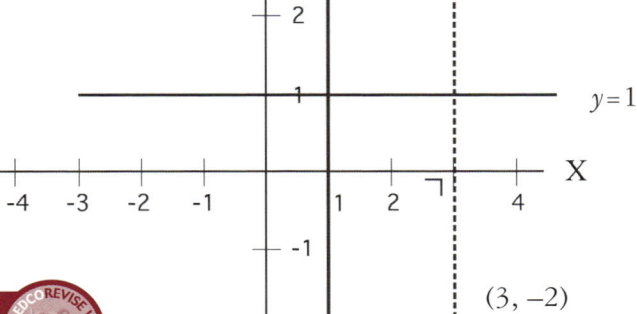

TOP TIPS

To perform an axial symmetry, go through the line at right angles and continue the same distance on the other side.

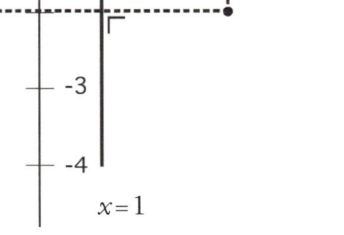

Answers:

(i) $S_x(3,-2) = (3,2)$
(ii) $(-1,-2)$ – diagram.
(iii) $(3,4)$ – diagram.

Example 23

Find the image of the point (2, 4) under axial symmetry in the line L: $x - 2y + 1 = 0$.

First, get the equation of a line K, through (2, 4) perpendicular to L:

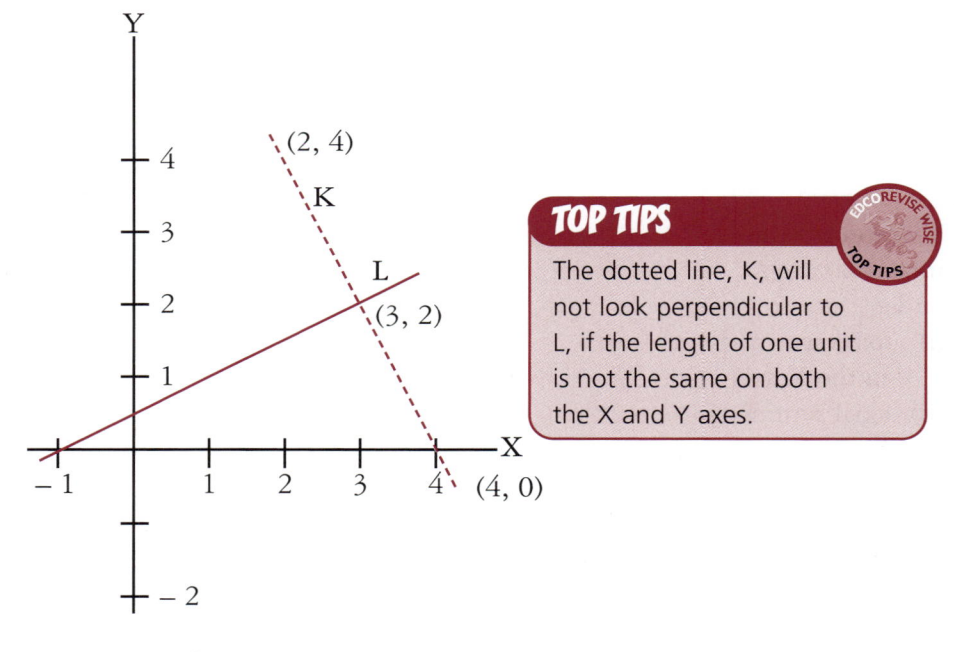

TOP TIPS

The dotted line, K, will not look perpendicular to L, if the length of one unit is not the same on both the X and Y axes.

Slope of L: $\dfrac{1}{2}$ $\Rightarrow$ slope of K: -2

$x_1 = 2$, $y_1 = 4$ and $m = -2$

Equation of K: $y - 4 = -2(x - 2)$
$y - 4 = -2x + 4$
$2x + y - 8 = 0$

CHAPTER 16
Geometry 1 : Proofs of the Theorems

●●● Learning Objectives

Be able to prove each of the following:
- Vertically opposite angles are equal in measure
- The measures of the three angles in a triangle add up to 180°
- An exterior angle of a triangle equals the sum of the two interior opposite angles in measure
- If two sides of a triangle are equal in measure, then the angles opposite these sides are equal in measure
- Opposite sides and opposite angles of a parallelogram are respectively equal in measure
- A diagonal bisects the area of a parallelogram
- The measure of the angle at the centre of a circle is twice the measure of the angle at the circumference, standing on the same arc
- A line through the centre of a circle, perpendicular to a chord, bisects the chord
- If two triangles are equiangular, then the lengths of corresponding sides are in proportion
- Pythagoras' theorem: In a right-angled triangle, the square of the length of the side opposite the right angle is equal to the sum of the squares of the lengths of the other two sides.

Notation

$|ab|$ is the distance from the point a to the point b.
$|\angle abc|$ is the measure of the angle formed by joining the point a to b and then to c.
Alternatively, put B in the angle in the diagram, then $|\angle B|$ is the measure of the angle.

Congruent triangles

The symbol for congruence is ≡, not =. When stating that two triangles are congruent, you must include one of the following: SSS, SAS, ASA or RHS.

TOP TIPS

Abbreviations used with congruent angles:
SSS – Side-Side-Side
SAS – Side-Angle-Side
ASA – Angle-Side-Angle
RHS – Right-Angle-Hypotenuse-Side

1 Vertically opposite angles are equal in measure

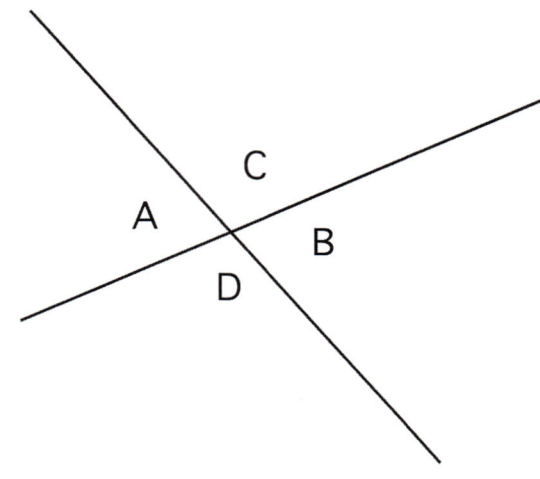

Given: Two intersecting lines with two pairs of vertically opposite angles A and B, C and D.

To prove: $|\angle A|=|\angle B|$ and $|\angle C| = |\angle D|$

Construction: None

Proof:
$|\angle A|+|\angle C|= 180°$ – straight angle
$|\angle B|+|\angle C|= 180°$ – straight angle
$\Rightarrow |\angle A|+|\angle C|= |\angle B|+|\angle C|$
$\Rightarrow |\angle A|=|\angle B|$

Similarly, we can prove that $|\angle C|=|\angle D|$

2 The measures of the three angles in a triangle add up to 180°

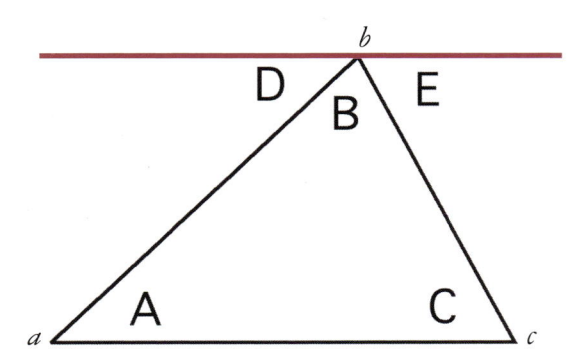

Given: A triangle *abc* with angles A, B and C inside the triangle.

To prove: $|\angle A|+|\angle B|+|\angle C| = 180°$

Construction: Through *b*, draw a line parallel to *ac*. Indicate angles D and E.

Proof:

$|\angle D|+|\angle B|+|\angle E| = 180°$ — straight angle

$|\angle D| = |\angle A|$ — alternate angles

∴ $|\angle C| = |\angle E|$ — alternate angles

$|\angle A|+|\angle B|+|\angle C| = 180°$

3 An exterior angle of a triangle equals the sum of the two interior opposite angles in measure

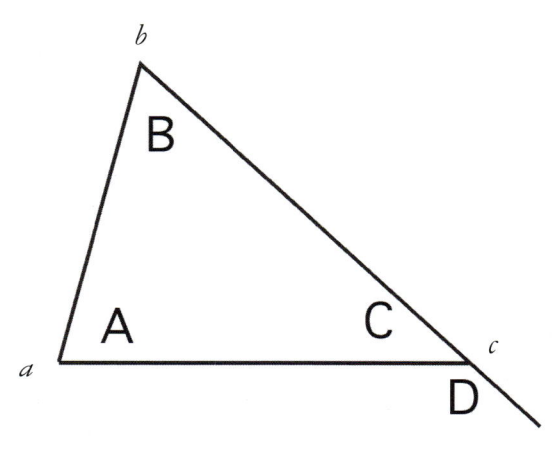

Given: A triangle abc, containing exterior angle D and two interior opposite angles A and B.

To prove: $|\angle D| = |\angle A| + |\angle B|$

Construction: None

Proof:

$|\angle C| + |\angle D| = 180°$ — straight angle

$|\angle C| + |\angle A| + |\angle B| = 180°$ — angles in a triangle add to 180°

$|\angle D| - |\angle A| - |\angle B| = 0$ — subtracting

$\therefore |\angle D| = |\angle A| + |\angle B|$

4 If two sides of a triangle are equal in measure, then the angles opposite these sides are equal in measure

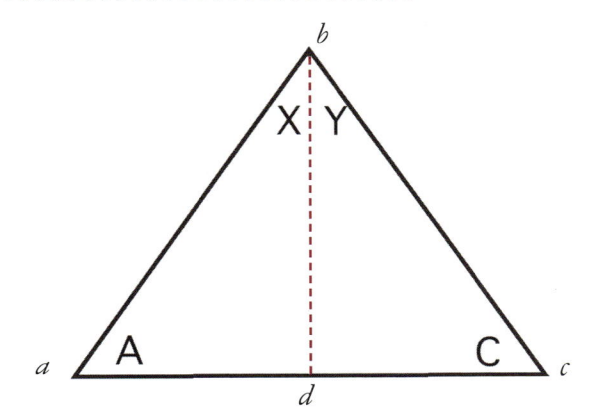

Given: A triangle abc, with $|ab|=|bc|$, angles A and C at the base of the triangle.

To prove: $|\angle A| = |\angle C|$

Construction: Draw the line segment bd, which bisects $\angle abc$ into X and Y.

Proof:

$|ab|=|bc|$ — given
$|\angle X|=|\angle Y|$ — construction
$|bd|=|bd|$

∴ $\triangle bad \equiv \triangle bcd$ — SAS

⇒ $|\angle A|=|\angle C|$ — corresponding parts

5 Opposite sides and opposite angles of a parallelogram are respectively equal in measure

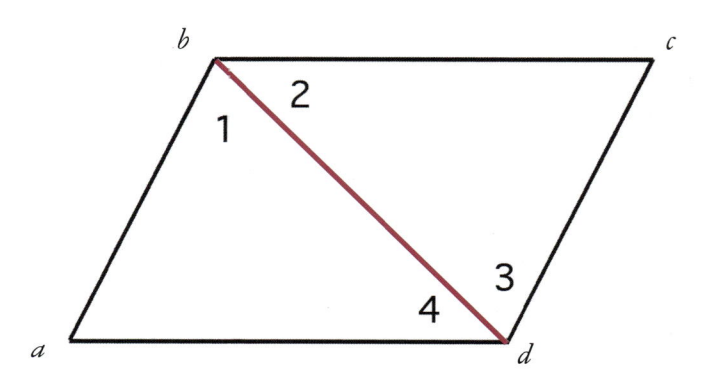

Given: Parallelogram $abcd$.

To prove: $|ab| = |cd|$, $|ad| = |bc|$, $|\angle bad| = |\angle bcd|$ and $|\angle abc| = |\angle adc|$

Construction: Join b to d and label angles 1, 2, 3 and 4.

Proof:

$|\angle 1| = |\angle 3|$	— alternate angles
$|\angle 2| = |\angle 4|$	— alternate angles
$|bd| = |bd|$	— common
$\therefore \; \triangle abd \equiv \triangle bcd$	— ASA
$\therefore \; |ad| = |bc|$	— corresponding sides
$|ab| = |dc|$	— corresponding sides
$|\angle bad| = |\angle bcd|$	— corresponding angles

Also $|\angle 1| + |\angle 2| = |\angle 3| + |\angle 4|$
$\therefore \; |\angle abc| = |\angle adc|$

6 A diagonal bisects the area of a parallelogram

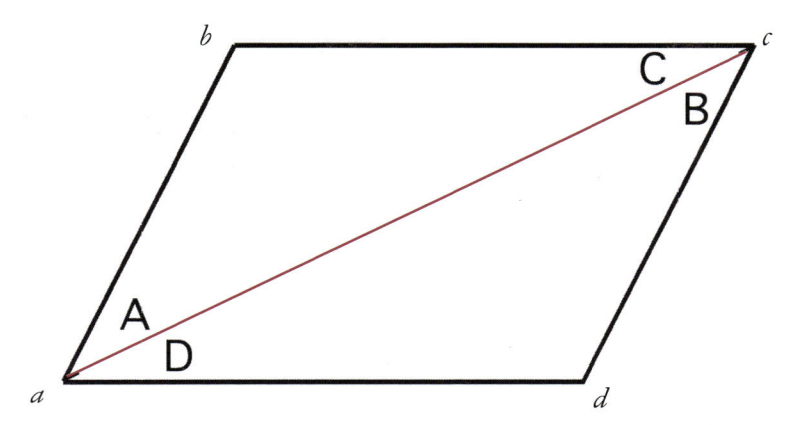

Given: A parallelogram *abcd*.

To prove: The area of the △ *abc* = the area of the △ *adc*.

Construction: Join *ac*. Indicate angles A, B, C and D.

Proof: $|\angle A| = |\angle B|$ — alternate angles
   $|ac| = |ac|$ — common
   $|\angle C| = |\angle D|$ — alternate angles

∴ △*abc* ≡ △*adc*   — ASA

∴ Area △*abc* = Area △*adc*

7 The measure of the angle at the centre of a circle is twice the measure of the angle at the circumference, standing on the same arc

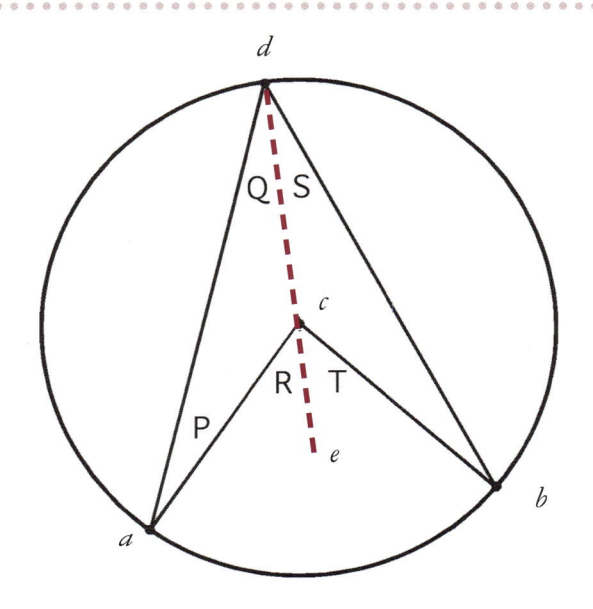

Given: Circle, centre c. $\angle acb$ at the centre of the circle, standing on the arc ab and $\angle adb$ at the circle, also standing on the arc ab.

To prove: $|\angle acb| = 2|\angle adb|$

Construction: Join dc and extend it to e. Indicate angles P, Q, R, S and T.

Proof:

$|ca| = |cd|$	— radius
$|\angle P| = |\angle Q|$	— isosceles triangle
$|\angle R| = |\angle P| + |\angle Q|$	— exterior angle
$|\angle R| = 2.|\angle Q|$	

Similarly, $|\angle T| = 2.|\angle S|$

$\therefore \quad |\angle R| + |\angle T| = 2.|\angle Q| + 2.|\angle S|$

$\Rightarrow \quad |\angle R| + |\angle T| = 2(|\angle Q| + |\angle S|)$

i.e. $|\angle acb| = 2.|\angle adb|$

Deduction 1: All angles at the circumference, standing on the same arc, are equal in measure

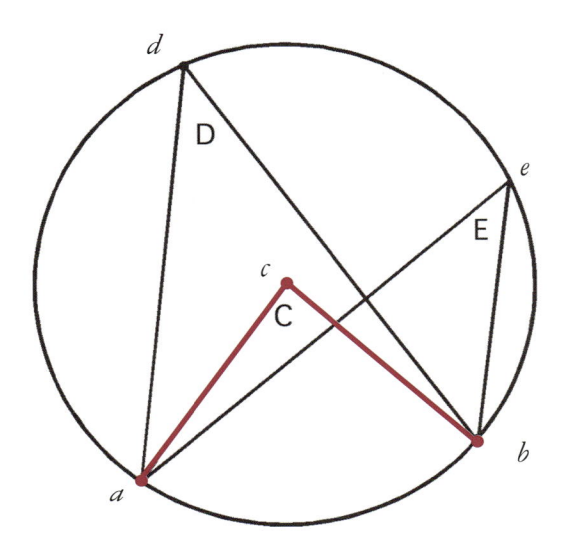

Given: Circle, centre c. $\angle adb$ and $\angle aeb$ at the circle, standing on the arc ab.

To prove: $|\angle adb| = |\angle aeb|$

Construction: Join ac and bc. Indicate angles C, D and E.

Proof:

$|\angle C| = 2.|\angle D|$	– angle at the centre is twice the angle at the circumference
$|\angle C| = 2.|\angle E|$	– angle at the centre is twice the angle at the circumference

$\therefore \quad 2.|\angle D| = 2.|\angle E|$

$\Rightarrow \quad |\angle D| = |\angle E|$

i.e. $\quad |\angle adb| = |\angle aeb|$

Deduction 2: An angle subtended by a diameter at the circumference is a right angle

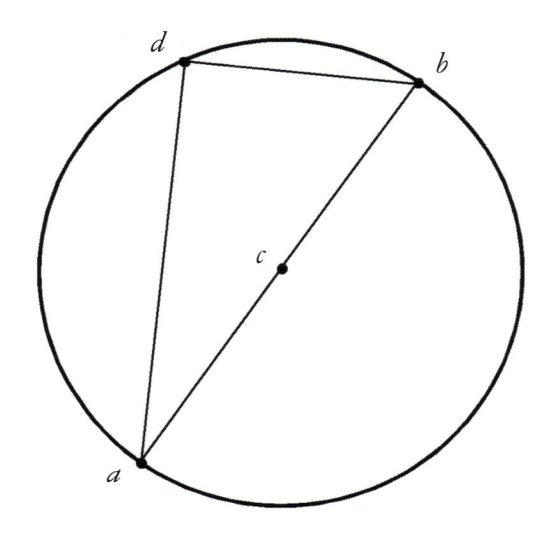

Given: Circle, centre c. Diameter $[ab]$. $\angle adb$ at the circle.

To prove: $|\angle adb| = 90°$

Construction: None

Proof:

$|\angle acb| = 2.|\angle adb|$ — angle at the centre is twice the angle at the circumference

$|\angle acb| = 180°$ — straight angle

$\Rightarrow \quad 2.|\angle adb| = 180°$

$\therefore \quad |\angle adb| = 90°$

Deduction 3: The sum of the opposite angles in a cyclic quadrilateral is 180°

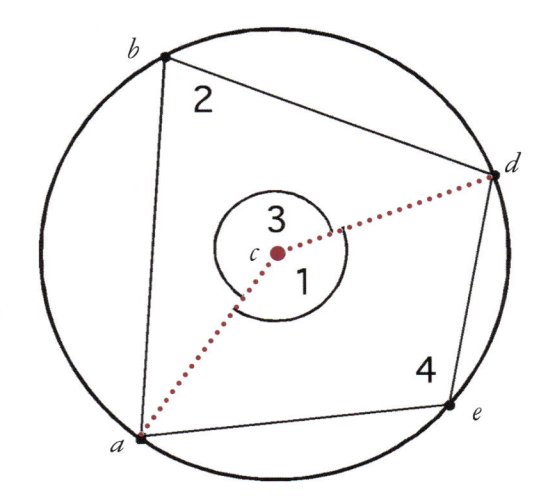

Given: Circle, centre c. Cyclic quadrilateral $abde$.

To Prove: $|\angle abd| + |\angle aed| = 180°$

Construction: Join ac and dc. Label angles 1, 2, 3 and 4.

Proof:

$|\angle 1| = 2|\angle 2|$ – angle at the centre is twice the angle at the circumference

$|\angle 3| = 2|\angle 4|$ – angle at the centre is twice the angle at the circumference

$\Rightarrow \quad |\angle 1| + |\angle 3| = 2|\angle 2| + 2|\angle 4|$

But $\quad |\angle 1| + |\angle 3| = 360°$ – angle in a circle

$\therefore \quad 2|\angle 2| + 2|\angle 4| = 360°$

$\Rightarrow \quad |\angle 2| + |\angle 4| = 180°$

$\Rightarrow \quad |\angle abd| + |\angle aed| = 180°$ Similarly, $|\angle bae| + |\angle bde| = 180°$

8 A line through the centre of a circle, perpendicular to a chord, bisects the chord

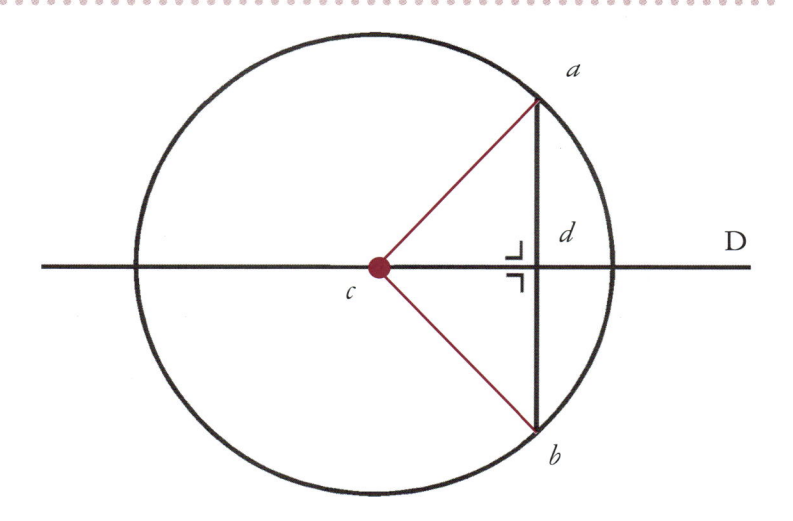

Given: A circle, centre c, a chord $[ab]$ and a line D, through c perpendicular to $[ab]$ and intersecting $[ab]$ at d.

To prove: $|ad| = |db|$

Construction: Join c to a and c to b.

Proof:

$\|\angle adc\| = \|\angle bdc\| = 90°$	– given
$\|ac\| = \|bc\|$	– radius
$\|dc\| = \|dc\|$	– common
$\therefore \quad \Delta adc \equiv \Delta bdc$	– RHS
$\Rightarrow \quad \|ad\| = \|db\|$	– corresponding sides

9 If two triangles are equiangular, then the lengths of the corresponding sides are in proportion

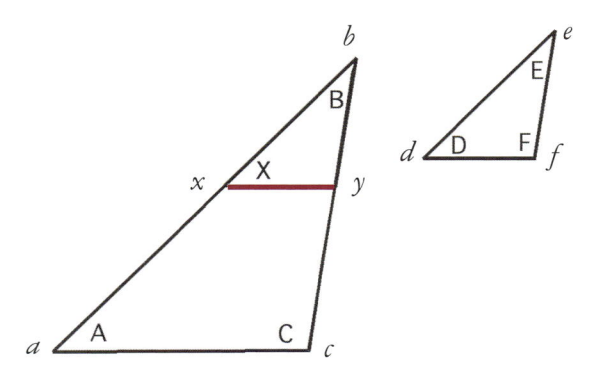

Given: Triangle abc and triangle def, where:
$|{<}A| = |{<}D|, |{<}B| = |{<}E|$, and $|{<}C| = |{<}F|$

To Prove: $\dfrac{|de|}{|ab|} = \dfrac{|ef|}{|bc|} = \dfrac{|df|}{|ac|}$

Construction: Mark a point x on $[ab]$, so that $|bx| = |de|$. Mark a point y on $[bc]$ so that $|by| = |ef|$. Join xy and label angle X.

Proof:

$|bx| = |ed|$	–	construction
$|by| = |ef|$	–	construction
$|\angle B| = |\angle E|$	–	given
∴ $\triangle bxy \equiv \triangle edf$	–	SAS
⇒ $|\angle X| = |\angle D|$	–	corresponding angles.

But $|\angle D| = |\angle A|$ ∴ $|\angle X| = |\angle A|$ ⇒ xy is parallel to ac, since corresponding angles are equal

⇒ $\dfrac{|bx|}{|ab|} = \dfrac{|by|}{|bc|}$

But $|bx| = |de|$ and $|by| = |ef|$

⇒ $\dfrac{|de|}{|ab|} = \dfrac{|ef|}{|bc|}$

Similarly we can prove that: $\dfrac{|ef|}{|bc|} = \dfrac{|df|}{|ac|}$

∴ $\dfrac{|de|}{|ab|} = \dfrac{|ef|}{|bc|} = \dfrac{|df|}{|ac|}$

10 Pythagoras' theorem

In a right-angled triangle, the square of the length of the side opposite the right angle is equal to the sum of the squares of the lengths of the other two sides.

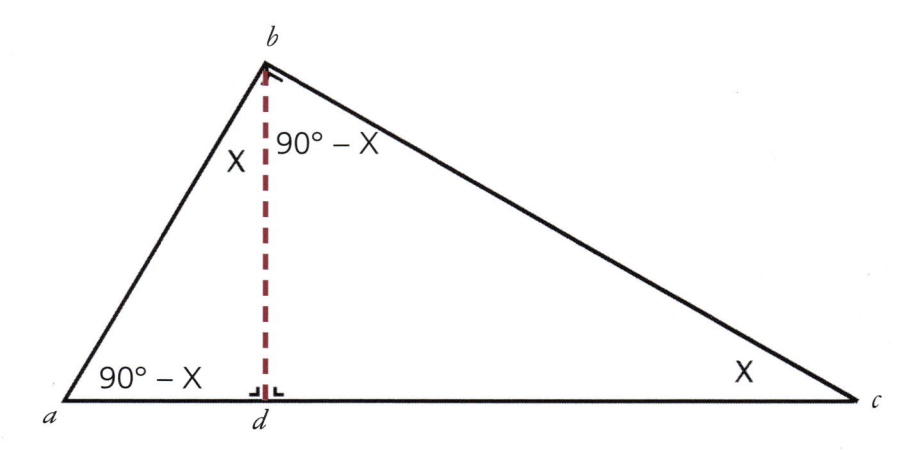

Given: Triangle abc, right angled at b.

To prove: $|ab|^2 + |bc|^2 = |ac|^2$

Construction: Draw $[bd] \perp ac$. Indicate angles X and 90° – X, as shown.

Proof: $\triangle abc$ and $\triangle abd$ are equiangular since they contain the angles X, 90° – X and 90°.

$$\therefore \quad \frac{|ab|}{|ac|} = \frac{|ad|}{|ab|} \quad \Rightarrow \quad |ab|^2 = |ac|.|ad|$$

$\triangle abc$ and $\triangle bdc$ are equiangular since they contain the angles X, 90° – X and 90°.

$$\therefore \quad \frac{|bc|}{|ac|} = \frac{|dc|}{|bc|} \quad \Rightarrow \quad |bc|^2 = |ac|.|dc|$$

$$\therefore \quad |ab|^2 + |bc|^2 = |ac|.|ad| + |ac|.|dc|$$
$$\Rightarrow \quad |ab|^2 + |bc|^2 = |ac|.(|ad| + |dc|)$$
$$\Rightarrow \quad |ab|^2 + |bc|^2 = |ac|.|ac|$$
$$\Rightarrow \quad |ab|^2 + |bc|^2 = |ac|^2$$

Key Points

- Memorise which diagrams go with which theorem.
- Practise reproducing the diagrams.
- Know which theorems involve a construction and what that construction is.
- If congruence is involved, be clear on which parts of the triangle are known to be equal and which parts you are trying to prove are equal.
- With congruence, always state one of the following: SSS, SAS, ASA or RHS.
- Study each theorem carefully and write it out approximately 1 hour after you have studied it.
- Write out the theorems at regular intervals.

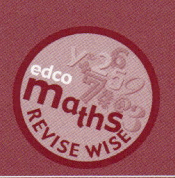

CHAPTER 17
Geometry 2: Sample Problems

Learning Objectives
- Key facts concerning lines and triangles
- Problems involving parallel lines and triangles
- Key facts concerning parallelograms
- Problems involving parallelograms
- Key facts concerning circles
- Problems involving circles
- Key facts concerning equiangular triangles
- Problems involving equiangular triangles
- Pythagoras' theorem
- Problems involving Pythagoras' theorem.

Key facts concerning lines and triangles

1 Vertically opposite angles are equal in measure.

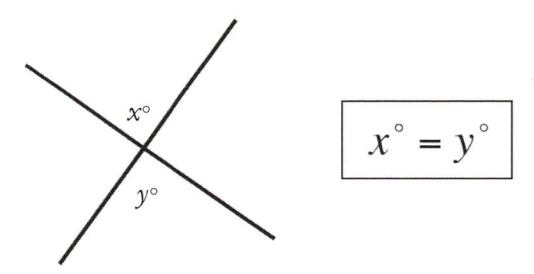

$$x° = y°$$

2 Straight line angles add up to 180°.

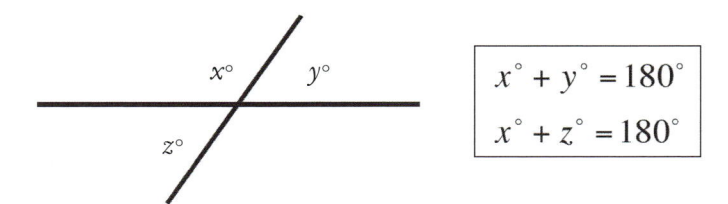

$$x° + y° = 180°$$
$$x° + z° = 180°$$

3 When parallel lines are cut by another line, alternate angles are equal in measure and corresponding angles are equal in measure.

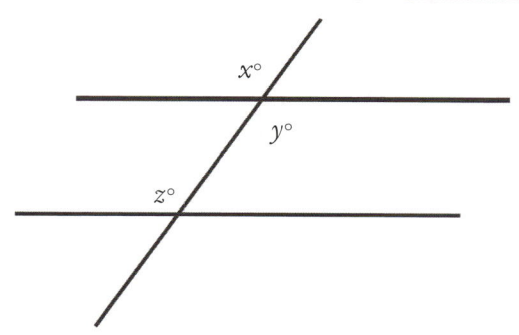

$x° = z°$ — corresponding
$y° = z°$ — alternate

4 The angles in a triangle add up to 180°.

5 The exterior angle in a triangle is equal in measure to the sum of the two interior opposite angles.

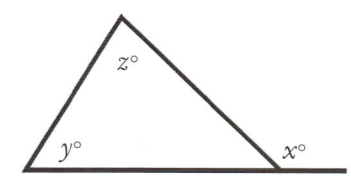

$x° = y° + z°$

6 If two sides of a triangle are equal in length, the angles opposite these sides are equal in measure.

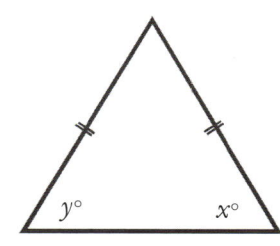

$x° = y°$

7 In an equilateral triangle (three sides equal in length) all angles are 60°.

Problems involving parallel lines and triangles

Example 1

L is parallel to M. Find the values of x, y and z.

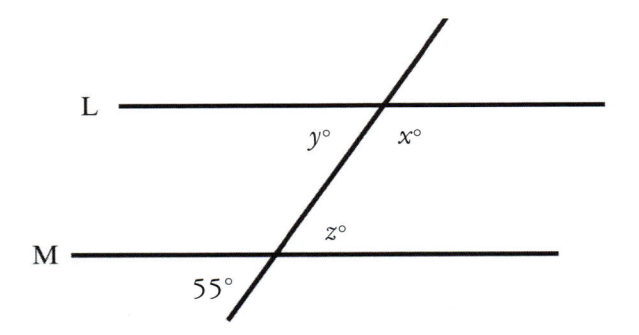

$z° = 55°$ — vertically opposite

$y° = 55°$ — corresponding angles

$x° + y° = 180° \Rightarrow x° = 125°$

Example 2

$|ab| = |bc|$. Find the values of x and y.

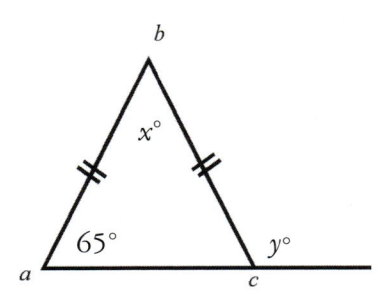

$|\angle acb| = 65°$ — base angles in an isosceles triangle are equal

$x° + 65° + 65° = 180°$ — angles in a triangle

$\Rightarrow x° = 50°$

$y° + 65° = 180°$ — straight angle

$\Rightarrow y° = 115°$

Example 3

The line *bd* is parallel to the line *ac*. Find $x°$ and $y°$.

$x° = 60°$ — alternate angles

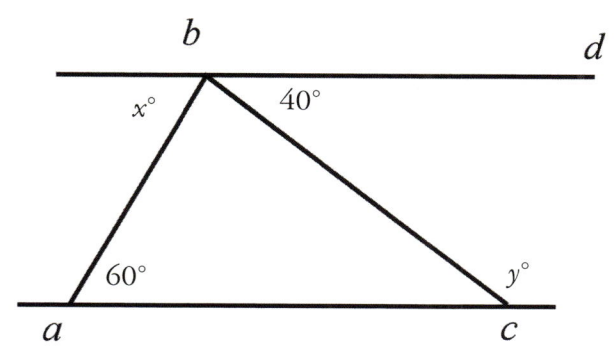

$|\angle bca| = 40°$ — alternate angles

$y° + 40° = 180°$ — straight angle

$\Rightarrow \quad y° = 140°$

TOP TIPS

Copy the diagram and fill in all angles that you know, not just the ones you are asked for.

Example 4

The lines L and M are parallel.

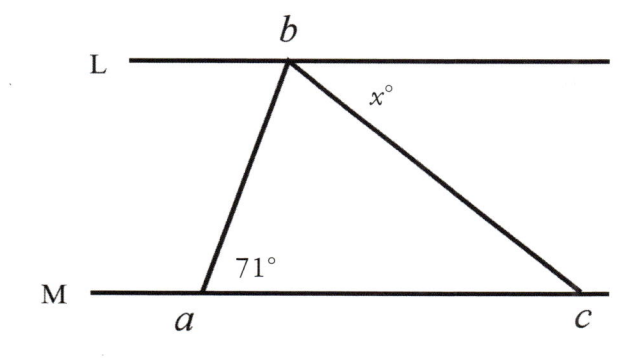

$|ac| = |bc|$.

Find $x°$.

$|ac| = |bc| \quad \Rightarrow \quad |\angle abc| = 71°$

$|\angle bca| + 71° + 71° = 180°$ — angles in a triangle

$\Rightarrow \quad |\angle bca| = 38°$

But $x° = |\angle bca| = 38°$ — alternate angles

Key facts concerning parallelograms

1 Diagonally opposite angles are equal in measure.

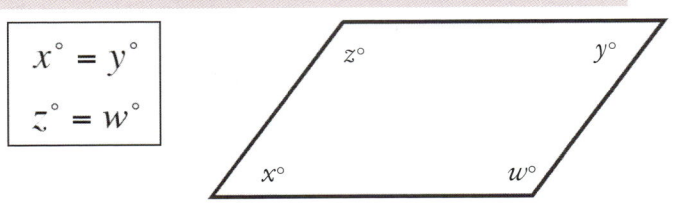

$$x° = y°$$
$$z° = w°$$

2 Adjacent angles add up to 180°.

$$y° + z° = 180° \text{ and } y° + w° = 180°$$

3 Opposite sides are equal in length.

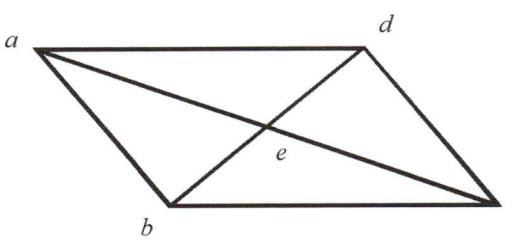

$$|ab| = |cd| \text{ and } |ad| = |bc|$$

4 The diagonals cut one another in half (bisect each other).

$$|ae| = |ce| \text{ and } |be| = |de|$$

5 When a diagonal is drawn, alternate angles are equal in measure. The diagonal does not bisect the corner angle unless the parallelogram is a rhombus (all sides are equal in length).

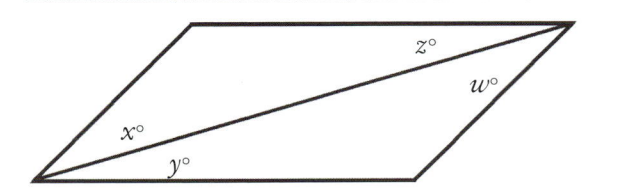

$$x° \neq y° \text{ and } z° \neq w°$$

$$x° = w° \text{ and } y° = z°$$

6 In a rhombus, the diagonals are perpendicular and they bisect the corner angles.

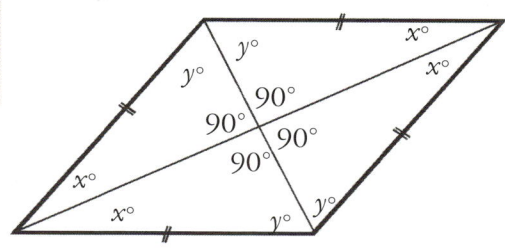

Problems involving parallelograms

Example 5

abcd is a parallelogram. Find $x°$ and $y°$.

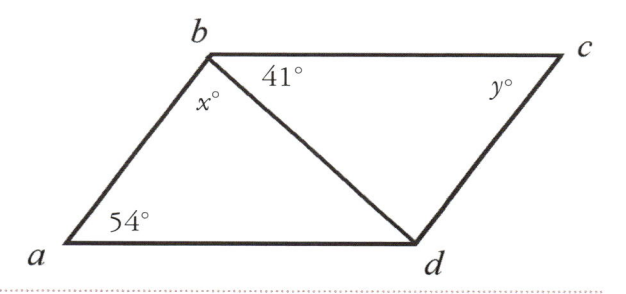

$x° + 41° + 54° = 180°$ — adjacent angles in a parallelogram add up to 180°

$\Rightarrow \quad x° = 85°$

$y° = 54°$ — opposite angles in a parallelogram are equal

Example 6

$abcd$ is a parallelogram. Find $x°$ and $y°$.

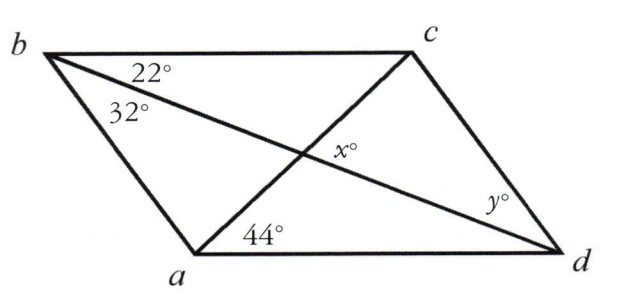

$y° = 32°$ — alternate angles

$|\angle bda| = 22°$ — alternate angles

$x° = |\angle bda| + 44°$ — exterior angle in a triangle
$x° = 22° + 44°$
$x° = 66°$

Example 7

$abcd$ is a rhombus. $|\angle ade| = 65°$

Find $|\angle dce|$.

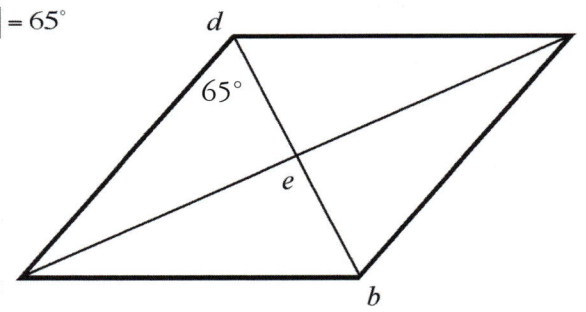

$|\angle dea| = 90°$ — the diagonals of a rhombus are perpendicular

$|\angle dae| = 25°$ — the angles in a triangle add to 180°

$|\angle dce| = |\angle dae|$ — $|da| = |dc|$

$|\angle dce| = 25°$

Example 8

abcd is a parallelogram.

de bisects ∠*adc*.

bf bisects ∠*abc*.

Prove that *de* is parallel to *fb*.

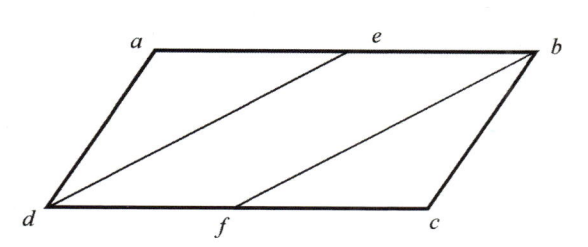

Opposite angles in a parallelogram are equal in measure. Therefore,

$|\angle ade| = |\angle edc| = |\angle fba| = |\angle fbc|$

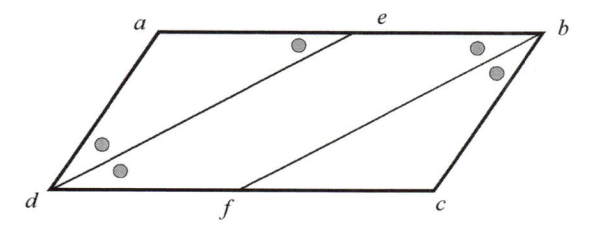

$|\angle aed| = |\angle edf|$ – alternate

∴ $|\angle aed| = |\angle fba|$

∴   *de* is parallel to *fb* – corresponding angles are equal

Example 9, Junior Certificate 2004

In the parallelogram *pqrs*, the points *t* and *w* are on the diagonal [*pr*] such that $|\angle pqt| = |\angle wsr|$.

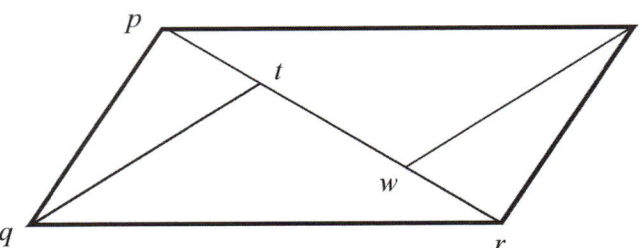

(i) Prove that $|pt| = |wr|$.
(ii) Hence, or otherwise, show that the triangles *psw* and *qtr* are congruent.

(i) Consider the triangles *pqt* and *wsr*.

$|\angle pqt| = |\angle wsr|$ — given
$|pq| = |sr|$ — opposite sides in a parallelogram are equal in length
$|\angle qpt| = |\angle wrs|$ — alternate angles

$\Delta pqt \equiv \Delta wsr$ — ASA

$|pt| = |wr|$ — corresponding sides

TOP TIPS

When asked to prove that two angles are equal in measure, check if they appear in triangles that look alike. If they do, then try to prove that the triangles are congruent.

(ii) Consider the triangles *psw* and *qtr*.

$|ps| = |qr|$ — opposite sides in a parallelogram are equal in length
$|\angle spw| = |\angle trq|$ — alternate angles
$|pw| = |pt| + |tw| = |wr| + |tw| = |tr|$ — $|pt| = |wr|$

$\Delta psw \equiv \Delta qtr$ — SAS

Example 10

abcd is a parallelogram. $e \in [ab]$.
de bisects $\angle adc$ and
ce bisects $\angle dcb$.
Prove that $|\angle dec| = 90°$

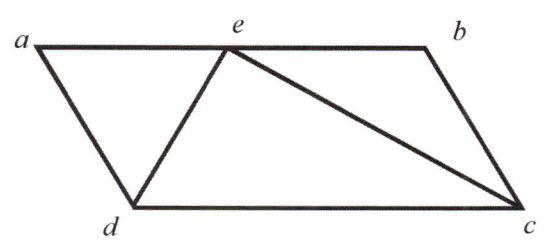

Let $|\angle ade| = X$ and let $|\angle bce| = Y$

Adjacent angles in a parallelogram add up to $180°$.

$\Rightarrow \qquad 2X + 2Y = 180°$

$\Rightarrow \qquad X + Y = 90°$

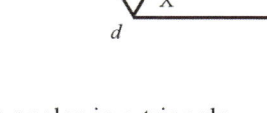

But $\quad X + Y + |\angle dec| = 180°$ — sum of the angles in a triangle

$\Rightarrow \qquad |\angle dec| = 90°$

Example 11

abcd is a parallelogram. *e* and *f* are points on $[bd]$ such that *ea* is parallel to *cf*.

Prove that $|df| = |eb|$.

Consider the triangles *abe* and *dfc*.

$|\angle abe| = |\angle fdc|$ — alternate angles

$|ab| = |dc|$ — opposite sides in a parallelogram

Now extend $[ae]$ to *g*, as shown.

$\qquad |\angle aeb| = |\angle feg|$ — vertically opposite

$\qquad |\angle feg| = |\angle dfc|$ — corresponding

$\Rightarrow \quad |\angle aeb| = |\angle dfc| \quad \Rightarrow \quad |\angle bae| = |\angle fcd|$

$\therefore \quad \triangle aeb \equiv \triangle dfg$ — ASA

$\Rightarrow \quad |eb| = |df|$ — corresponding sides

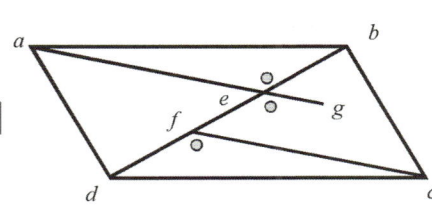

Key facts concerning circles

1. The measure of the angle at the centre, standing on an arc, is twice the measure of the angle at the circumference, standing on the same arc.

$$\boxed{|\angle aob| = 2|\angle acb|}$$

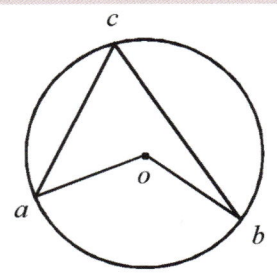

2. All angles at the circumference, standing on the same arc, are equal in measure.

$$\boxed{|\angle adb| = |\angle acb|}$$

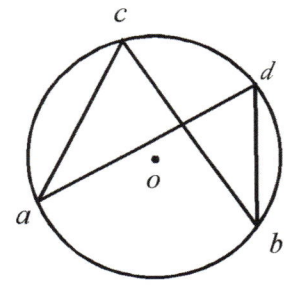

3. The angle at the circumference, standing on a diameter, is 90°.

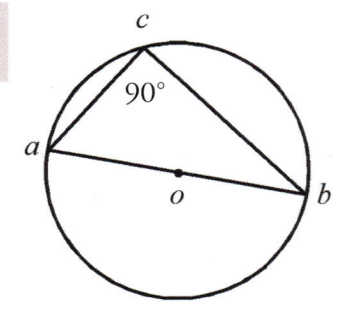

4. Opposite angles in a cyclic quadrilateral add up to 180°. (A cyclic quadrilateral is a four-sided figure formed by joining four points on the circumference.)

$$\boxed{x° + y° = 180°}$$

$$\boxed{z° + w° = 180°}$$

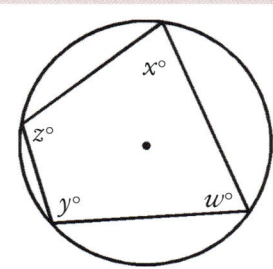

5 A line through the centre of a circle, perpendicular to a chord, bisects the chord. (A chord is a line segment joining two points on the circumference.)

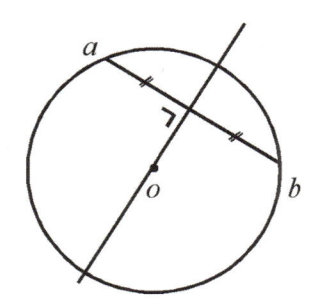

Problems involving circles

Example 12

c is the centre of the circle.
Find $x°$.

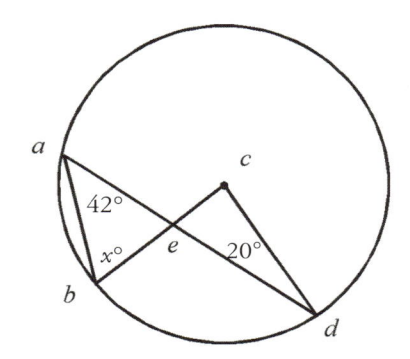

$\lvert \angle bcd \rvert = 84°$	–	the angle at the centre is twice the angle at the circle standing on the same arc (bd)
$\lvert \angle ced \rvert = 76°$	–	the angles in a triangle add up to $180°$
$\lvert \angle bed \rvert = 104°$	–	straight line angles add up to $180°$
$\lvert \angle bed \rvert = x° + 42°$	–	exterior angle in a triangle

$$104° = x° + 42°$$
$$x° = 62°$$

Example 13

c is the centre of the circle.
Find $x°$.

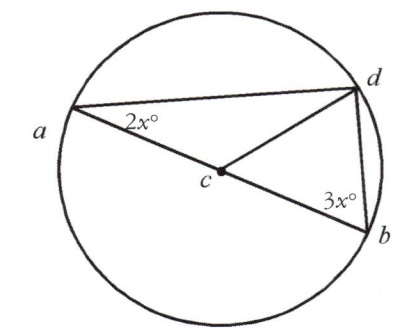

$|\angle adc| = 2x°$ — $|ac| = |cd|$ = radius

$|\angle bdc| = 3x°$ — $|bc| = |dc|$ = radius

$|\angle adb| = 5x° = 90°$ — angle in a semi-circle is 90°

$\Rightarrow \quad x° = 18°$

Example 14

c is the centre of the circle.
Find $x°$.

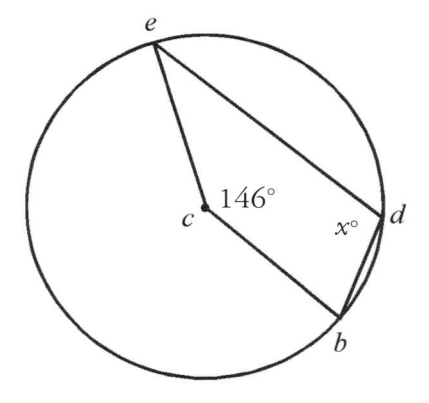

$|\text{reflex}\angle ecb| + 146° = 360°$ — angles in a circle

$|\text{reflex}\angle ecb| = 214°$

$|\text{reflex}\angle ecb| = 2|\angle edb|$ — angle at the centre is twice the angle at the circle standing on the same arc (eb)

$2x° = 214°$

$x° = 107°$

Example 15, Junior Certificate 2004

A circle, centre c, has a chord $[ab]$ of length 8.
d is a point on $[ab]$ and cd is perpendicular to ab.
$|cd| = 3$.

Find the length of a diameter of the circle.

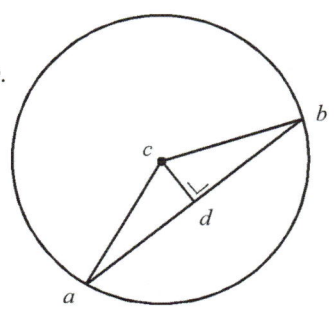

A line through the centre, perpendicular to a chord, cuts the chord in half.

Therefore, $|ad| = 4$

Using Pythagoras theorem, $|ac|^2 = 3^2 + 4^2 = 25$
$\Rightarrow \quad |ac| = 5 =$ the radius

Therefore, the length of a diameter is 10.

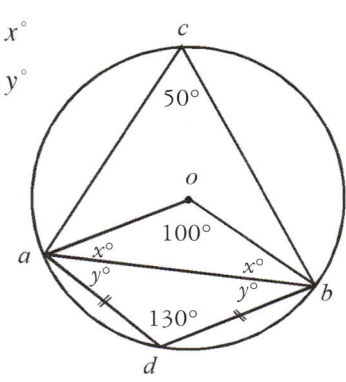

Example 16, Junior Certificate 2004

a, d, b, c are points on a circle, as shown.
o is the centre of the circle.
$|\angle acb| = 50°$ and $|ad| = |db|$.
Find

(i) $\quad |\angle aob|$

(ii) $\quad |\angle adb|$

(iii) $\quad$ By joining a to b, or otherwise, find $|\angle oad|$.

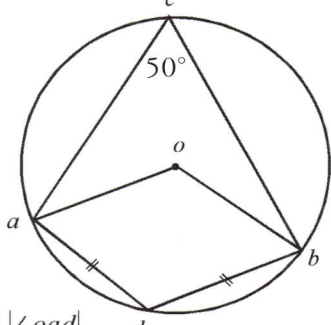

(i) $\quad |\angle aob| = 100°$ — the angle at the centre is twice the angle at the circle, standing on the same arc (ab)

(ii) $\quad |\angle adb| + 50° = 180°$ — opposite angles in a cyclic quadrilateral
$\quad |\angle adb| = 130°$

(iii) Join a to b.

$|oa| = |ob| =$ radius $\quad \Rightarrow \quad |\angle oab| = |\angle oba| = x°$
$|ad| = |bd|$ – given $\quad \Rightarrow \quad |\angle dab| = |\angle dba| = y°$

$2x° = 80° \quad \Rightarrow \quad x° = 40°$
$2y° = 50° \quad \Rightarrow \quad y° = 25°$

$|\angle oad| = x° + y° = 65°$

Example 17, Junior Certificate 2003

a, d, b, c are points on a circle, as shown.

$[ab]$ is a diameter of the circle.

$|ab| = 12$ cm and $|ac| = |cb|$.

(i) Write down $|\angle bca|$, giving a reason for your answer.

(ii) Find $|\angle cdb|$.

(iii) Find $|bc|$.

(iv) Find the area of $\triangle abc$.

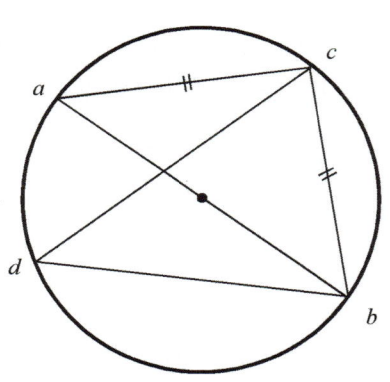

(i) $|\angle bca| = 90°$ — the angle at the circle standing on a diameter is 90°

(ii) $|\angle cdb| = |\angle cab|$ — angles at the circle standing on the same arc are equal in measure

$|\angle cab| = 45°$ — $|ca| = |cb|$
$|\angle cdb| = 45°$

(iii) Let $x = |bc|$

$x^2 + x^2 = 12^2$ — Pythagoras' theorem
$2x^2 = 144$
$x^2 = 72$
$x = \sqrt{72} = 6\sqrt{2}$

(iv) Area $\triangle abc$ = $\frac{1}{2}\sqrt{72} \times \sqrt{72}$

= $\frac{1}{2}(72)$

= 36

Key facts concerning equiangular triangles

1. Equiangular triangles are triangles that contain the same angles. One of them could be regarded as a 'scaled down' version of the other.

   For example, these two triangles are equiangular.

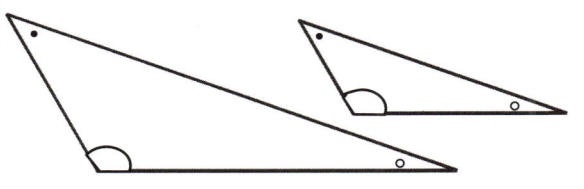

2. If a triangle is cut by a line, parallel to one of the sides, the two triangles are equiangular.

   The triangles *abc* and *dec* are equiangular.

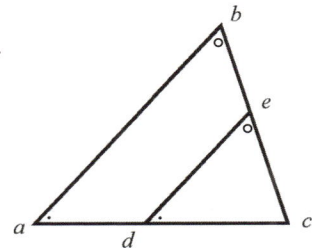

3. To prove that two triangles are equiangular, you must identify two angles in one triangle that you know to be equal to two angles in the other triangle. You must also explain how you know that they are equal.

4. If two triangles are equiangular, then the corresponding sides are proportional. This means when sides that are opposite the same angle are divided, the answer is the same each time.

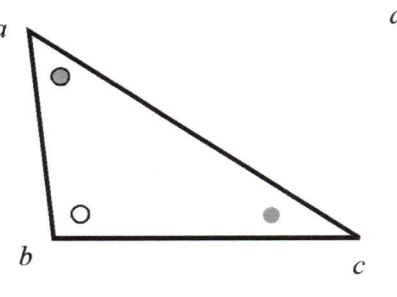

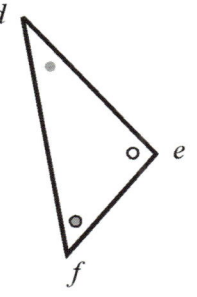

   $$\frac{|ab|}{|ef|} = \frac{|ac|}{|df|} = \frac{|bc|}{|de|}$$

5. Equiangular triangles are also called **similar** triangles.

6. Equiangular triangles must not be confused with **congruent** triangles. Equiangular triangles are usually different in size, whereas congruent triangles are identical in every way.

Problems involving equiangular Triangles

Example 18

The triangles *abc* and *xyz* are equiangular.

$|\angle acb| = |\angle xzy|$ and $|\angle abc| = |\angle xyz|$

$|ab| = 6, |bc| = 5, |xy| = 4$

Find $|yz|$.

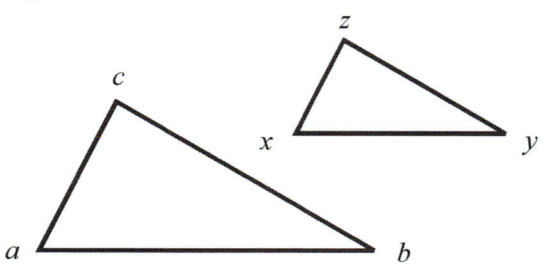

$\dfrac{|yz|}{|bc|} = \dfrac{|xy|}{|ab|}$ — corresponding sides are proportional

$\dfrac{|yz|}{5} = \dfrac{4}{6}$

$|yz| = \dfrac{5 \times 4}{6} = \dfrac{20}{6} = \dfrac{10}{3}$

Example 19

abcd is a parallelogram. *cb* is extended to *f* and *fd* intersects *ab* at *e*.

$|ad| = 8, |eb| = 4$ and $|bf| = 3$

Find $|ae|$.

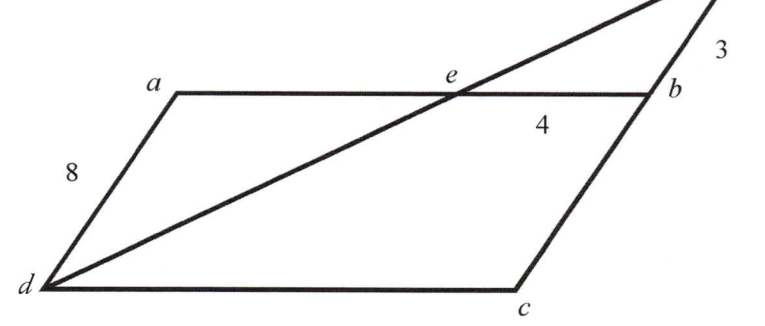

$|\angle aed| = |\angle feb|$ — vertically opposite

$|\angle ade| = |\angle efb|$ — alternate ⇒ Δade and Δebf are equiangular

∴ $\dfrac{|ae|}{|eb|} = \dfrac{|ad|}{|bf|}$ — corresponding sides are proportional

$\dfrac{|ae|}{4} = \dfrac{8}{3}$ ⇒ $|ae| = \dfrac{32}{3}$

Example 20

o is the centre of the circle shown and $[ab]$ is a diameter.

(i) Prove that the triangles ace and deb are equiangular
(ii) Hence, find the radius of the circle.

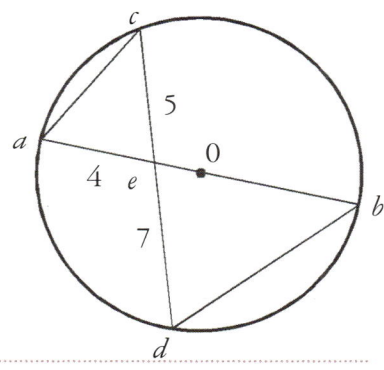

(i) $|\angle acd| = |\angle abd|$ –   at the circle, standing on the same arc ad

      $|\angle aec| = |\angle deb|$ –   vertically opposite

      Therefore, the triangles ace and deb are equiangular.

(ii) $\dfrac{|eb|}{|ce|} = \dfrac{|de|}{|ae|}$ –   corresponding sides are proportional.

$\Rightarrow \quad \dfrac{|eb|}{5} = \dfrac{7}{4}$

$\Rightarrow \quad |eb| = \dfrac{35}{4} = 8\dfrac{3}{4}$

$|ab| = 4 + 8\dfrac{3}{4} = 12\dfrac{3}{4}$ (the diameter) $\quad\Rightarrow\quad$ radius $= 6\dfrac{3}{8}$

Example 21

de is parallel to bc.
$|ae| = 3$ and $|ec| = 4$.

Find $\dfrac{|de|}{|bc|}$.

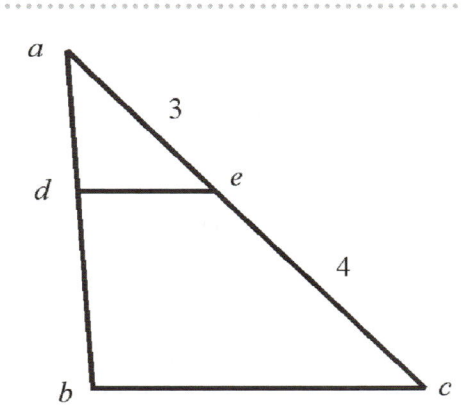

| $\angle ade| = |\angle abc|$ –   corresponding

$|\angle dae| = |\angle bac|$ –   same angle

∴ Δade and Δabc are equiangular

$\Rightarrow \quad \dfrac{|de|}{|bc|} = \dfrac{|ae|}{|ac|} = \dfrac{3}{7}$

Example 22

In the triangle abc the line de is parallel to ac. The point e divides $[bc]$ in the ratio 3 : 2.

Find $\dfrac{\text{area of } \Delta abc}{\text{area of } \Delta bde}$ as a fraction in its simplest form.

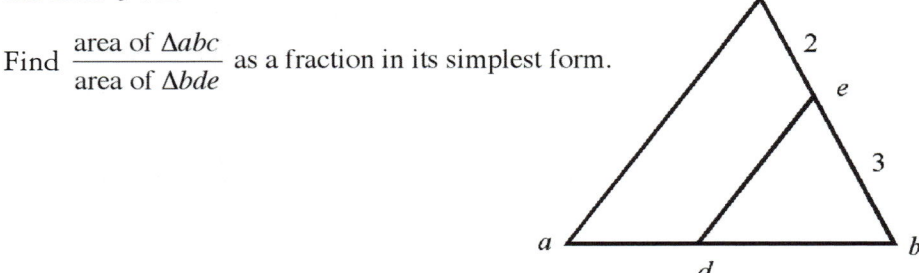

The point d divides $[ab]$ in the ratio 3 : 2 since de is parallel to ac.

Using the formula from trigonometry for the area of a triangle, $\dfrac{1}{2}ab\sin C$

$$\dfrac{\text{area of } \Delta abc}{\text{area of } \Delta bde} = \dfrac{\tfrac{1}{2}|ab|.|bc|\sin\angle abc}{\tfrac{1}{2}|bd|.|be|\sin\angle abc}$$

$$= \dfrac{|ab|}{|bd|} \cdot \dfrac{|bc|}{|be|}$$

$$= \dfrac{5}{2} \cdot \dfrac{5}{2}$$

$$= \dfrac{25}{4}$$

Example 23

The triangle abc is right angled at b. The line bd is perpendicular to ac.

Prove that the triangle abd and the triangle bcd are equiangular.

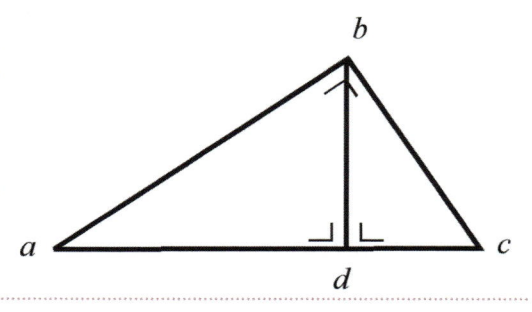

Let $|\angle dab| = X°$ $\Rightarrow$ $|\angle abd| = 90° - X°$
$\Rightarrow$ $|\angle dbc| = X°$
$\Rightarrow$ $|\angle bcd| = 90° - X°$

The $\triangle abd$ and the $\triangle bdc$ are equiangular since they each contain the angles 90°, X° and 90° − X°.

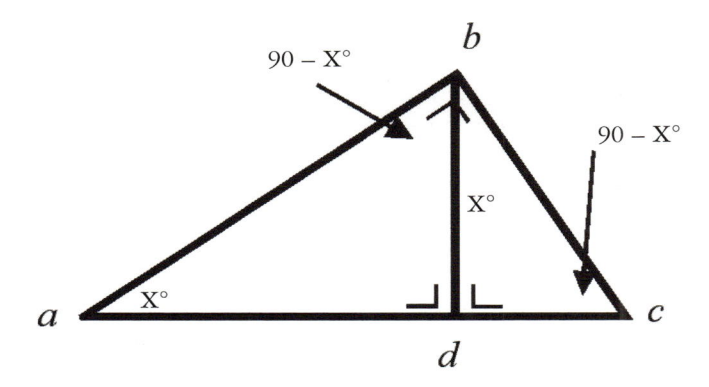

Pythagoras' theorem

Only in a right-angled triangle, the square of the hypotenuse (the side opposite the right angle) is equal to the sum of the squares of the other two sides.

That is, $|ab|^2 + |bc|^2 = |ac|^2$

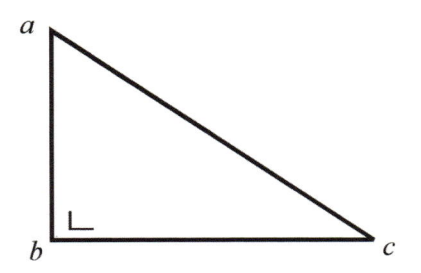

Problems involving Pythagoras' theorem

Example 24

The triangle abc is right angled at b. The line bd is perpendicular to ac.

Prove that $|ab|^2 + |dc|^2 = |bc|^2 + |ad|^2$

TOP TIPS

If you are not sure where to start, look at the diagram and write down any result you know to be true.

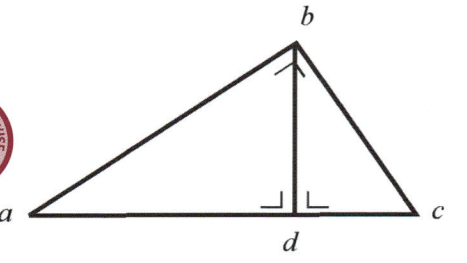

The key to this problem is to involve $[bd]$, the side shared by the two inner triangles, even though $|bd|$ is not mentioned in the question.

The triangle abd is right angled $\Rightarrow$ $|ad|^2 + |bd|^2 = |ab|^2$

$\Rightarrow$ $|bd|^2 = |ab|^2 - |ad|^2$

The triangle bdc is right angled $\Rightarrow$ $|bd|^2 + |dc|^2 = |bc|^2$

$\Rightarrow$ $|bd|^2 = |bc|^2 - |dc|^2$

$\therefore$ $|ab|^2 - |ad|^2 = |bc|^2 - |dc|^2$

$\Rightarrow$ $|ab|^2 + |dc|^2 = |bc|^2 + |ad|^2$

Example 25

The triangle pqr is right angled at q. s is a point on $[pq]$ and t is a point on $[qr]$.

Prove: $|pt|^2 + |sr|^2 = |st|^2 + |pr|^2$.

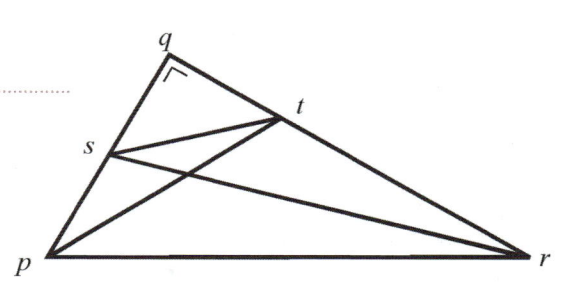

The triangle *pqt* is right angled $\Rightarrow$ $|pt|^2 = |pq|^2 + |qt|^2$

The triangle *qsr* is right angled $\Rightarrow$ $|rs|^2 = |qs|^2 + |qr|^2$

$\therefore$ $|pt|^2 + |rs|^2$ $= |pq|^2 + |qt|^2 + |qs|^2 + |qr|^2$

$\qquad \qquad \qquad = |qs|^2 + |qt|^2 + |pq|^2 + |qr|^2$

$\qquad \qquad \qquad = |st|^2 + |pr|^2 \qquad -$ since Δqst and Δpqr are right angled

Pythagoras' theorem is often combined with the fact that a line through the centre of a circle, perpendicular to a chord, bisects the chord. See Example 15.

Key Points

Lines and triangles
- Vertically opposite angles are equal in measure.
- Straight line angles add up to 180°.
- When parallel lines are cut by another line, alternate angles are equal in measure and corresponding angles are equal in measure – know which is which!
- The angles in a triangle add up to 180°.
- The exterior angle in a triangle is equal in measure to the sum of the two interior opposite angles.
- If two sides of a triangle are equal in length, the angles opposite these sides are equal in measure.
- In an equilateral triangle (three sides equal in length), all angles are 60°.

Parallelograms
- Diagonally opposite angles are equal in measure.
- Adjacent angles add up to 180°.
- Opposite sides are equal in length.
- The diagonals cut one another in half (bisect each other).
- When a diagonal is drawn, alternate angles are equal in measure. The diagonal does not bisect the corner angle unless the parallelogram is a rhombus (all sides are equal in length).
- In a rhombus, the diagonals are perpendicular and they bisect the corner angles.

Circles
- The measure of the angle at the centre, standing on an arc, is twice the measure of the angle at the circumference, standing on the same arc.
- All angles at the circumference, standing on the same arc, are equal in measure.

- The angle at the circumference, standing on a diameter, is 90°.
- Opposite angles in a cyclic quadrilateral add up to 180°. A cyclic quadrilateral is a four-sided figure formed by joining four points on the circumference.
- A line through the centre of a circle, perpendicular to a chord, bisects the chord. A chord is a line segment joining two points on the circumference.

Equiangular triangles
- Equiangular triangles are triangles that contain the same angles.
- If a triangle is cut by a line, parallel to one of the sides, the two triangles are equiangular.
- To prove that two triangles are equiangular, you must identify two angles in one triangle that you know to be equal to two angles in the other triangle.
- If two triangles are equiangular, then the corresponding sides are proportional.
- Equiangular triangles are also called similar triangles.
- Equiangular triangles are not the same as congruent triangles. Equiangular triangles usually differ in size, whereas congruent triangles are identical in every way.

Pythagoras' theorem
- Only in a right-angled triangle, the square of the hypotenuse (the side opposite the right angle) is equal to the sum of the squares of the other two sides.

CHAPTER 18
Geometry 3: Transformations

Learning Objectives
- To recognise the effects of a translation
- To recognise the effects of a central symmetry
- To recognise the effects of an axial symmetry
- To recognise the effects of a rotation.

Effects of a translation

Example 1

Illustrate the image of the figure shown under the given translation.

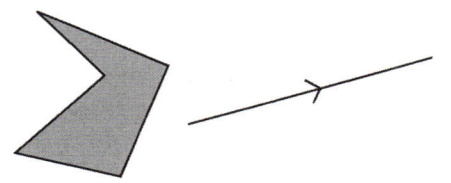

Notice that the image looks exactly like the original.

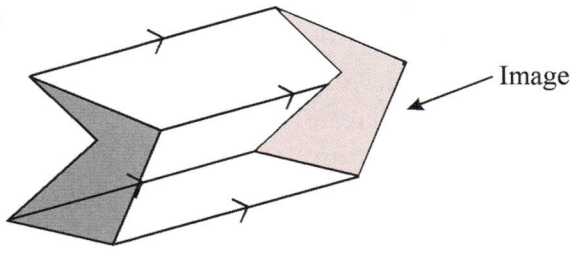

Image

Effects of a central symmetry

Example 2

Illustrate the image of the given figure under central symmetry through p.

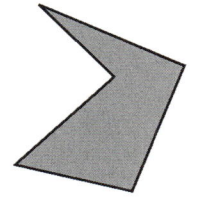

Notice that the original object has been rotated about p through an angle of 180°.

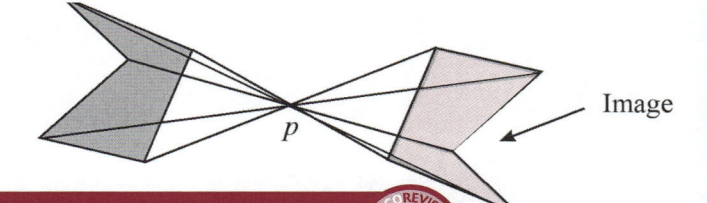

> **TOP TIPS**
>
> Turn the page containing the original object upside down to see what the image should look like.

Effects of an axial symmetry

Example 3

Illustrate the image of the given object under axial symmetry in the line L.

> **TOP TIPS**
>
> Notice that the original object would fit exactly onto its image if the page were folded along the line L.

Notice also that it is not possible to create the image by rotating the original object. This is the easiest way to recognise an axial symmetry.

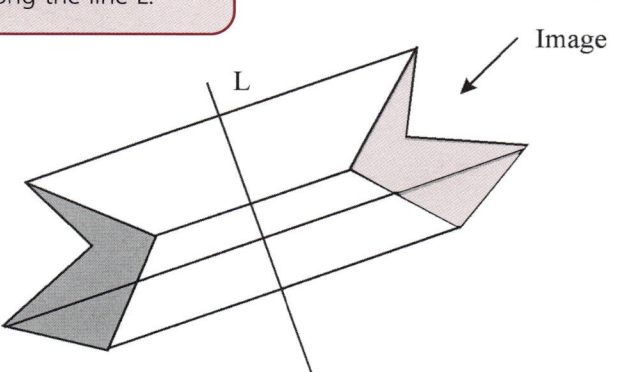

Effects of a rotation

Example 4

Illustrate the image of the given object under a rotation, centre p, through 90°.

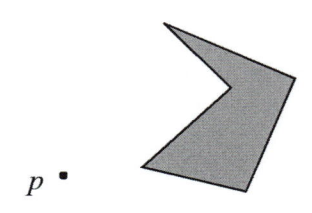

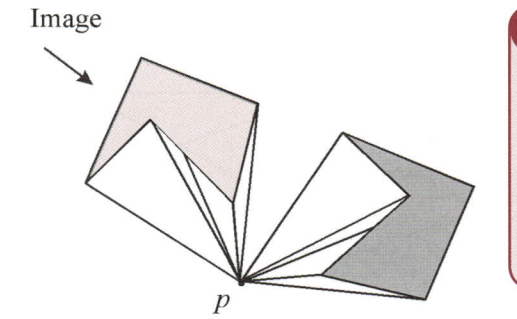

CHAPTER 18: GEOMETRY 3: TRANSFORMATIONS

Image

TOP TIPS

Notice that the appearance of the image can be predicted by turning the page on its side in an anti-clockwise direction (rotation through 90°).

Transformations

Example 5

Each of the objects A, B, C and D below is the image of the figure under one of the following transformations: translation, central symmetry, axial symmetry and rotation through 90°.

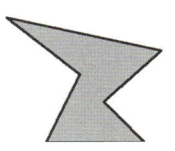

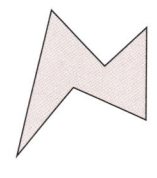

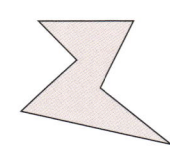

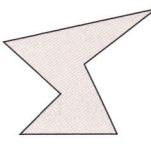

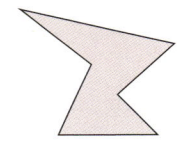

A   B   C   D

State which transformation applies to which object.

A: Rotation through 90°. Turn the page on its side in an anti-clockwise direction.

B: Central symmetry. Turn the page upside down.

C: Axial symmetry. It is impossible to create this object by rotation – try turning the page!

D: Translation. The image looks exactly like the original.

Example 6

The parallelogram *defg* is the image of *abcd* under central symmetry in *d*.

Write down:
(i) the image of *d* under central symmetry in *y*.
(ii) the image of [*ax*] under the translation $\vec{cg}$.
(iii) a transformation that maps △ *bxc* onto △ *fye*.
(iv) the image of [*bx*] under the translation $\vec{bx}$.

(i) *f*.
(ii) [*ey*].
(iii) Central symmetry in *d*.
(iv) [*xd*].

Example 7, Junior Certificate 2003

The diagram shows a regular hexagon. (A regular hexagon has six equal sides and six equal angles.)

(i) How many axes of symmetry has the hexagon?
(ii) Copy the diagram into your answer book and draw in the axes of symmetry.
(iii) [*ad*] and [*cf*] intersect at *o*. What is the measure of the angle of the rotation, about *o*, which maps *a* onto *c*?
(iv) Describe one transformation which maps [*af*] onto [*cd*].

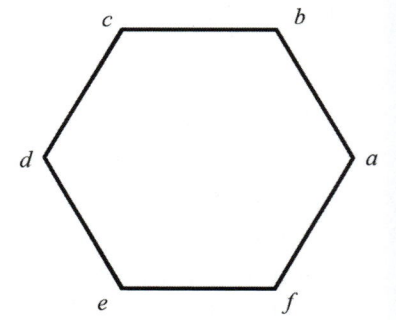

(i) The hexagon has six axes of symmetry.

(ii)

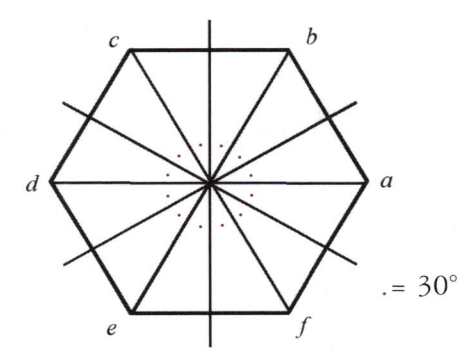

. = 30°

(iii) 120°
(iv) Axial symmetry in the line *be*.
   Other possible answers:
   • Central symmetry in *o*, the point of intersection of the axes of symmetry.
   • The translation $\vec{ac}$ or $\vec{fd}$.
   • Rotation of 180° about *o*.

Key Points

- The image of a translation looks exactly like the original.
- In a central symmetry the original object is rotated about a point through an angle of 180°. The appearance of the image can be seen by turning the page with the original upside down.
- In axial symmetry, the original object fits exactly onto its image if the page is folded along the line of symmetry.
- In a rotation, the appearance of the image can be predicted by turning the page on its side in an anti-clockwise direction (rotation through 90°).

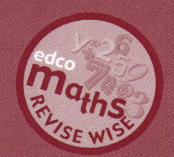

CHAPTER 19
Geometry 4: The Constructions

●●● Learning Objectives

- To construct a triangle given the lengths of the three sides
- To construct a triangle given the lengths of two sides and the measure of the angle where they meet
- To construct a triangle given the length of one side and the measure of two angles
- To construct a triangle given a right angle, the length of the hypotenuse, and the length of another side
- To construct the perpendicular bisector of a line segment
- To construct the circumcircle of a triangle
- To construct the bisector of an angle
- To construct the incircle of a triangle
- To divide a line segment into a specified number of equal parts.

1 A triangle, given the lengths of the three sides

Construct a triangle abc where $|ab|=6$ cm, $|bc|=4$ cm and $|ac|=5$ cm

Step 1

Draw a rough diagram showing the information given.

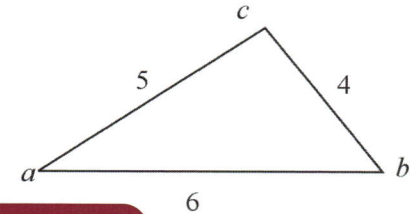

TOP TIPS
Always choose a side whose length you know as base.

Step 2

Draw a horizontal line longer than 6 cm. Label one endpoint a.

With a radius of 6 cm, place the compass at a and draw an arc to cut the line at b, as shown.

Step 3

With a radius of 5 cm, place the compass at a and draw an arc, as shown.

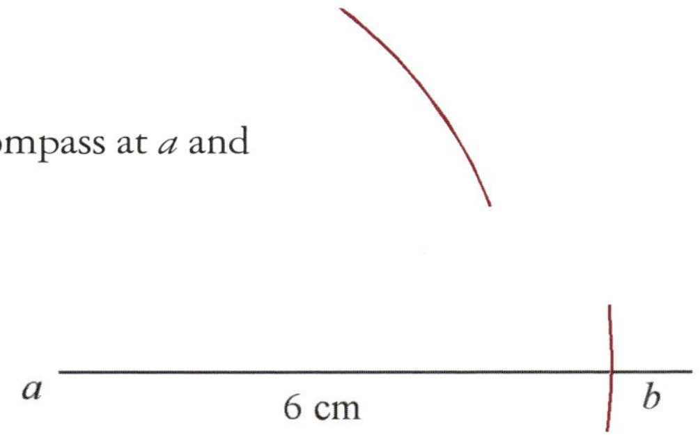

> **TOP TIPS**
> Construction lines should be lightly drawn but clearly visible. Work in pencil.

Step 4

With a radius of 4 cm, place the compass at b and draw an arc to intersect the first arc at c.

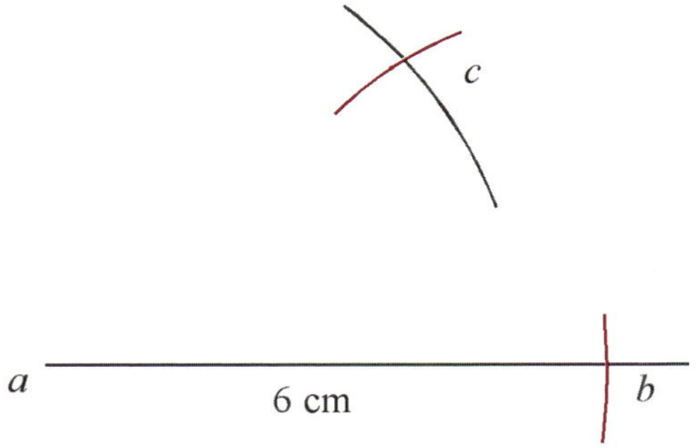

Step 5

Complete the triangle abc and show the lengths 5 cm and 4 cm.

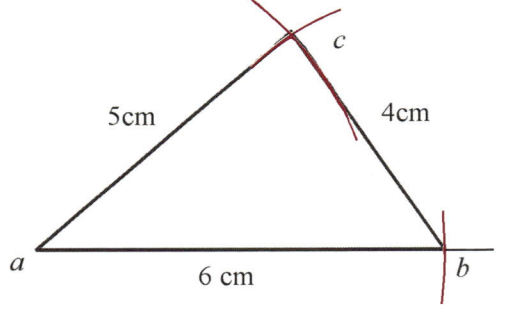

2 A triangle, given the lengths of two sides and the measure of the angle where they meet

Construct a triangle abc where $|ab| = 5$ cm, $|bc| = 3\cdot 5$ cm and $|\angle abc| = 50°$

Step 1

Draw a rough diagram showing the information given.

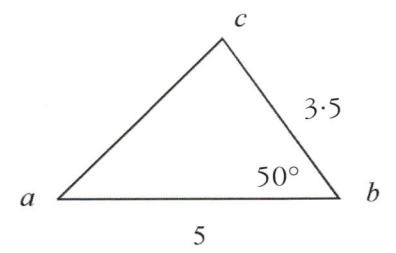

Step 2

Draw a horizontal line longer than 5 cm. Label one endpoint *a*. With a radius of 5 cm, place the compass at *a* and draw an arc to cut the line at *b*, as shown.

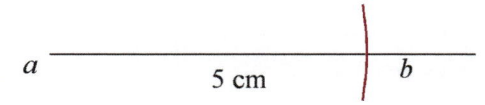

Step 3

Place the protractor at *b* and draw a line longer than 3·5 cm, forming a 50° angle with [*ab*].

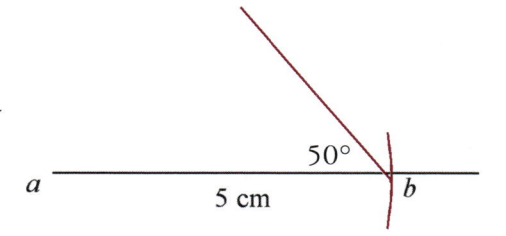

Step 4

Using a radius of 3·5 cm, place the compass at *b* and draw an arc to intersect the previous line, as shown.

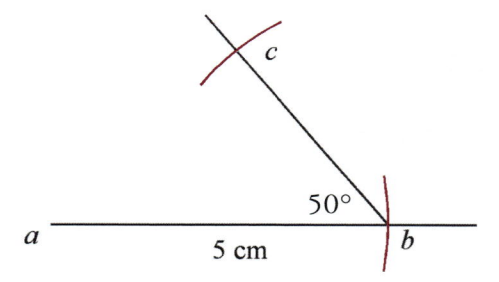

Step 5

Complete the triangle *abc* and show the given information.

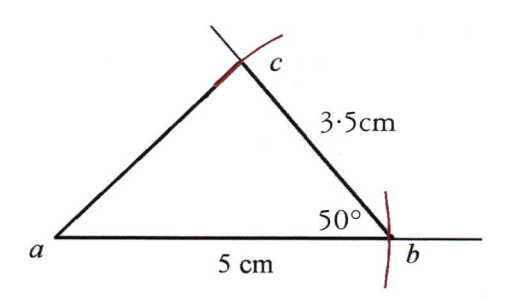

3 A triangle, given the length of one side and the measure of two angles

Construct a triangle abc where $|ab| = 5$ cm, $|<abc| = 35°$ and $|<bac| = 65°$.

TOP TIPS
If two angles are given, you can find the third.

Step 1

Draw a rough diagram showing the information given.

Step 2

Draw a horizontal line longer than 5 cm. Label one endpoint a. With a radius of 5 cm, place the compass at a and draw an arc to cut the line at b, as shown.

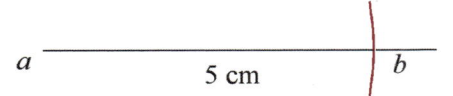

Step 3

Place the protractor at b and draw a line, forming a 35° angle with $[ab]$.

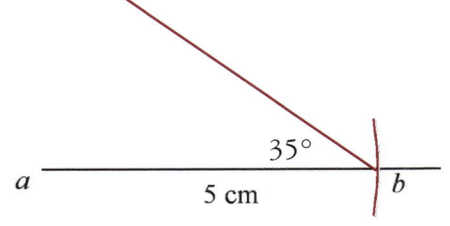

Step 4

Place the protractor at a and draw a line, forming a 65° angle with $[ab]$, intersecting the previous line at c.

This is the required triangle.

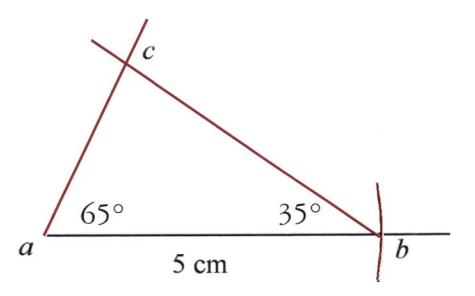

4 A triangle, given a right angle, the length of the hypotenuse, and the length of another side

Construct the triangle abc where $|\angle cab| = 90°$, $|bc| = 6$ cm and $|ab| = 5$ cm.

Step 1

Draw a rough diagram showing the information given.

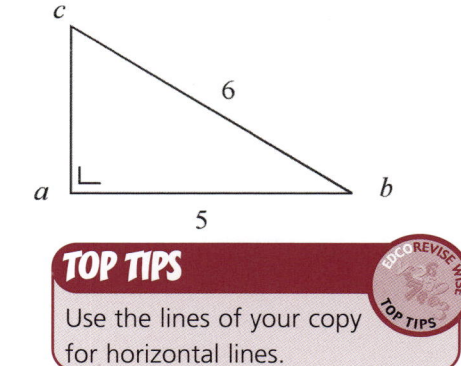

Step 2

TOP TIPS
Use the lines of your copy for horizontal lines.

Draw a horizontal line longer than 5 cm. Label one endpoint a. With a radius of 5 cm, place the compass at a and draw an arc to cut the line at b, as shown.

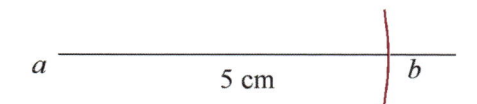

Step 3

Place the protractor at a and draw a line, forming a 90° angle with $[ab]$.

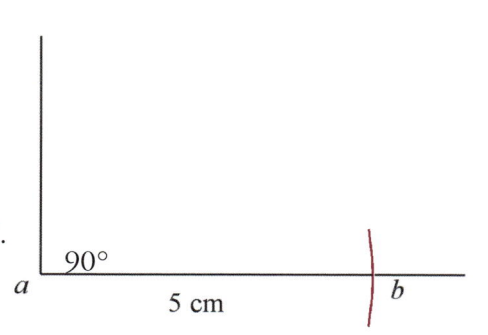

Step 4

Using a radius of 6 cm, place the compass at b and draw an arc to intersect the previous line at c.

Join c to b to complete the triangle.

This is the required triangle.

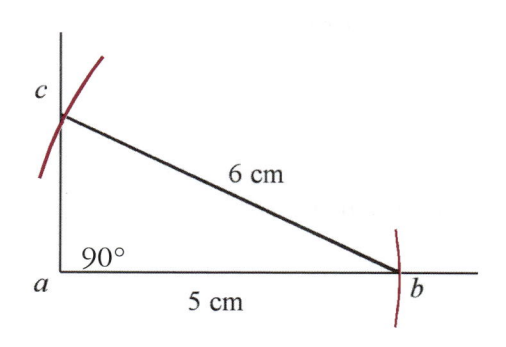

5 The perpendicular bisector of a line segment

Step 1

Draw the line segment [ab].

Place the compass at a and, using a radius greater than half the length of [ab], draw an arc, as shown.

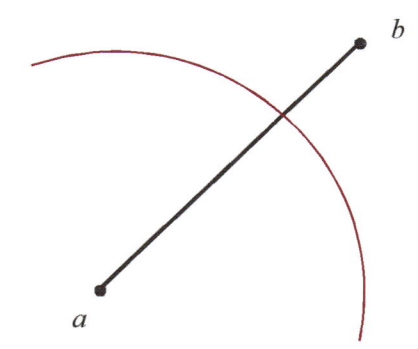

Step 2

Using the same radius, place the compass at b and draw a second arc that cuts the first one twice.

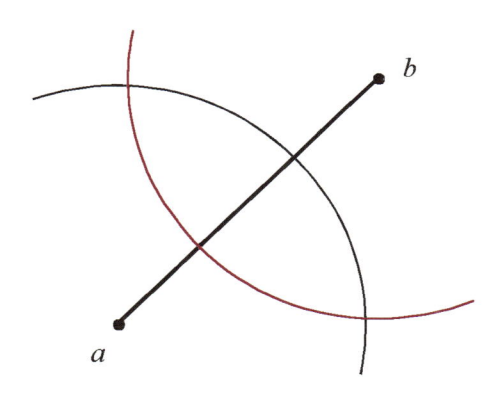

Step 3

Draw the line L through the points of intersection of the arcs, as shown.

L is the perpendicular bisector of [ab].

Every point on L is the same distance from a as it is from b.

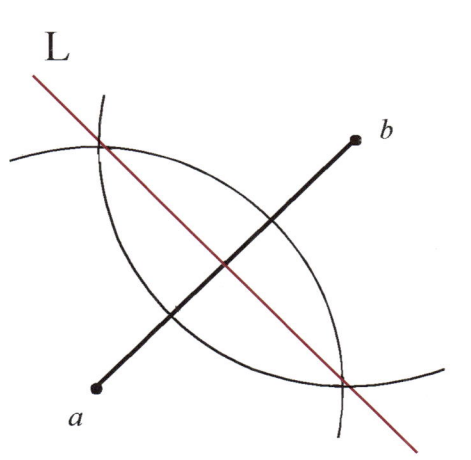

6 The circumcircle of a triangle

Step 1

Construct the triangle *abc*.

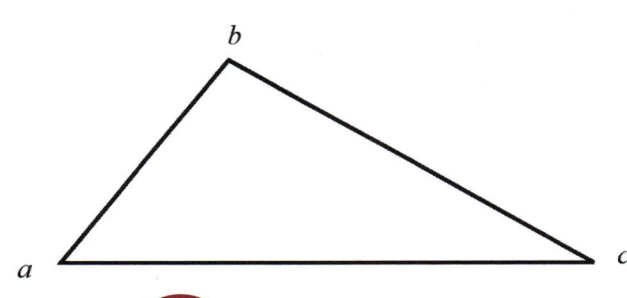

TOP TIPS

For the circumcircle we use the perpendicular bisectors of the sides.

Step 2

Construct L, the perpendicular bisector of [*ab*].

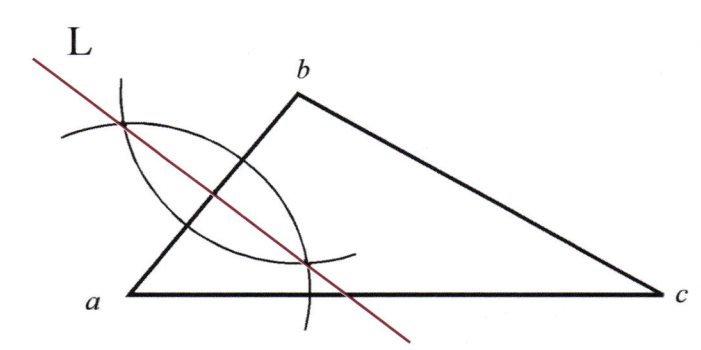

Step 3

Construct M, the perpendicular bisector of [*bc*]. To avoid confusion, use a larger radius than the radius used to construct L.

Call *d* the point of intersection of L and M.

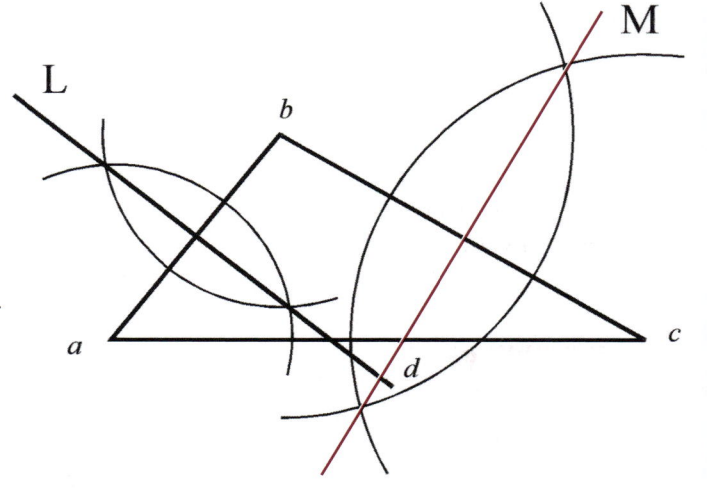

Step 4

Place the compass at d and using $|ad|$ as radius, draw a circle.

The circle should pass through a, b and c and is called the circumcircle of the triangle.

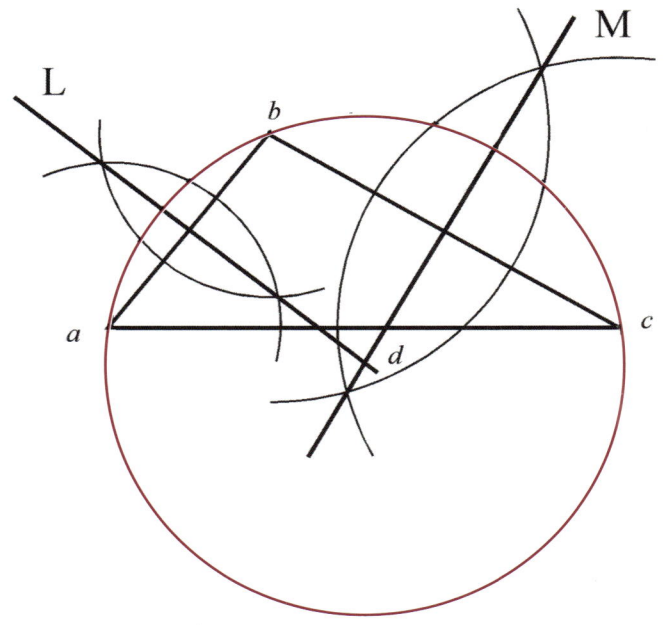

7 The bisector of an angle

Step 1

Construct the angle abc.

If the size of the angle is not specified in the question, make it roughly 70°, as shown.

Step 2

With b as centre and using any length as radius, draw an arc that cuts the arms of the angle at x and y, as shown.

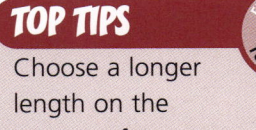

TOP TIPS

Choose a longer length on the compass for greater accuracy.

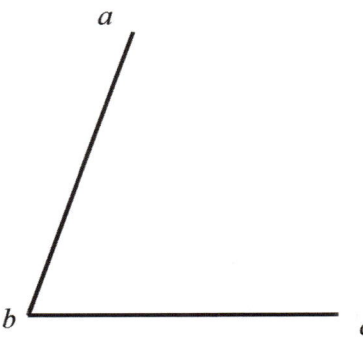

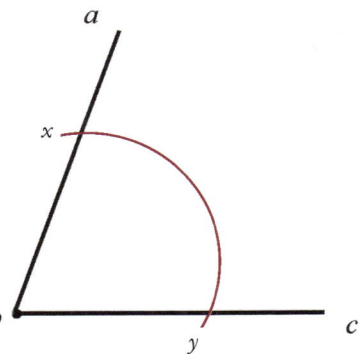

Step 3

Using the same radius, place the compass at x and draw an arc, inside the angle, as shown.

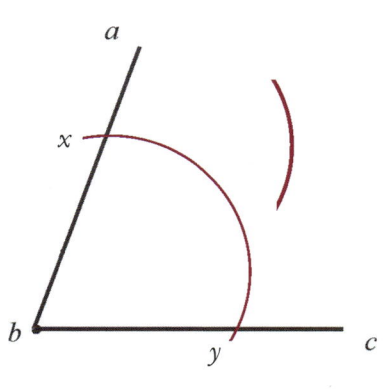

Step 4

Using the same radius, place the compass at y and draw an arc to intersect the previous one at d, as shown.

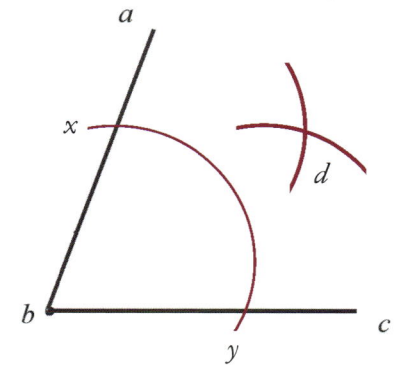

Step 5

Draw a line L from b through d.

L is the bisector of the angle abc.

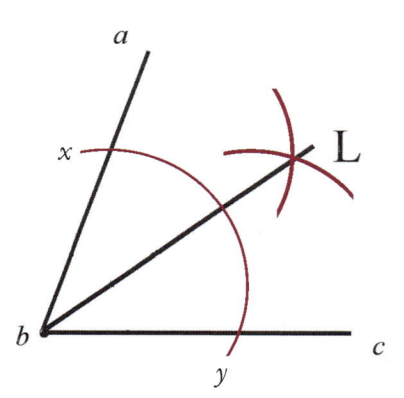

8 The incircle of a triangle

TOP TIPS

For the incircle use the bisectors of the angles.

Step 1

Construct a triangle abc.

The size of the triangle may be specified in the question.

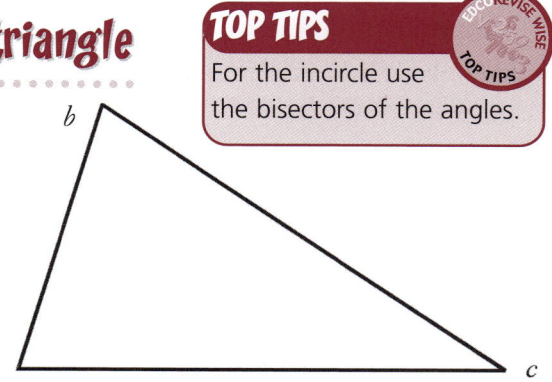

Step 2

Construct L, the bisector of the angle *bac*.

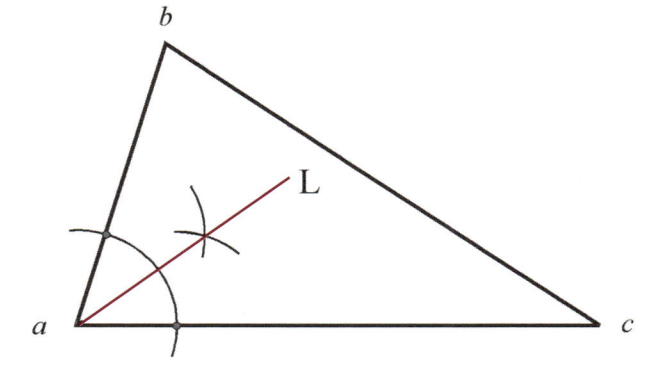

Step 3

Construct M, the bisector of the angle *bca*.

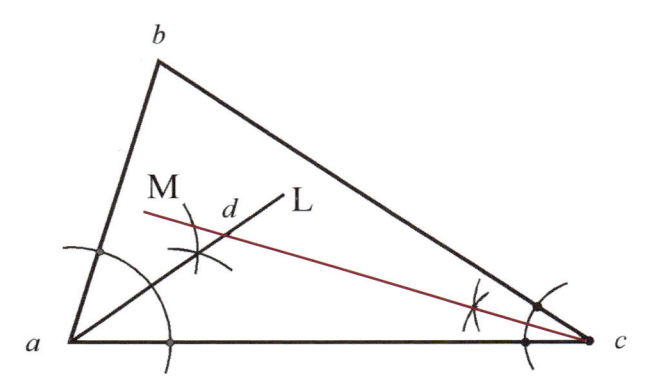

Step 4

Draw a dotted line *de* perpendicular to *ac*.

With *d* as centre and |*de*| as radius, draw a circle. The circle should touch the three sides of the triangle.

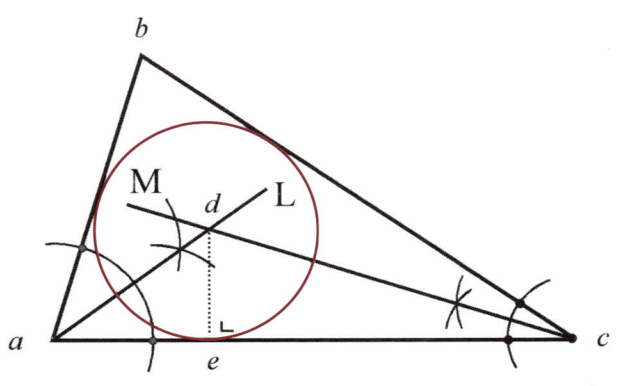

This circle is called the incircle of the triangle.

9 To divide a line segment into a specified number of equal parts

Draw a line segment and divide it into four equal parts.

Step 1

Draw a horizontal line segment [ab].

Step 2

Draw a line segment [ac] at least 7 cm long, as shown.

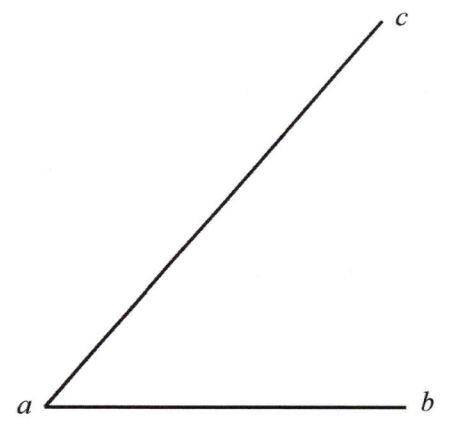

Step 3

With a radius of roughly 1.5 cm, place the compass at a and draw an arc, intersecting [ac] at w.

With the same radius, place the compass at w and mark x. Place the compass at x and mark y. Finally, place the compass at y and mark z.

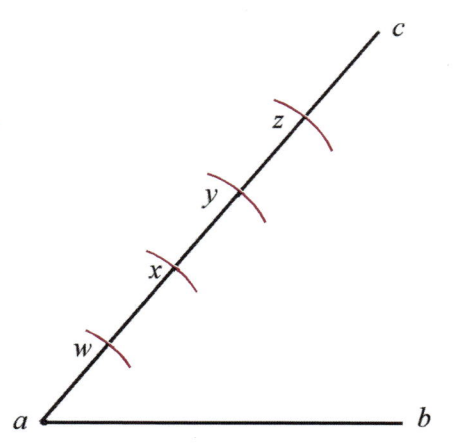

Step 4

Join z to b and draw lines through y, x and w parallel to zb, intersecting $[ab]$ at c, d and e.

c, d and e divide $[ab]$ into four equal parts.

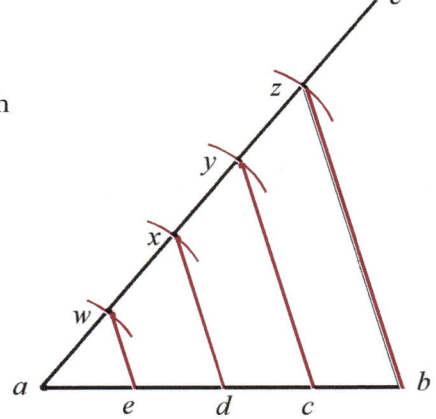

Key Points

- Begin all constructions with a rough diagram, clearly labelled.
- The base of a triangle should always be a side whose length you know.
- Construction lines should be lightly drawn but clearly visible.
- Do not erase any construction lines.
- A circumcircle goes around a triangle and its centre is found using the perpendicular bisectors of the sides.
- An incircle is inside a triangle and its centre is found using the bisectors of the angles.

CHAPTER 20
Trigonometry

●●● Learning Objectives

- Reading sin, cos or tan from a diagram
- Using Pythagoras' theorem
- Constructing an angle
- Using the calculator
- Solving right-angled triangles
- Finding a missing side in a right-angled triangle
- Practical problems
- Compass bearings
- Trigonometry problems with compass bearings
- The area of a triangle
- The Sine Rule
- Solving non-right-angled triangles
- The Unit Circle
- Trigonometric equations.

Introduction

A right-angled triangle is a triangle that contains a 90° angle. Each side in a right-angled triangle is given a special name, either **opposite**, **adjacent** or **hypotenuse**.

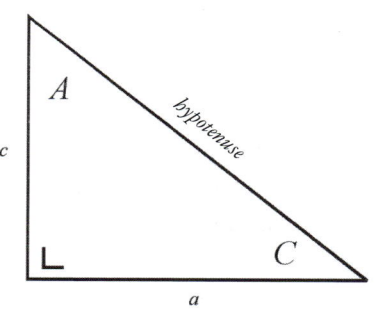

The side opposite the right angle is the hypotenuse. It is always the longest side. The names given to the other two sides vary, as shown in the diagram.

Opposite the angle A

Adjacent to the angle C

We usually use a capital letter to represent an unknown angle and the corresponding lowercase letter for the length of the opposite side.

CHAPTER 20: TRIGONOMETRY

Every fraction that can be formed using two sides of a right-angled triangle has a special name. The three fractions that we use are called **sin, cos** and **tan**.

$$\sin A = \frac{\text{opposite}}{\text{hypotenuse}} \qquad \cos A = \frac{\text{adjacent}}{\text{hypotenuse}} \qquad \tan A = \frac{\text{opposite}}{\text{adjacent}}$$

Reading sin, cos or tan from a diagram

Example 1

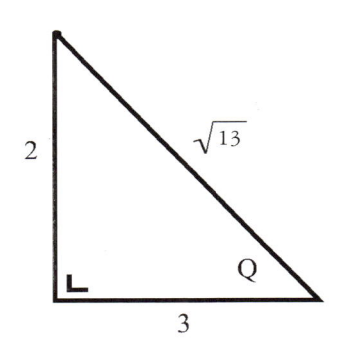

In the triangle on the right:

The side opposite Q is 2.
The side adjacent to Q is 3.
The hypotenuse is $\sqrt{13}$.

Therefore: $\sin Q = \dfrac{2}{\sqrt{13}}, \quad \cos Q = \dfrac{3}{\sqrt{13}}$ and $\tan Q = \dfrac{2}{3}$

Example 2

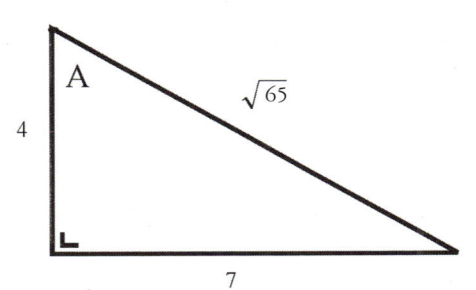

The side opposite A is 7.
The side adjacent to A is 4.
The hypotenuse is $\sqrt{65}$.

Therefore:
$\sin A = \dfrac{7}{\sqrt{65}}, \quad \cos A = \dfrac{4}{\sqrt{65}}, \quad \tan A = \dfrac{7}{4}$

Using Pythagoras' theorem

Given two sides of a right-angled triangle, use Pythagoras' theorem to find the third.

Example 3

Find x.

Using Pythagoras: $x^2 = 3^2 + 4^2$
$x^2 = 25$
$x = 5$

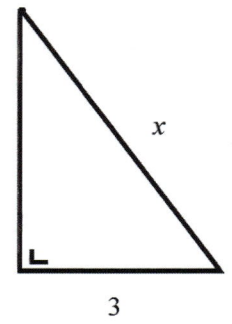

Example 4

Find x and then write down the value of tanA.

We proceed as in Example 3.

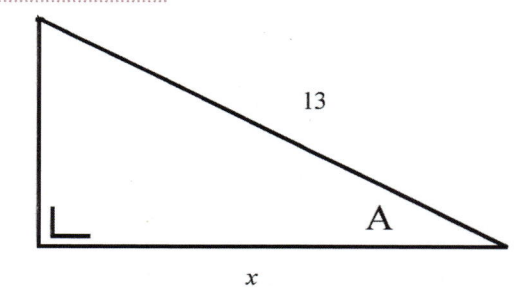

$x^2 + 5^2 = 13^2$
$x^2 = 144$ $\therefore \tan B = \dfrac{12}{5}$
$x = 12$

If we are given the sin, cos or tan of an angle, then we know two sides of a right-angled triangle containing that angle. We can then proceed as in Example 4 to find the other ratios.

Example 5

$\cos A = \dfrac{8}{17}$. Find sinA and tanA.

Begin by drawing a right-angled triangle showing the angle A and sides of length 8 and 17. Now, use Pythagoras' theorem to find the third side.

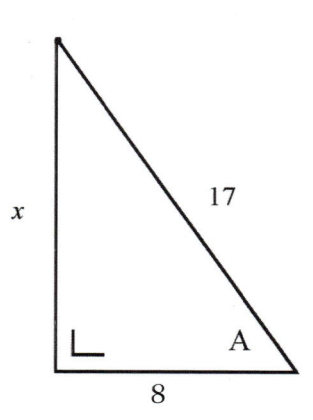

CHAPTER 20: TRIGONOMETRY

$$x^2 + 8^2 = 17^2$$
$$x^2 = 289 - 64$$
$$x^2 = 225$$
$$x = 15$$

$$\sin A = \frac{15}{17}$$

$$\tan A = \frac{15}{8}$$

Sometimes in a question like the one above, there is some work to be done in order to get the sin, cos or tan as a fraction.

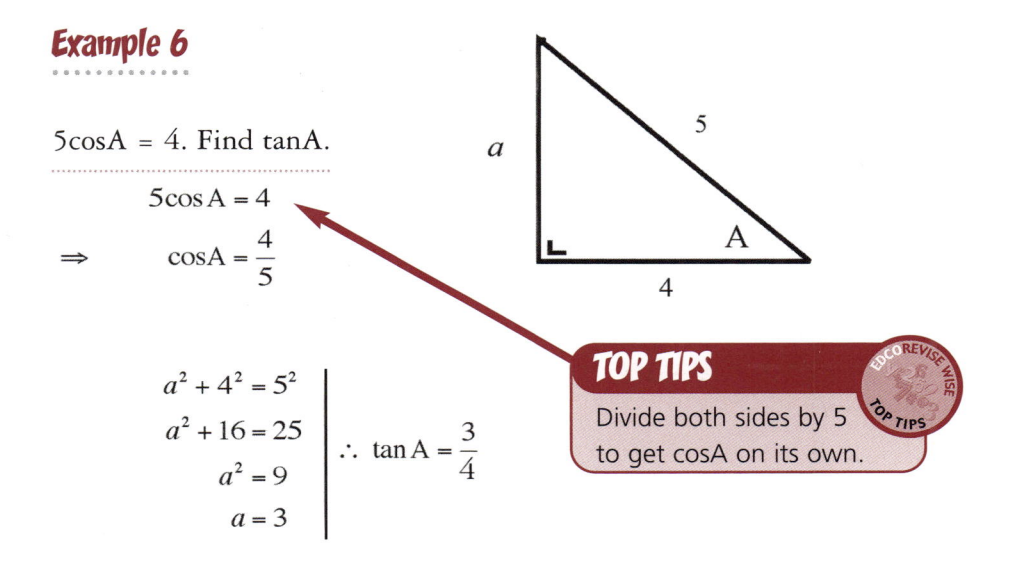

Example 6

$5\cos A = 4$. Find $\tan A$.

$$5\cos A = 4$$
$$\Rightarrow \cos A = \frac{4}{5}$$

$$a^2 + 4^2 = 5^2$$
$$a^2 + 16 = 25$$
$$a^2 = 9$$
$$a = 3$$

$$\therefore \tan A = \frac{3}{4}$$

TOP TIPS

Divide both sides by 5 to get cosA on its own.

Constructing an angle

When asked to construct an angle, **construct a right-angled triangle** that contains the required angle.

You will be given the sin, cos or tan of the angle, so you will know the lengths of two sides.

Example 7

Construct the angle X if $\sin X = \frac{3}{7}$.

1. Draw a rough sketch first. The side opposite X must be 3 and the hypotenuse must be 7.

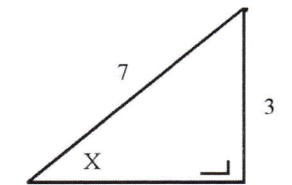

2. Construct a right angle at some point, p. Place a compass at p and with a radius of 3 units (cm or inches) mark a point q along the vertical. The length from p to q is 3 units.

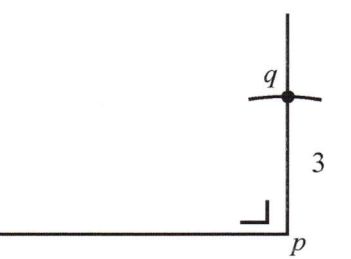

3. Place the compass at q and with a radius of 7 units (the same units as before) mark a point r on the horizontal. Join q to r and put an X in the $\angle qrp$. This is the required angle.

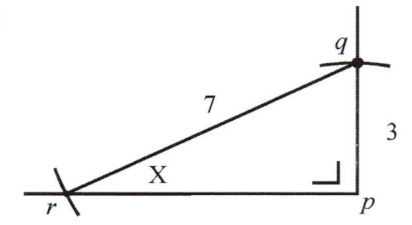

Using the calculator

The calculator can give us the sin, cos or tan of any angle as a decimal.

Example 8

Use the calculator to find sin 30°.

Press calculator keys as follows:

| sin | 3 | 0 | = |

TOP TIPS

Always have the calculator in degree mode – you should see **deg** on the display. If you see **rad** or **grad**, press the DRG key until the display changes to deg.

The answer should be 0·5 since $\sin 30° = \dfrac{1}{2} = 0·5$

A degree can be divided into 60 equal parts called minutes. The angle 30°25' is 30 degrees and 25 minutes. This is keyed into the calculator as follows:

| 3 | 0 | D°M'S | 2 | 5 |

The angle 30·25° does not involve minutes. This is 30·25 degrees and is keyed into the calculator as follows:

| 3 | 0 | . | 2 | 5 |

We can also use the calculator to identify an angle when we know the sin, cos or tan of the angle.

The current exam trend is to use decimals rather than minutes.

Example 9

$\sin A = 0·2$. Find the measure of the angle A to the nearest degree.

$\sin A = 0·2 \Rightarrow A = \sin^{-1} 0·2$ (the angle whose sin is 0·2).

| 2ndF | sin | ·5 | = |

The calculator gives 11·53695903°. Therefore, $A = 12°$, to the nearest degree.

Solving right-angled triangles

We can now use the calculator to find an angle in a right-angled triangle if we know two sides.

Example 10

Find the measure of the angle A, to the nearest degree.

$\tan A = \dfrac{7}{6} \qquad A = \tan^{-1} \dfrac{7}{6}$

$\tan^{-1} \dfrac{7}{6}$ is the acute angle whose tan is $\dfrac{7}{6}$.

To find it press: | 2ndF | tan | 7 | $a^b/_c$ | 6 | = |

The calculator gives: 49·39870535

Answer: $A = 49°$

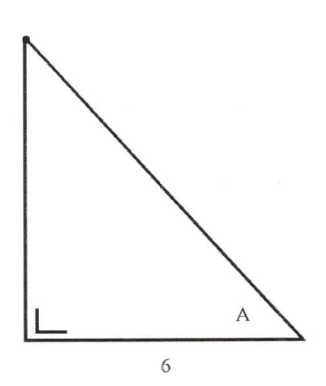

Example 11

Find the measure of the angle B to the nearest degree.

$\cos B = \dfrac{\sqrt{17}}{6}$

$\Rightarrow \quad B = \cos^{-1} \dfrac{\sqrt{17}}{6}$

When using the calculator to find $\cos^{-1} \dfrac{\sqrt{17}}{6}$ the $a\raisebox{0.2ex}{$b$}\!/\!\raisebox{-0.2ex}{$c$}$ key does not work as there is a square root involved. Instead, press:

| 2ndF | cos | (| √ | 1 | 7 | ÷ | 6 |) | = |

The calculator gives 46·59236927°. Therefore, B = 47°, to the nearest degree.

Finding a missing side in a right-angled triangle

If we know two sides, we can use Pythagoras' theorem to find the third.

If we know one side and an angle, then we can find the other two sides using sin, cos or tan.

Example 12

Find the values of x and y correct to one decimal place.

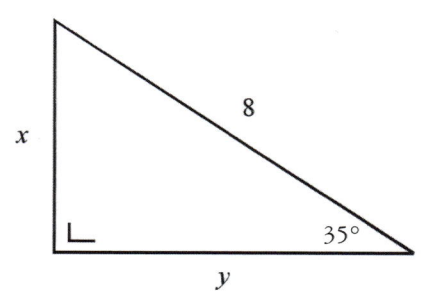

x is opposite the angle 35° and we know that the **hypotenuse** is 8, so we use **sin** to find x.

$$\sin 35° = \frac{x}{8}$$

$\Rightarrow \quad 8\sin 35° = x$

$\Rightarrow \quad 4 \cdot 5886 = x$

$\Rightarrow \quad x = 4 \cdot 6$

> **TOP TIPS**
> Cross-multiply to get x on its own

y is adjacent to the angle 35° and we know that the **hypotenuse** is 8, so we use **cos** to find y.

$$\cos 35° = \frac{y}{8}$$

$\Rightarrow \quad 8\cos 35° = y$

$\Rightarrow \quad 6 \cdot 5532 = y$

$\Rightarrow \quad y = 6 \cdot 6$

Example 13

Find the value of x correct to two decimal places.

6 is adjacent to the angle 48·4° and x is the hypotenuse, so we use cos.

$$\cos 48 \cdot 4° = \frac{6}{x}$$

$x \cos 48 \cdot 4° = 6$

$x = \dfrac{6}{\cos 48 \cdot 4°} = 9 \cdot 037148836$

$x = 9 \cdot 04$, correct to two decimal places.

> **TOP TIPS**
> When x is on the bottom we cross multiply and then divide, to get x on its own.

Practical problems

Angles of **elevation** or **depression** are always made with the **horizontal**.

Example 14

A tree 12 m high casts a shadow of 15 m on horizontal ground.
What is the angle of elevation of the sun, to the nearest degree?

Let E be the angle of elevation.

$\tan E = \dfrac{12}{15} = 0\cdot 8000$

$E = \tan^{-1} 0\cdot 8$
$E = 38\cdot 65980825$
$E = 39°$, to the nearest degree

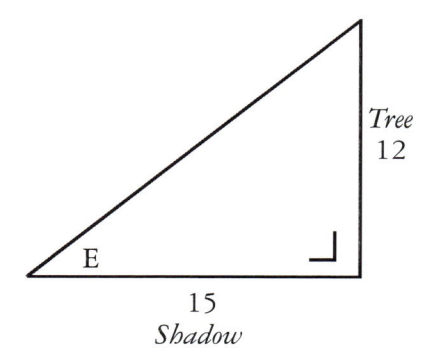

Example 15

From the top of a cliff 50 m high the angle of depression of a boat at sea is 27·2°. How far is the boat from the base of the cliff? Give your answer correct to two decimal places.

When using tan, it is a little easier if we use the angle opposite the required side.

$\tan 62\cdot 8° = \dfrac{x}{50}$

$50(\tan 62\cdot 8°) = x$
$50(1\cdot 945789558) = x$
$97\cdot 28947788 = x$
$x = 97\cdot 29$, correct to two decimal places

Compass bearings

The diagram shows the directions North, South, East, West, Northeast, etc. In trigonometry, however, we often deal with more precise directions.

For example, E56°S.

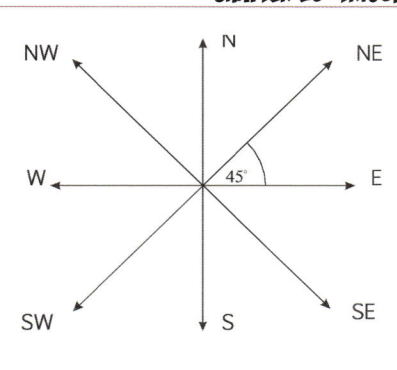

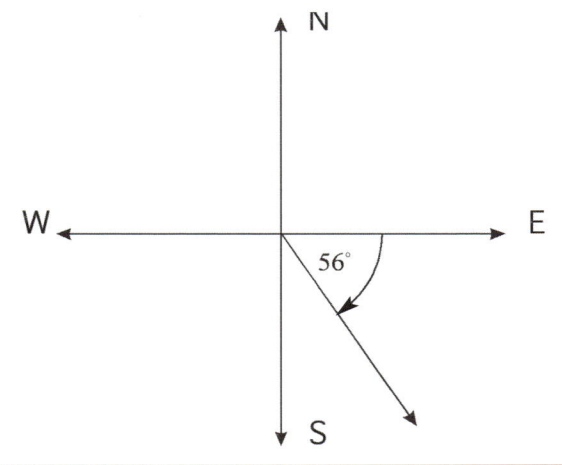

To illustrate this direction, begin by showing North, South, East and West. Then, go east and swing an arc to the south. Put 56° in the arc.

Trigonometry problems with compass bearings

Example 16

Two ships, A and B, leave a port at the same time. A sails N43°E at 15 km/hr, while B sails S47°E at 20 km/hr. What is the distance between them after 2 hours?

A has travelled for 2 hours at 15 km/hr and has therefore travelled 30 km. Similarly, B has gone 40 km.

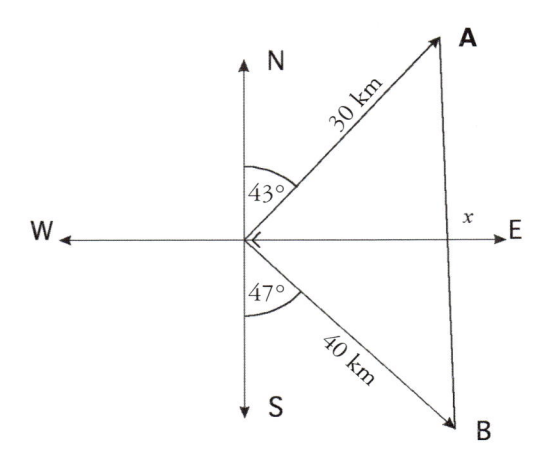

As you can see from the diagram, the distance between A and B is along the hypotenuse of a right-angled triangle and can, therefore, be obtained using Pythagoras' theorem:

$$x^2 = 30^2 + 40^2$$
$$x^2 = 900 + 1600$$
$$x^2 = 2500$$
$$x = 50$$

Answer: The distance between the ships is 50 km.

The area of a triangle

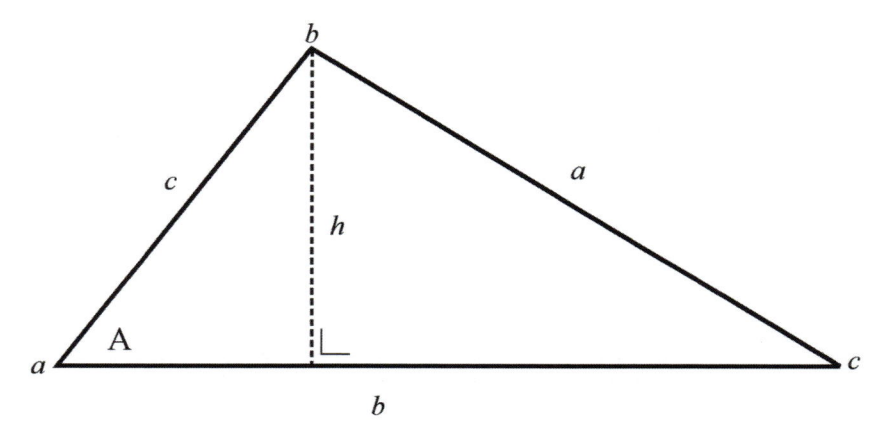

Consider the triangle abc with sides a, b and c, as shown above. From the point b draw the perpendicular height of the triangle, h.

We know from geometry that the area of a triangle is 'half the base multiplied by the perpendicular height'.

Therefore: area $\triangle abc = \dfrac{1}{2}bh$

But: $\sin A = \dfrac{h}{c}$ $\Rightarrow$ $h = c \sin A$

Therefore: $\triangle abc = \dfrac{1}{2}bc \sin A$

i.e. area $\triangle abc$ = 'half the product of two sides multiplied by the sin of the angle where they meet'.

The previous formula can be applied to any of the sides in the triangle, so we can find three different expressions for the area of the above triangle:

$$\text{area } \Delta abc = \frac{1}{2}bc\sin A = \frac{1}{2}ac\sin B = \frac{1}{2}ab\sin C$$

The Sine Rule

We have seen from our work on the area of a triangle that:

$$\frac{1}{2}bc\sin A = \frac{1}{2}ac\sin B = \frac{1}{2}ab\sin C$$

Now, dividing each expression by $\frac{1}{2}abc$, we get:

$$\frac{\frac{1}{2}bc\sin A}{\frac{1}{2}abc} = \frac{\frac{1}{2}ac\sin B}{\frac{1}{2}abc} = \frac{\frac{1}{2}ab\sin C}{\frac{1}{2}abc}$$

From which it follows that:

$$\boxed{\frac{\sin A}{a} = \frac{\sin B}{b} = \frac{\sin C}{c}}$$

This result is known as the Sine Rule and its importance is that it enables us to solve triangles that do not contain a right angle.

Note 1: The Sine Rule applies to **all** triangles, including right-angled triangles.

Note 2: We can invert each fraction, to get

$$\boxed{\frac{a}{\sin A} = \frac{b}{\sin B} = \frac{c}{\sin C}}$$

You should use this version of the Sine Rule when trying to find a side.

Note 3: In order to use the Sine Rule to solve a triangle, we must know the length of one side, the measure of its opposite angle and either another side or another angle.

Solving non-right-angled triangles

Example 17

Find $|ac|$, correct to one decimal place.

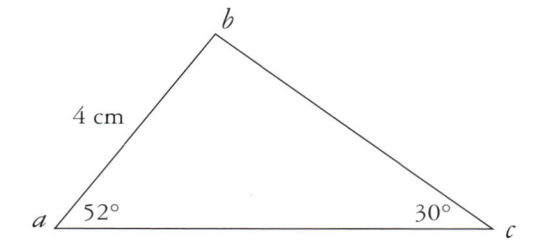

$$\frac{|ac|}{\sin 52°} = \frac{4}{\sin 30°}$$

$$|ac| = \frac{4 \sin 52°}{\sin 30°}$$

$$|ac| = 6·304$$

$$|ac| = 6·3, \text{ correct to one decimal place}$$

Example 18

Find the measure of the angle A, to the nearest degree.

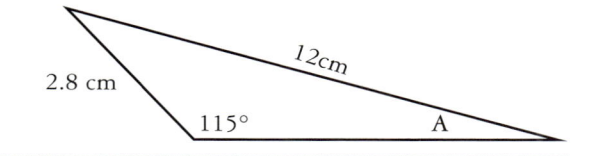

$\dfrac{\sin A}{2 \cdot 8} = \dfrac{\sin 115°}{12}$

$\sin A = \dfrac{2 \cdot 8 \, \sin 115°}{12}$

$\sin A = 0 \cdot 211471817$

A = 12°, to the nearest degree.

Example 19, Junior Certificate 2006

abc is an isosceles triangle with $|ab| = |ac| = 9$

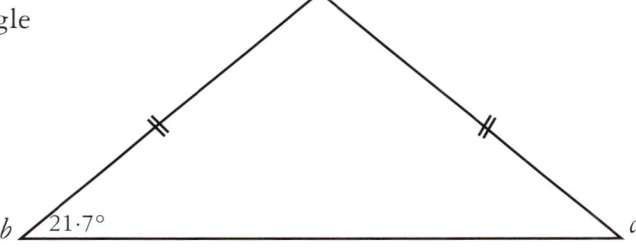

Given that $|\angle abc| = 21 \cdot 7°$, calculate the area of the triangle abc, giving your answer correct to two decimal places.

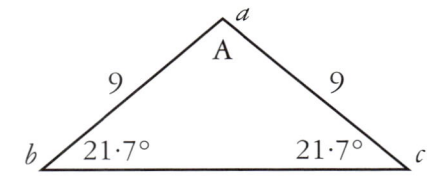

A + 21·7° + 21·7° = 180°
A = 136·6°

TOP TIPS

To get the area of a triangle we need two sides and the angle where they meet.

Area abc = $\dfrac{1}{2}$ (9)(9) sin 136·6°

= 27·82704419

= 27·83, correct to two decimal places

Example 20

d and e are points on a riverbank 80 m apart and f is a point on the opposite bank as shown in the diagram. $|\angle fde| = 38°$ and $|\angle fed| = 65°$

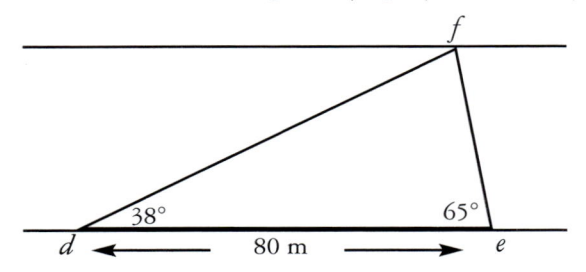

(i) Find $|ef|$, correct to the nearest metre.

(ii) Find the width of the river as measured from f, correct to the nearest metre.

(i) $|\angle dfe| = 180° - 38° - 65°$

$= 77°$

$$\frac{|ef|}{\sin 38°} = \frac{80}{\sin 77°}$$

$$|ef| = \frac{80 \sin 38°}{\sin 77°}$$

$= 50 \cdot 54847209$

$= 51$ m, correct to the nearest metre

(ii) Let x be the width of the river.

$\sin 65° = \dfrac{x}{51}$

$51 \sin 65° = x$

$x = 46$ m, correct to the nearest metre.

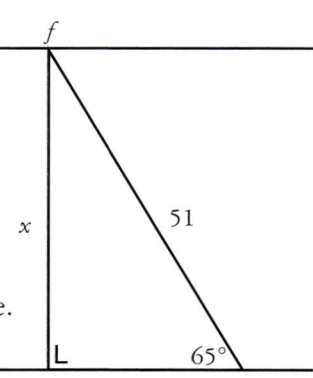

CHAPTER 20: TRIGONOMETRY

Example 21

$|ab| = 85$, $|cd| = 24$
$|\angle adc| = 90°$
$|\angle acd| = 50°$

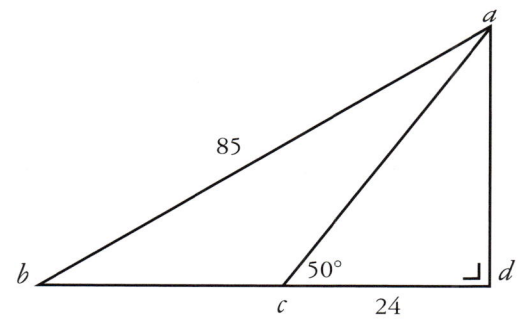

(i) Find $|ad|$, correct to one decimal place.

(ii) Find $|\angle abd|$, correct to the nearest degree.

(i) $\tan 50° = \dfrac{|ad|}{24}$

  $24 \tan 50° = |ad|$

  $|ad| = 28 \cdot 60208622$

  $|ad| = 28 \cdot 6$, correct to one decimal place

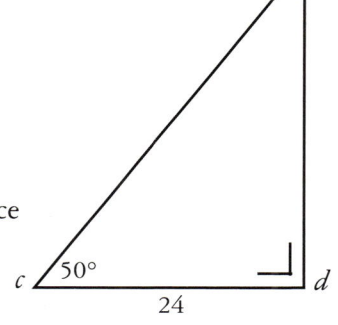

(ii) $\sin \angle abd = \dfrac{28 \cdot 6}{85}$

  $\sin \angle abd = 0 \cdot 336470588$

  $|\angle abd| = 19 \cdot 66198849°$

  $= 20°$, to the nearest degree

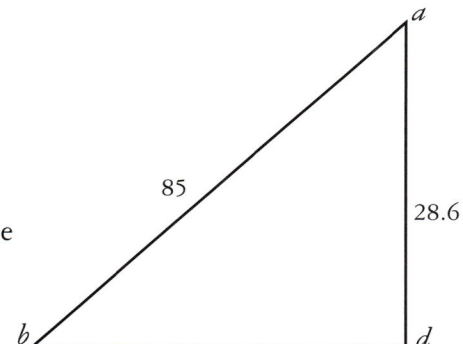

211

The Unit Circle

Consider the following right-angled triangle:

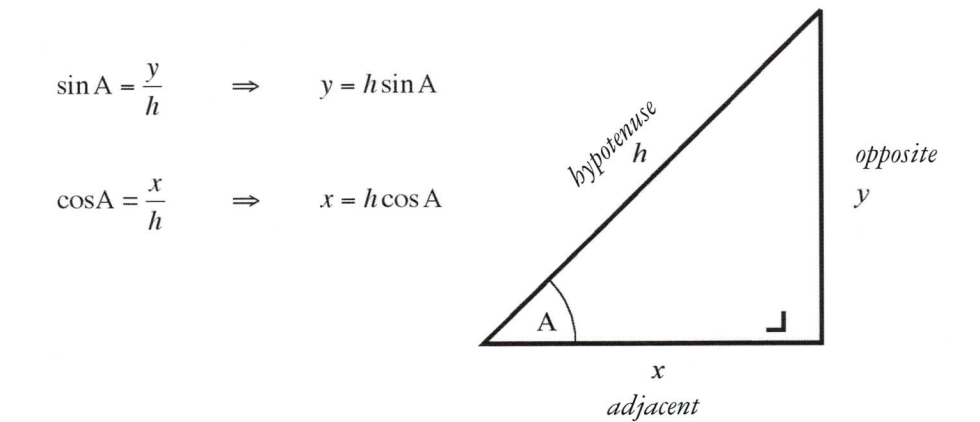

$\sin A = \dfrac{y}{h} \quad \Rightarrow \quad y = h \sin A$

$\cos A = \dfrac{x}{h} \quad \Rightarrow \quad x = h \cos A$

Therefore, in any right-angled triangle, the length of the adjacent can be found by multiplying the hypotenuse by the cosine of the angle, and the length of the opposite can be found by multiplying the hypotenuse by the sin of the angle.

Now consider the following circle, centre and radius of 1 unit. It is referred to as the **unit circle**.

Draw a line from the origin which makes an angle A with the positive sense of the X axis and let (x, y) be the coordinates of the point p where the line cuts the circle.

Then, applying the above result, $x = \cos A$ and $y = \sin A$, since the hypotenuse has a length of 1 unit.

Therefore, the coordinates of the point p are the cosine and sine of the angle A.

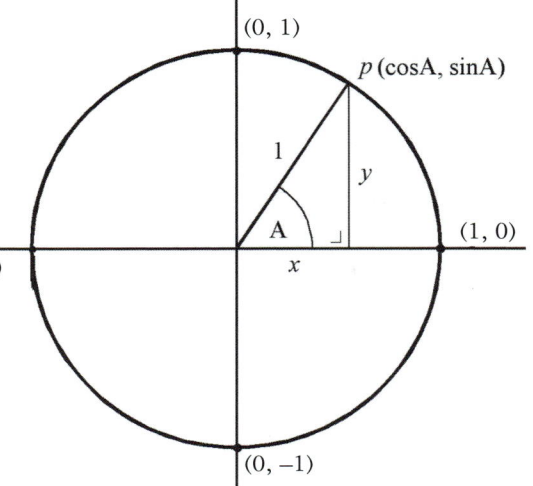

The importance of this result is that it gives a meaning to the cos, sin and tan of angles bigger than 90° and less than 0°.

The following diagram shows how we can use the unit circle to estimate the cosine and sine of the angle 120°.

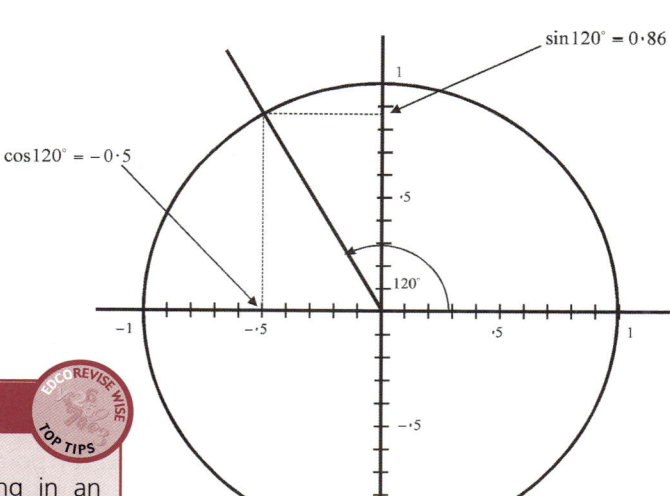

sin 120° = 0·86
cos 120° = −0·5

TOP TIPS

Positive angles are obtained by rotating in an **anti-clockwise** direction, starting at the point (1, 0). Negative angles are obtained by rotating in a clockwise direction.

Note: Although we cannot read the tan of an angle directly from the unit circle, we can get it by dividing the sine by the cosine.

$$\text{i.e.} \quad \tan A = \frac{\sin A}{\cos A}$$

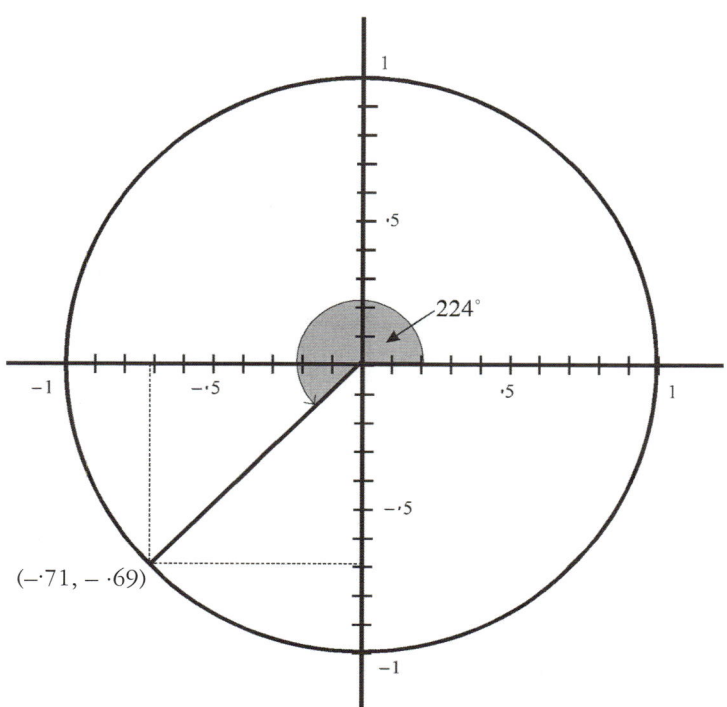

224°

(−·71, −·69)

Every point on the unit circle represents an infinite set of angles. For instance, the point p in the diagram represents the angle 224°, but it also represents 584°, 944°, −136°, −496°, etc. That is, the point p represents the angles (224° ± multiples of 360°).

The coordinates of the point p are the cosine and the sine, in that order, of the angles represented by p. Therefore:

$\cos 224° = -\cdot 71$ $\sin 224° = -\cdot 69$
$\cos 584° = -\cdot 71$ $\sin 584° = -\cdot 69$
$\cos(-136°) = -\cdot 71$ $\sin(-136°) = -\cdot 69$, etc.

We can use the unit circle to read **exactly** the cos and sin of the angles 0°, 90°, 180°, 270° and 360°.

In the diagram below, the point a represents 0° and 360°. The point b represents 90°. The point c represents 180°, and the point d represents 270°.

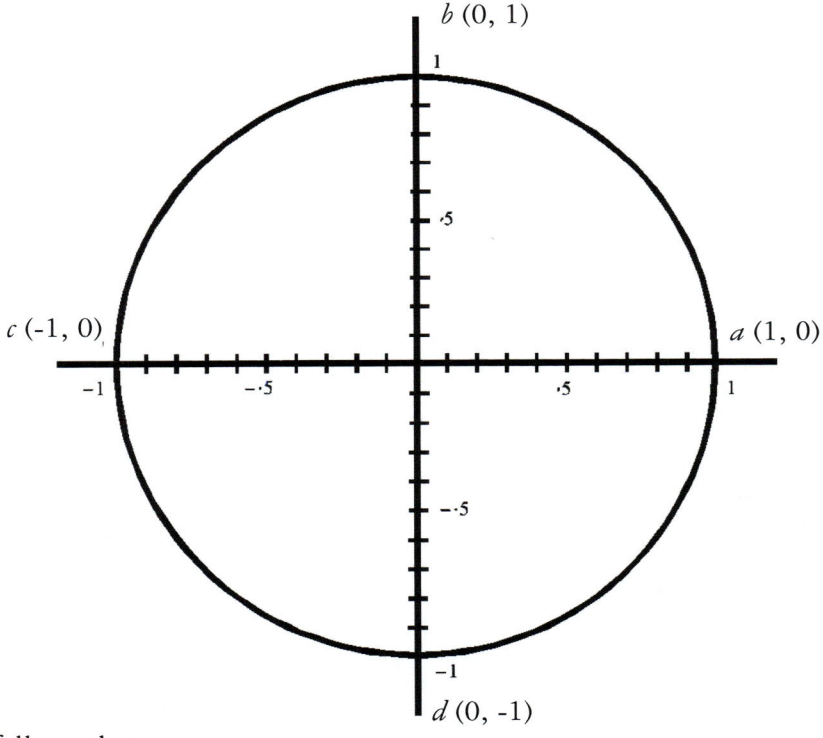

It follows that:

	Cos	Sin	Tan
0° and 360°	1	0	0
90°	0	1	Undefined
180°	−1	0	0
270°	0	−1	Undefined

Remember that tan is obtained by dividing sin by cos.

The following diagram summarises the positive ratios in each quadrant:

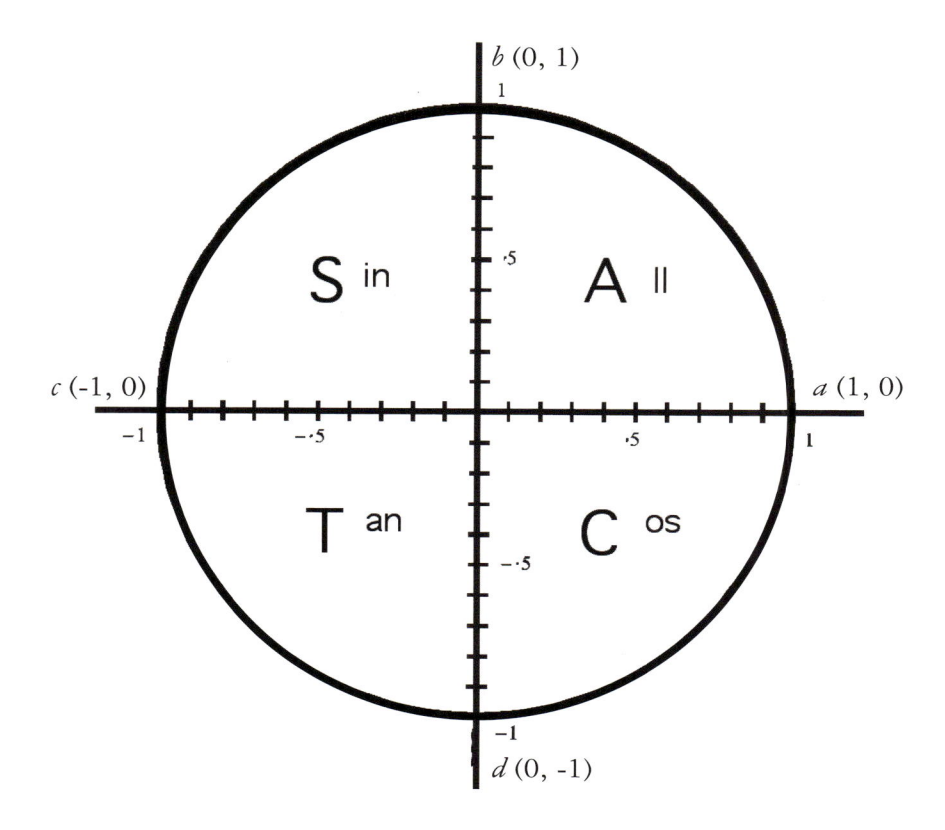

Trigonometric equations

A trigonometric equation arises when we know the sin, cos or tan of an angle and we must find the angle. As demonstrated above, there will be an infinite number of solutions but we are usually asked for solutions between 0° and 360°.

Key Points

- A right-angled triangle is a triangle that contains a 90° angle. Each side in a right-angled triangle is given a special name, either opposite, adjacent or hypotenuse.
- Every fraction that can be formed using two sides of a right-angled triangle has a special name. The three fractions that we use are called sin, cos and tan.
- When given two sides of a right-angled triangle, use Pythagoras' theorem to find the third.
- When asked to construct an angle, construct a right-angled triangle that contains the required angle.
- The calculator can give us the sin, cos or tan of any angle as a decimal.
- Use the calculator to find an angle in a right-angled triangle if two sides are known.
- Angles of elevation or depression are always made with the horizontal line.
- The area of a triangle is half the product of two sides multiplied by the sin of the angle where they meet.
- The Sine Rule enables us to solve non-right-angled triangles.
- When using the Sine Rule to solve a triangle, the length of one side, the measure of its opposite angle and either another side or another angle must be known.
- When the centre of a circle is (0, 0) and the radius is one unit, the circle is referred to as the unit circle.
- A trigonometric equation arises when we know the sin, cos or tan of an angle and we must find the angle. There are usually two solutions between 0° and 360°.
- The unit circle gives meaning to the sin and cos of angles bigger than 90° and of negative angles.

CHAPTER 21
Statistics

Learning Objectives

- Definitions of mode, mean and median
- To find the mean from a frequency table
- Given the mean, to find a missing figure from a frequency table
- Using mid-interval values in a grouped frequency table, to estimate the mean
- How to construct and use pie charts
- Given a grouped frequency table, to construct a histogram
- Given a histogram, to complete a grouped frequency table
- Given a grouped frequency table, to complete a cumulative frequency table
- Given a cumulative frequency table, to complete a grouped frequency table
- To draw a cumulative frequency curve (Ogive)
- To estimate the median of a cumulative frequency curve
- To estimate the interquartile range in a cumulative frequency curve
- Other uses of a cumulative frequency curve.

Statistics definitions

In a list of numbers there are three different **central value** numbers that you may be asked to identify:

Mode: This is the one which occurs most frequently.

Mean: This is another word for the average. It is obtained by adding all the numbers and then dividing by the amount of numbers.

Median: If the numbers are arranged in order, the median is the one in the middle.

Note: If we are given an even amount of numbers, there will be two in the middle, and in this case the median is the average of these two.

Example 1

Identify the mode, the mean and the median of the following numbers:

2, 3, 6, 4, 2, 4, 6, 7, 8, 6, 5, 6, 7, 5, 4, 3, 6, 2, 1, 3

Solution:
We will begin by arranging the numbers in order:
1, 2, 2, 2, 3, 3, 3, 4, 4, 4, 5, 5, 6, 6, 6, 6, 6, 7, 7, 8

The **mode** is 6, since it occurs most often.

The **mean** is $\dfrac{1+6+9+12+10+30+14+8}{20} = \dfrac{90}{20} = 4 \cdot 5$

The **median** is $\dfrac{4+5}{2} = 4 \cdot 5$ since the two middle numbers are 4 and 5.

Frequency table

The set of figures in Example 1 could be presented as follows:

Number	1	2	3	4	5	6	7	8
Frequency	1	3	3	3	2	5	2	1

TOP TIPS

6 has the biggest frequency and is therefore the mode.

This is called a frequency table. The top row lists all the different numbers that appear and the bottom row lists the frequency of each number, i.e. how often each number appears.

Notice that the frequency table presents the numbers in order, starting with the smallest.

To get the mode, look for the biggest frequency. The mode is the number above it, in this case 6.

$$\text{Mean} = \dfrac{1 \cdot 1 + 2 \cdot 3 + 3 \cdot 3 + 4 \cdot 3 + 5 \cdot 2 + 6 \cdot 5 + 7 \cdot 2 + 8 \cdot 1}{1+3+3+3+2+5+2+1} = \dfrac{90}{20} = 4 \cdot 5$$

To get the median we begin by adding the frequencies to see how many numbers are listed. In this case there are 20, so the median is the average of the tenth and eleventh numbers. Add the frequencies and we can see that the tenth number is 4 and the eleventh is 5, so the median is 4.5.

Example 2

The mean of 1, 2, 5, 7 and x is 6. Find x.

Solution:
If the mean of 5 numbers is 6, then the numbers must add up to 30.

$$\therefore \quad x + 1 + 2 + 5 + 7 = 30$$
$$\Rightarrow \quad x + 15 = 30$$
$$\Rightarrow \quad x = 15$$

Example 3

If the means from the following table is 3, find x.

Number	1	2	3	4	5
Frequency	8	10	12	x	4

Solution:

$$\text{Mean} = \frac{1 \cdot 8 + 2 \cdot 10 + 3 \cdot 12 + 4x + 5 \cdot 4}{8 + 10 + 12 + x + 4}$$

$$= \frac{8 + 20 + 36 + 4x + 20}{x + 34}$$

$$= \frac{4x + 84}{x + 34}$$

But we are given that the mean is 3.

$$\therefore \quad \frac{4x + 84}{x + 34} = \frac{3}{1}$$
$$\Rightarrow \quad 4x + 84 = 3x + 102$$
$$\Rightarrow \quad 4x - 3x = 102 - 84$$
$$\Rightarrow \quad x = 18$$

Grouped frequency table

When a large amount of data is collected, it is not usually practical to display the results using a frequency table, since there is likely to be a large variety of results. Instead, we divide the results into intervals and present them using a **grouped** frequency table.

The following table illustrates the ages of 100 people in a survey:

Age	0–10	10–20	20–40	40–60	60–100
Number of people	8	34	20	31	7

Note: 10–20 includes 10 but not 20.

The difficulty with the above information is that we do not know the precise age of anyone surveyed. For instance, we know that there are 31 people in the 40–60 category, but they could all be under 50 or all over 50.

We cannot **calculate** the mean in a grouped frequency table, but we can **estimate** it by assuming **mid-interval values**. This means that we assume that everyone in the 0–10 category is aged 5, everyone in the 40–60 category is aged 50, etc.

Example 4

With the aid of the above table, estimate the mean, using mid-interval values.

Mid-interval	5	15	30	50	80
Age	0–10	10–20	20–40	40–60	60–100
Number of people	8	34	20	31	7

Note: The mid-interval is the average of the two numbers in each category.

$$\text{Mean} = \frac{5 \cdot 8 + 15 \cdot 34 + 30 \cdot 20 + 50 \cdot 31 + 80 \cdot 7}{8 + 34 + 20 + 31 + 7}$$

$$= \frac{3260}{100}$$

$$= 32 \cdot 6$$

Pie charts

A pie chart is a circle, divided into sectors, which is used to represent a set of figures.

The angle in each sector is calculated as follows:

1 Add all the numbers – call this number a
2 Divide 360° by a to get $b°$
3 Multiply each number by $b°$ to convert it to degrees.

Example 5

The following table compares the number of new cars registered on a certain day. Represent these figures by a pie chart.

Manufacturer	Audi	Toyota	Ford	Mercedes	Peugeot
Number of cars	8	26	18	5	15

Add the numbers: $8 + 26 + 18 + 5 + 15 = 72$

$$\frac{360°}{72} = 5°$$

Multiply each number by 5°.

Manufacturer	Audi	Toyota	Ford	Mercedes	Peugeot
Number of cars	8	26	18	5	15
Angle in sector	40°	130°	90°	25°	75°

Now draw the pie chart:

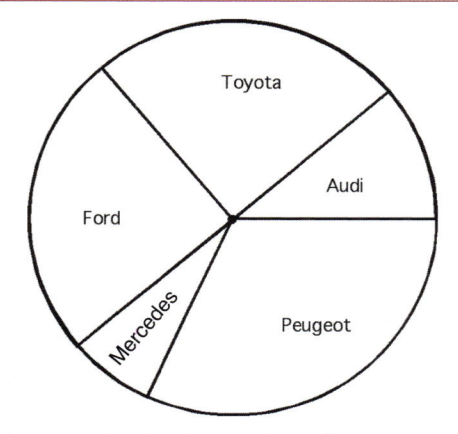

You may be given a pie chart and asked to identify the number that is represented by a particular sector.

Example 6

The following pie chart illustrates the results of a survey on how a group of people travel to work. If 45 people in the survey said that they cycle to work then,

(i) How many people in the survey said that they walk?
(ii) How many people were surveyed?

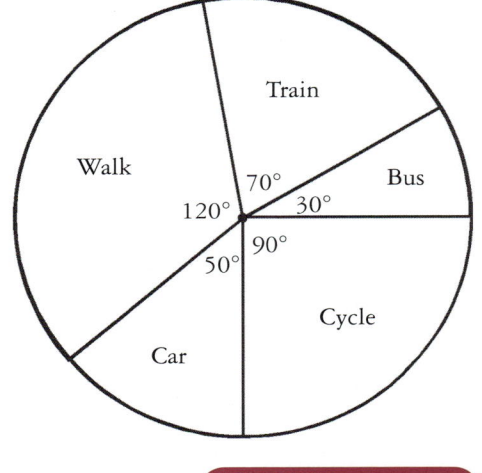

(i) 90° represents 45 people.
∴ 2° represents 1 person.
Divide each angle by 2° to convert it to people.
120° ÷ 2° = 60, so 60 people walk to work.
(ii) 360° ÷ 2°, so 180 people were surveyed.

TOP TIPS
The total number in the survey is represented by 360°.

Solution: Therefore, 60 people said that they walked to work and 180 people were surveyed.

Histogram

A histogram is a picture, similar to a bar chart, used to present a set of figures. However, there are no spaces between the bars and the bars may be different in width.

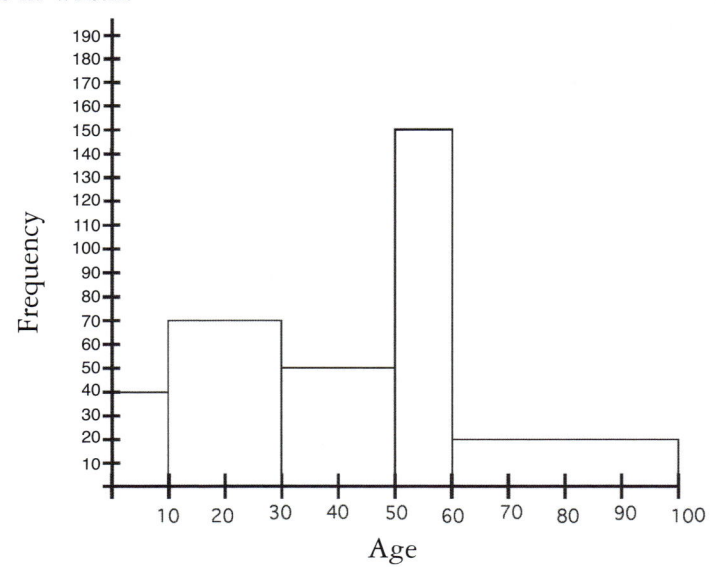

When representing information in a grouped frequency table by a histogram, it is important to remember that the **area** of each bar must represent the frequency, **not the height**.

Given a grouped frequency table, to construct a histogram

If the bars have different widths, the heights of the bars must be calculated as follows:

1 Add a new row at the top of the grouped frequency table, called width
2 Add a new row at the bottom, called height
3 Write in the width of each bar (subtract the numbers in the intervals)
4 Multiply each frequency by the smallest width and then divide by its own width to get the height for each bar.

Example 7

Represent the following test results on a histogram:

Marks	10–20	20–30	30–50	50–70	70–100
Number of students	4	6	18	22	15

Width	10	10	20	20	30
Marks	10–20	20–30	30–50	50–70	70–100
Number of students	4	6	18	22	15
Height	4	6	9	11	5

The smallest width is 10.

$$\frac{4 \times 10}{10} = 4$$

$$\frac{6 \times 10}{10} = 6$$

$$\frac{18 \times 10}{20} = 9$$

$$\frac{22 \times 10}{20} = 11$$

$$\frac{15 \times 10}{30} = 5$$

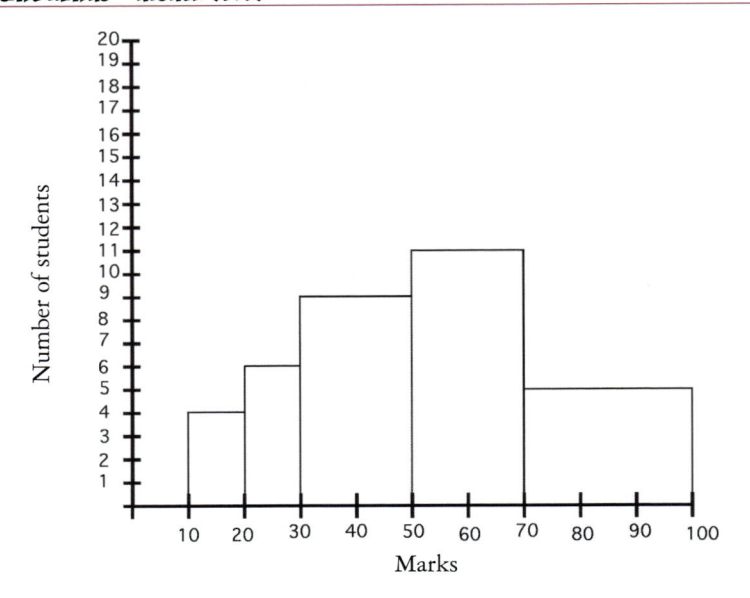

Given a histogram, to complete a grouped frequency table

One of the frequencies is always given.

1 Calculate the area of each bar
2 Divide the given frequency into the area of the corresponding bar
3 Divide each of the other areas by the answer to find their frequency.

Example 8

The following histogram illustrates the number of days missed by a number of students: Complete the following grouped frequency table:

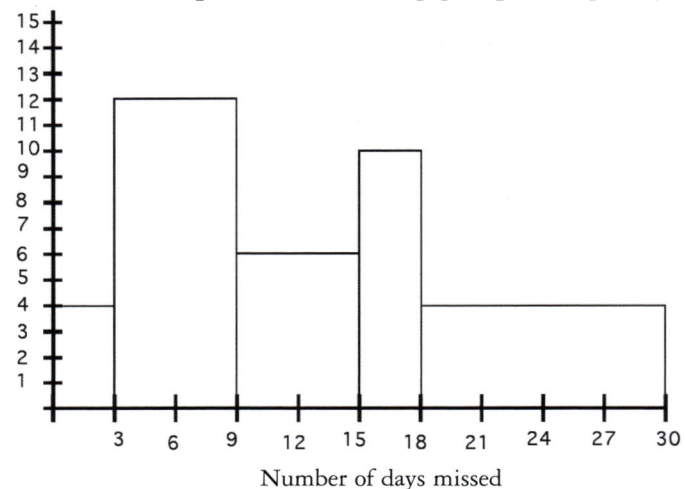

Number of days missed	0–3	3–9	9–15	15–18	18–30
Number of students		36			

72 ÷ 36 = 2

Bar	Width	Height (from graph)	Area	Frequency Area÷2
0–3	3	4	12	6
3–9	6	12	72	36
9–15	6	6	36	18
15–18	3	10	30	15
18–30	12	4	48	24

Answer:

Number of days missed	0–3	3–9	9–15	15–18	18–30
Number of students	6	36	18	15	24

Cumulative frequency table

The following cumulative frequency table shows the amount of time taken by 30 students to solve a maths problem:

Time in minutes	<2	<4	<6	<8	<10
Number of students	1	6	8	19	30

Therefore, 19 students took less than 8 minutes to solve the problem. This figure includes the 8 students who took less than 6 minutes, etc. We can conclude that 11 students took between 6 and 8 minutes.

TOP TIPS
This figure is always the total number surveyed.

Example 9

Convert the following frequency table to a cumulative frequency table:

Goals scored	0–20	20–40	40–60	60–80	80–100	100–120
Number of teams	2	6	5	3	3	1

The number of teams who scored less than 20 goals includes 1 category, 0–20. This number is 2.

The number of teams who scored less than 40 goals includes 2 categories, 0–20 and 20–40. (2 + 6 = 8)

The number of teams who scored less than 60 goals includes 3 categories, 0–20, 20–40 and 40–60. (2 + 6 + 5 = 13)

The number of teams who scored less than 80 goals includes 4 categories, 0–20, 20–40, 40–60 and 60–80. (2 + 6 + 5 + 3 = 16)

The number of teams who scored less than 100 goals includes 5 categories, 0–20, 20–40, 40–60, 60–80 and 80–00. (2 + 6 + 5 + 3 + 3 = 19)

The number of teams who scored less than 120 goals includes 6 categories, 0–20, 20–40, 40–60, 60–80, 80–100 and 100–120. (2 + 6 + 5 + 3 + 3 + 1 = 20)

Answer:

Goals scored	<20	<40	<60	<80	<100	<120
Number of teams	2	8	13	16	19	20

When converting back from a cumulative frequency table to a grouped frequency table, use the following result:

> The number in the a to b category = number $<b$ − number $<a$.

Example 10

Convert the following cumulative frequency table to a grouped frequency table:

Goals scored	<20	<40	<60	<80	<100	<120
Number of teams	1	3	7	14	8	20

$0 - 20$ and <20 are the same: 1
$20 - 40 \ = \ <40 - <20 \ = \ 2$
$40 - 60 \ = \ <60 - <40 \ = \ 4$
$60 - 80 \ = \ <80 - <60 \ = \ 7$
$80 - 100 = \ <100 - <80 = 4$
$100 - 120 = \ <120 - <100 = 2$

Answer:

Goals scored	0–20	20–40	40–60	60–80	80–100	100–120
Number of teams	1	2	4	7	4	2

Cumulative frequency curve (Ogive)

This is a graph used to present the figures in a **cumulative** frequency table.

Example 11

Draw a cumulative frequency curve to represent the following:

Time in minutes	<2	<4	<6	<8	<10
Number of students	1	6	8	19	30

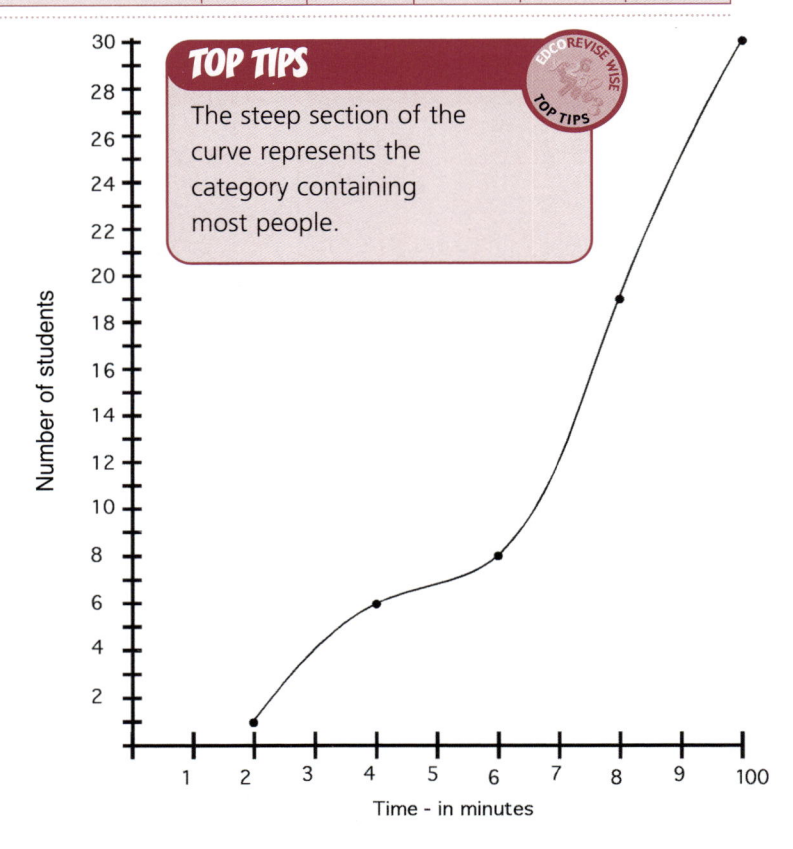

TOP TIPS

The steep section of the curve represents the category containing most people.

TOP TIPS

Bottoms Up! The bottom numbers in the table go up the side of the graph.

Using a cumulative frequency curve

Example 12

Using the curve in the previous example, estimate:

(i) The median
(ii) The interquartile range
(iii) The number of students who took less than 5 minutes to solve the problem
(iv) The number of students who took more than 5 minutes
(v) The number of students who took between 5 and 7 minutes.

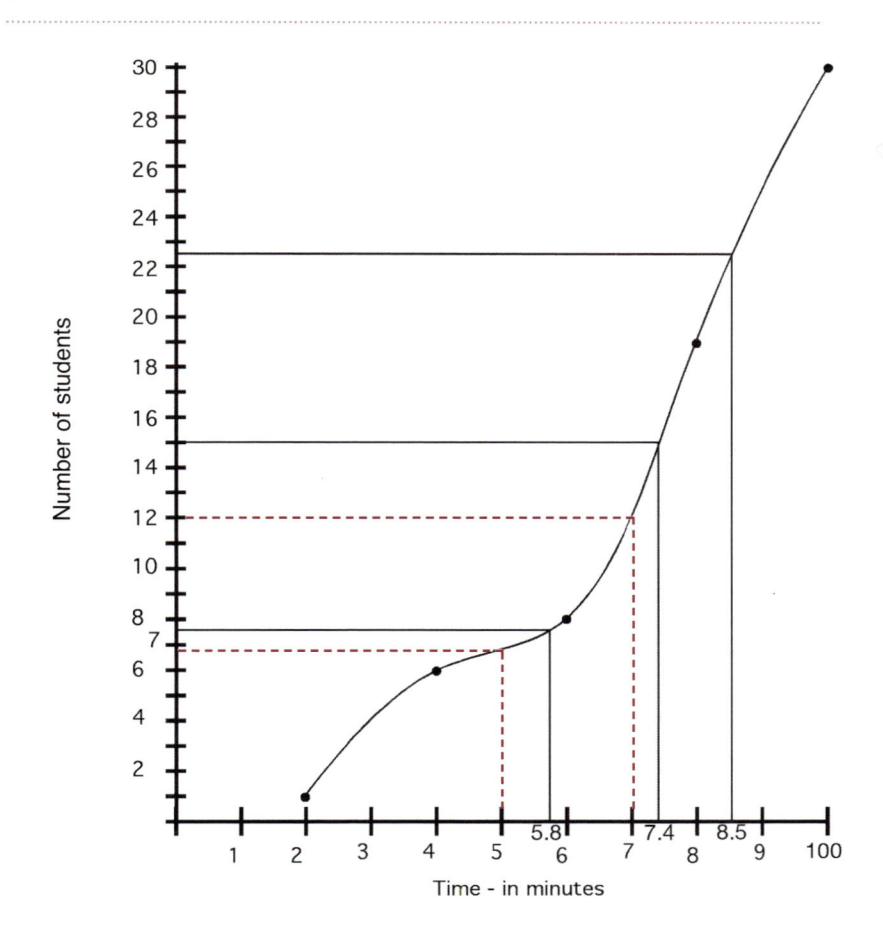

(i) To get the median, go halfway up the side, across and down, to 7.4. The median is approximately 7.4.

(ii) To get the interquartile range, go quarter and three-quarter the way up the side, across and down to 5.5 and 8.5. Then subtract the answers: the interquartile range is 2.7.

(iii) To estimate the number of students who took less than 5 minutes to solve the problem, go to 5 on the horizontal, go up to the graph and across to 7. Approximately 7 students took less than 5 minutes.

(iv) To estimate the number of students who took more than 5 minutes to solve the problem, repeat the above, but then subtract the answer from the total number of students: 30 − 7 = 23. Therefore, approximately 23 students took more than 5 minutes.

(v) To estimate the number of students who took between 5 and 7 minutes, go to 5 and 7 on the horizontal, go up and across and then subtract the answers. 15 − 7 = 8, therefore, approximately 8 students took between 5 and 7 minutes.

Key Points

- The mode is the number which occurs most frequently in a list of numbers.
- The mean or average is got by adding all the numbers and then dividing by the amount of numbers.
- If a list of numbers is arranged in order, the median is the one in the middle, or in an even set of figures, the average of the two in the middle.
- In a frequency table the top row lists all the different numbers that appear and the bottom row lists the frequency of each number, i.e. how often each number appears. The table presents the numbers in order, starting with the smallest.
- When a large amount of data is collected the results are divided into intervals and presented in a grouped frequency table.
- The mean in a grouped frequency table cannot be calculated, but it can be estimated by assuming mid-interval values. The mid-interval is the average of the two numbers in each interval.
- A pie chart is a circle, divided into sectors, which is used to represent a set of figures. There is no space between the bars and the bars may differ in width.
- A histogram is a picture, similar to a bar chart, used to present a set of figures. There is no space between the bars and the bars may differ in width.
- When representing information in a grouped frequency table by a histogram, the area of each bar must represent the frequency not the height.
- A cumulative frequency table is based on a grouped frequency table, but each interval has an upper limit only, e.g. <40.
- A cumulative frequency curve (Ogive) is a graph used to present the figures in a cumulative frequency table.
- A cumulative frequency curve can be used to estimate the median and the interquartile range.

CHAPTER 22
Examination Section

Useful information to learn

Preparation for an examination begins with your day-to-day work, both in the classroom and at home. The key to success is consistent work over a long period of time, not last-minute cramming! Here are some tips on how to prepare for the Junior Certificate Higher Level Maths examination.

1. Classwork — new material

When the teacher is doing something new in class, ask yourself:
- Do I understand what is going on?
- Is there something I need to memorise?
- Is the teacher using words that I don't understand?
- Will I recognise when to use this method?
- Are there other problems where this method could be used?

If you need help, ask your teacher. If you find it difficult too ask questions in class, then try asking your teacher after class. Alternatively, ask a friend or a parent. But it is important to ... **ask someone!**

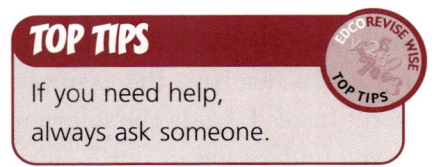

TOP TIPS
If you need help, always ask someone.

It is important to have a notebook in class where you can record:
- Words, whose meaning you must discover and learn
- Formula that must be memorised
- Material you need to revise
- Mistakes you make.

2. Classwork — correcting homework

Always be conscious of the following:
- What topic is under discussion?
- What aspect of that topic is under discussion?

- On which question in the examination does this usually appear?
- Is this material totally new or is it linked to earlier material that may need revision?

When homework is being corrected, compare the solution with your work. If you made a mistake, always identify exactly where you went wrong. It is very common for students to be shown the correct solution and still not to know what mistake they made. If you are not sure where you went wrong, **ask your teacher**.

If you had no idea how to go about the question for homework, then you should try the question again as part of the next homework. Do not assume that you can now solve the problem just because you have been shown the solution!

3. Homework

Before attempting written work, check your notes to see if there is something you need to memorise. If there is, then do this first.

When it comes to doing questions, always begin by reading the question carefully so that you know exactly what you are trying to do and will recognise the question when it appears again.

If you are having difficulties…

If you do not see how to go about the problem, look for a similar problem in your textbook, school notes or in this book. Do not have the example visible beside you while you do your homework! Instead, study the solution in the example carefully and when you think you understand it, put it away and try the homework. If you get stuck, go through the same procedure again.

Watch out for little differences in the way questions are worded. Two questions can look very similar but require different methods of solution. Also, two questions may be worded differently, but have exactly the same method of solution.

For example, students often confuse:

Factorise: $2x^2 - 5x - 3$

with

Solve for x: $2x^2 - 5x - 3 = 0$

Always attempt a question

If you have no idea how to do a question, still make some attempt! It is essential if you are to pick up attempt marks in an examination that you develop the habit of making an attempt at all questions. Do anything you can do with the information provided, regardless of what you were asked to do.

For example:
- In a geometry problem you could draw the diagram and fill in any lengths or angles that you know.
- If you see a right-angled triangle, try applying Pythagoras' theorem.
- In area/volume, if you know the radius and height of a cylinder then you can find the volume.
- In coordinate geometry, if you are asked for the equation of a line, find some slope and some point and apply the equation of a line formula.
- In trigonometry, to find a side or angle in a triangle, try applying the sine rule.

If you are sure what to do...

When it comes to questions that you know how to do, the following tips will help you avoid needless errors:

TOP TIPS

- Present all your work clearly, one step at a time.
- Do 'rough work' neatly on the page, not in your head.
- Double-check awkward calculations using the calculator.
- Look for ways to check your answer **without** looking up the answer in the book. You must establish habits that can be used in an examination
- Having solved the problem, read the question again to ensure that you did exactly what you were asked to do.

4. Revision

Revision should become a habit in mathematics. You will regularly encounter a problem that requires some information or a method that was last seen months before.

The key to studying a topic properly is to be aware of the different types of problems that you must be able to solve. The examples that are demonstrated in this book should prove helpful in that regard. Make a list of different types and this can be used as a checklist leading up to the examination to ensure that your revision is comprehensive.

Make a list of **facts**, **formulae**, **keywords**, **proofs** and **constructions** that must be memorised. Return regularly to this list.

Next, you must identify 'problem areas'. These can be solutions that you do not understand or questions that you do not recognise how to begin. You will need help with these! Ideally, ask your teacher. Alternatively, ask someone who can help. Now you need practice!

> **TOP TIPS**
> Memorise facts, formulae, keywords, proofs and constructions.

Practise... Practise... Practise

Go through the examples in this book and try them without looking at the solution. If you do not get it right, study the solution carefully and put an asterisk beside the question to remind you that you had difficulty with it. Also, keep a record of mistakes that you make. Keeping a record ensures first of all that you identify where you made your mistake but also helps you to avoid that mistake again.

Regularly return to problems that you have done before to ensure that you have not forgotten how to do them.

In particular, the constructions and the proofs of theorems should be written out regularly. However, do not read through the solution and then immediately write it out. This can give you a false sense of security. If you need to read over the solution, do so. Then do some other homework and after an hour or so try writing out the proof. Eventually, you must be able to write out the proof or construction without looking at it in advance.

Use the study plan at the back of this book to help you revise.

5. Preparing for the examination

- Identify the amount of time available for the revision of maths. Then make out a timetable showing exactly what you are going to revise, when you are going to do it, and how much time you are going to spend on it.
- The sooner you start, the more comprehensive your preparations will be.
- If you haven't time to cover everything, prioritise.
- Study previous papers carefully so you know what type of question to expect. In particular, watch out for questions that appear regularly and ensure that you know how to do them.
- Jot down key points/formulae, etc. to memorise. This should be the last thing you look at before you go into the examination.
- Get up early on the morning of the examination. Have a good breakfast and ensure that you have everything you will need, in particular, a working calculator.
- Arrive at the examination centre in plenty of time and study your key points.

6. Doing the examination

- Be calm!
- As soon as you receive the question paper, write on it any key points/formulae that you may forget.
- Do not read through the entire paper first! There is no choice on the paper so there is no point. Go to your favourite question and begin it immediately.
- Read the questions carefully. Pay attention to every detail.
- Be aware of time. You have on average 25 minutes per question.
- If you get stuck on part of a question, leave a space and come back to it when you have everything else done.
- You may make more than one attempt at a question and the best attempt will be marked. If you make more than one attempt, put a single line through cancelled work.

- When going back over problems that you had trouble with, check how much time is left and divide it evenly between these problems. Make sure that you have made some attempt at every question.
- If you have time left, go back over your work looking for errors. Do not leave early!

7. After the examination

- Do not discuss what you have done – it cannot be changed.
- Focus on your next examination.

Good Luck!

Study Plan

Date				
Time				
Section to be revised				

Date				
Time				
Section to be revised				

Date				
Time				
Section to be revised				

Date				
Time				
Section to be revised				

Date				
Time				
Section to be revised				

Date				
Time				
Section to be revised				

Night before exam

Sections to be revised

Study Plan

Date				
Time				
Section to be revised				
Date				
Time				
Section to be revised				
Date				
Time				
Section to be revised				
Date				
Time				
Section to be revised				
Date				
Time				
Section to be revised				
Date				
Time				
Section to be revised				
Night before exam				
Sections to be revised				

Study Plan

Date				
Time				
Section to be revised				
Date				
Time				
Section to be revised				
Date				
Time				
Section to be revised				
Date				
Time				
Section to be revised				
Date				
Time				
Section to be revised				
Date				
Time				
Section to be revised				

Night before exam	
Sections to be revised	

Study Plan

Date
Time
Section to be revised

Date
Time
Section to be revised

Date
Time
Section to be revised

Date
Time
Section to be revised

Date
Time
Section to be revised

Date
Time
Section to be revised

Night before exam
Sections to be revised